DATE DUE

JE - 1 '10			

DEMCO 38-296

MUSIC AND POETRY
OF THE
ENGLISH RENAISSANCE

Da Capo Press Music Reprint Series

GENERAL EDITOR
FREDERICK FREEDMAN
VASSAR COLLEGE

MUSIC AND POETRY
OF THE
ENGLISH RENAISSANCE

By Bruce Pattison

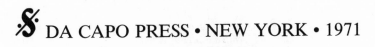 DA CAPO PRESS • NEW YORK • 1971

A Da Capo Press Reprint Edition

This Da Capo Press edition of
Music and Poetry of the English Renaissance
is an unabridged republication of the first
edition published in London in 1948.

Library of Congress Catalog Card Number 70-127278

SBN 306-71298-9

Published by Da Capo Press
A Division of Plenum Publishing Corporation
227 West 17th Street, New York, N. Y. 10011

MUSIC AND POETRY
OF THE ENGLISH RENAISSANCE

BRUCE PATTISON

MUSIC AND POETRY OF THE ENGLISH RENAISSANCE

METHUEN & CO. LTD. LONDON

36 Essex Street, Strand, W.C.2

First published in 1948

CATALOGUE NO. 3963/U

THIS BOOK IS PRODUCED IN COMPLETE
CONFORMITY WITH THE AUTHORIZED
ECONOMY STANDARDS

PRINTED IN GREAT BRITAIN

TO MY WIFE

PREFACE

THE age of Shakespeare and Jonson is also the age of Byrd and Dowland. A great period of English poetry coincides with the most splendid period of English music. The fact must be significant for the history of the English lyric ; but little attempt has been made to examine in detail the points of contact between the two arts, and to show precisely how each affected the development of the other. This book tries to demonstrate that the relationship between them was not only intimate but such as could have existed at no other time ; that environment and tradition kept poets and composers in close touch ; that literary points of view helped to shape musical forms, and that the structure and content of lyric poetry owed much to music. By illustrating a few aspects of the influence of one art on the other, it is hoped to make some contribution towards the understanding of how the Renaissance mind approached the creation and enjoyment of music and poetry.

A study of this kind naturally depends on a good deal of previous scholarship. Particularly every student of the period must be grateful to Dr. E. H. Fellowes for his editing of the madrigal and lutanist volumes. Without reliable texts a work like the present would be impossible. Where I could I have acknowledged the assistance of other scholars in making information easily accessible : a general acknowledgement must cover them all now. Since almost all the literature and all the music of the Renaissance period are relevant to such a study as this, I cannot claim to have completely covered the ground in even a general way. I have tried merely to isolate what seemed to me significant tendencies, leaving the details to be filled in later. Even so, the preparation of this volume has covered several years, and the writing of it has been much interrupted and distracted by other duties. The bulk of the work was done before the war, during which I had no time to think much about either literature or music. Now conditions are not very favourable to checking the results of my pre-war researches. I must, therefore, ask indulgence for any errors and oversights that have crept into the large amount of material I have tried to manipulate.

I must take this opportunity to thank several people who have been of help to me in my work.   The idea of studying the relations between poetry and music was first suggested to me by Prof. W. L. Renwick, for whose many kindnesses I cannot adequately express my gratitude.   Prof. W. G. Whittaker, under whom I studied music, and Prof. E. J. Dent, my supervisor at Cambridge, helped to put me on the right path and greatly encouraged my investigations.   Finally, I can but mention the very great help and encouragement I have had from my wife at all stages of the work : without her constant aid the book would never have been published at all.

BRUCE PATTISON

UNIVERSITY COLLEGE
    LONDON, W.C.1

CONTENTS

CHAPTER I

MUSIC IN SIXTEENTH-CENTURY SOCIETY

MUSIC played an important part in Renaissance philosophy. Before Descartes had reduced the physical universe to a mass of particles in motion, and Newton had postulated the force of gravitation as the arbiter of those particles, rhythm was the principle invoked to explain the creation and movements of the heavenly bodies. Sun, moon and stars whirled round the earth to the music of the spheres, which governed their speeds and motions and prevented their colliding. The universe, in fact, was nothing else than a huge choral dance, as Sir John Davies was quick to explain when he wished to defend the terrestrial pleasure of dancing.

> Dauncing (bright Lady) then began to be,
> When the first seedes whereof the world did spring,
> The Fire, Ayre, Earth, and water—did agree,
> By Loues perswasion,—Natures mighty King,—
> To leaue their first disordered combating ;
> And in a daunce such measure to obserue,
> As all the world their motion should preserue.
>
> Since when, they still are carried in a round,
> And changing, come one in anothers place ;
> Yet doe they neyther mingle nor confound,
> But euery one doth keepe the bounded space
> Wherein the Daunce doth bid it turne or trace ;
> This wondrous myracle did Loue deuise,
> For dauncing is Loues proper exercise.[1]

This rhythmic conception of the universe the Renaissance owed to Greek philosophy, and with it was adopted a Greek analogy between celestial order and human affairs. The study of astronomy was supposed to reveal the principles on which public and private life should be conducted. As the heavens were preserved from chaos by the harmonious movements of the planets, so the state could prosper only when the different interests in it danced to a common tune. Hence Sir Thomas Elyot decrees that the tutor of his young noble

shall commende the perfecte understandinge of musike, declaringe howe necessary it is for the better attaynynge the knowlege of a publike weale : whiche, as I before haue saide, is made of an ordre of astates and degrees,

---

[1] *Orchestra* (1596), ed. R. S. Lambert (Stanton Press), pp. 11–12.

and, by reason thereof, conteineth in it a perfect harmony : whiche he shall afterwarde more perfectly understande, whan he shall happen to rede the bokes of Plato, and Aristotle, of publike weales : wherein be written diuers examples of musike and geometrye.   In this fourme may a wise and circumspecte tutor adapte the pleasant science of musike to a necessary and laudable purpose.[1]

Personal character, too, was a harmony of varied qualities, and there were private as well as public reasons why every gentleman should learn music, which maintained the contradictory parts of the personality in ordered relationship and so stimulated to virtuous action and serene contemplation.

For I shall enter [says the Count in Castiglione's *Courtyer*] in a large sea of the praise of Musicke, and call to rehearsall how much it hath alwaies beene renowned among them of olde time, and counted a holy matter : and how it hath beene the opinion of most wise Philosophers, that the worlde is made of musike, and the heavens in their moving make a melodie, and our soule is framed after the verie same sort and therefore lifteth up it selfe, and (as it were) reviveth the vertues and force of it selfe with Musicke. . . .   And I remember I have understoode that Plato and Aristotle will have a man that is wel brought up, to be also a Musition : and declare with infinite reasons the force of musicke to bee to very great purpose in us, and for many causes (that should be too long to rehearse) ought necessarily to be learned from a mans childhood, not onely for the superficiall melodie that is heard, but to be sufficient to bring into us a new habite that is good, and a custome inclining to vertue, which maketh the minde more apt to the conceiving of felicitie, even as bodely exercise maketh the bodie more lustie, and not onely hurteth not civil matters and warrelike affaires, but is a great stay to them.[2]

Fortified by such counsels, the nobility of the sixteenth century devoted itself to music with more fervour than any class at any other time in English history.   It is true that doubts were expressed about excessive attention to the arts.   Ascham feared ' moch Musick marreth mens maners '.[3]   He and Elyot both emphasized that a gentleman must not try to become a really skilled performer on instruments : he must remember that affairs claimed first notice. But good taste in music was everywhere approved, and patronage of composers and performers by the great was regarded as an obligation of gentility.   We cannot take the ideal for the actual, but the existence of such a standard, backed by philosophical and

---

[1] *The Boke Named the Governour,* Everyman ed., p. 28.
[2] Trans. Sir Thomas Hoby, Everyman ed., pp. 75–6.
[3] *The Scholemaster* (1570), The First Booke, ed. J. E. B. Mayor, p. 82.

educational precept, must have meant that music occupied a higher
place in the consideration of educated Elizabethans than it did
among educated people of later generations. It was no small
incentive to be taught

> The man that hath no music in himself,
> Nor is not moved with concord of sweet sounds,
> Is fit for treasons, stratagems, and spoils. [1]

The complete gentleman of the courtesy books is not only a man
of affairs, a soldier, and a courtier, but capable of intelligent criticism
of literature and music. The young lady of the period must sing
and play the lute or virginals. So unanimous an opinion about
the desirability of music in a complete education must mean that
many educated people tried to learn it. To be fashionable one
had to be musical. Gallants and dandies affected an interest in
music along with the other outward marks of breeding. Jonson's
Fastidious Brisk is always drawing attention to his fine ear, and
when he visits his mistress he declares her bass viol out of tune
merely to impress her with his acute sense of pitch.[2] Even such
affectation presupposes a general standard of musical taste and
performance.

The court set a good example. It had a tradition of musical
patronage. The Chapel Royal from an early date won the admira-
tion of all foreign visitors. Henry VI, himself a distinguished
composer, had gathered round him a group of able musicians.
Henry VII, although inclined to parsimony, did not stint his chapel,
and Henry VIII, again a composer and performer himself, maintained a large staff of secular musicians in his household. He
played the lute well, and sang his part at sight, and he saw that
his children were taught music early. Mary was presented to the
King of France as a player on the virginals when she was only
eleven, and Elizabeth impressed Sir James Melville by her performance on that instrument. The regular establishment of the
last Tudor sovereign included between sixty and seventy musicians,
organized in seven classes, and in addition an organist and player
on the virginals. The wind classes were recorders, flutes, hautboys,
and sackbuts ; the strings viols, violins, and lutes. The lutanists'
duties included singing, and they were of higher rank than the
rest, being often composers of their own songs as well as arrangers
of consort music.

The great houses emulated the court. Music was so necessary

[1] *Merchant of Venice*, V, i.
[2] *Every Man Out of his Humour*, III, iii.

a part of great state that Sir Francis Drake took with him on a voyage round the world a band of instrumentalists, in order to impress strange peoples with the splendour of English civilization. The Earl of Northumberland in 1512 kept a chapel establishment of ten men (increased by two in 1514) and six boys, the men taking it in turn to play the organ. For secular purposes he had his trumpeters and players on the lute, rebec, and tabret.[1]   No doubt the Reformation curtailed expenditure on private devotions ; but the secular musicians remained. Many a minor Count Orsino could call on his instrumentalists and singers to test whether music were the food of love. If the household did not retain plenty of musicians on its permanent staff, outside help was employed for special occasions.[2]   A troupe of players belonging to a nobleman would sometimes give its services to another mansion when its employer did not require it.[3]   Besides playing, there was also a certain amount of teaching to be done. By serving as pages young gentlemen learned courtly behaviour, and knowledge of music was an important part of such training.[4]   Wealthier and more cultured homes, therefore, often employed not only performers but directors of music, who arranged entertainments and taught the children. Many great Elizabethan composers earned a living in this way. John Dowland was for a time lutanist to Lord Howard de Walden. The great madrigal com-

---

[1] *Northumberland Household Book*, ed. Percy, p. 47.

[2] In the Belvoir Castle accounts, for instance, are entries such as : ' Given, 23rd. October, 1620, to the musicq *per* Mr Ellis, when the Lord Marquis Buckingham, Marcus Hambleton, Lord Crumbwell and others weire at Belvoir, x *s*.' (*MSS. at Belvoir Castle*, Hist. MSS. Comm., IV, 522).

[3] In the same accounts : ' Geven, the xvij*te* Januarie, 1591, to iiij meusisons, beinge my Lord Welowbie men, by my Ladys com., ij *s*.

' Geven, the, xv*te* Marche, 1590, to Sir Thomas Stanope his musisons, iij *s*. iiij *d*.

' Geven, the xxv*te* Maye, 1591 to my Lord Comberland musisons, by my Ladys com, iij *s*. iiij *d*.

' Geven, the xxv*te* Maye, 1591, to Sir Thomas Stanope his musisions, by my Ladys com, vj *s*.

' Geven, the xj*th* day of Aprill, 1594, to Sir Henry Cavndyge musitians iij *s*. iiij *d*.

' Geven the same tyme [i.e. 3 Sept., 1594], unto my Lord Wyllobees musicians bein at Belvoire tow dayes, by my Ladyes commandement, xl *s*.' (ib., IV, 399, 400, 407).

[4] In the same accounts (1557–8) : ' Gyvyn to Weston for the teachyng of Rycherd, my Lade page, to playe on the Lute, x *s*. . . .   Apryll xxvj—Payde to Weston for teachyng my Lordes page to playe on the lute, x *s*.' (ib., IV, 381, 383).

poser, John Wilbye, for many years served the Kytson family at Hengreave Hall, and there are extant comparatively full details of the provision for music there. Two inventories, taken in 1602–3 and in 1621, show an impressive stock of instruments and part-books.[1] There is perhaps some reason to suppose that the Kytsons were an exceptionally musical family; but many other houses might have possessed similar facilities on a smaller scale. Although it would be foolish to give the impression that every Elizabethan family was a centre of sweetness and light, there is plenty of evidence that the new nobility of the sixteenth century, aping the Italian princelets in the splendour of their new residences, were anxious to include culture as part of their magnificence; and, in an age which symbolized important functions by richness of adornment and elaborate ceremonial, a large musical establishment was a natural expression of their concern for the values of civilized life.

This aristocratic patronage of music was not a new thing. Nobility had involved the encouragement of minstrelsy throughout the middle ages. The replacement of the wild medieval warlords by a more civilized landed gentry, however, meant a rise in the status of the secular musician and a greater chance for sophisticated music to be produced. The despoilers of the monasteries deflected polyphonic ingenuity from sacred to secular composition. Energies that had been bound to the service of the Church were released for the satisfaction of the usurping power. The madrigal succeeded the motet.

There was, moreover, a widening public apart from the aristocracy. A middle class of tradesmen and yeomen was beginning to influence the cultural life of the nation, as it was beginning to make itself felt politically through the Puritan movement. The development of printing conferred on this class the opportunity of imitating the cultural standards of its social superiors. The reading public was as yet too small for publishers to specialize the appeal of their books. Plays, poems, pamphlets, sermons, romances, and music were all directed at the same heterogeneous mass of readers, for to succeed books had to interest a large proportion of the limited literate classes. The very fact that a considerable number of musical volumes could be printed is evidence of a widespread demand for music. The great houses no doubt appreciated the convenience of print; but they did not depend on the publishers for the means of making music. It was the

[1] Reproduced by E. H. Fellowes, *The English Madrigal*, pp. 12–13.

literate class below them that benefited most.   Between 1590 and
1620 some forty volumes of madrigals alone were issued from the
press.   This is only a portion of the total musical output of the
three decades, but it is significant.   We have no information as
to the sales of any of the volumes ; we can only assume that
philanthropy did not maintain the flow of new editions.   Yet the
madrigal was not native to England, and it never became in any
sense a popular form of music.   We can only conclude that there
was a very general love of singing.   Instrumental ability was
widely diffused too ; but the English genius has always excelled
at vocal music, and madrigal volumes could only have been used
by people who liked singing together quite difficult music.   It
must be remembered that there were no public concerts until the
end of the seventeenth century.   Madrigals are for performers,
not listeners ; they are for the home, not for the public hall.   If
the Elizabethans bought volumes of madrigals, it must have been
because a large number of them sang in the family circle.[1]   ' 'Tis
a singing age,' comments one of the characters in a play by Fletcher ;
and we must agree that it seems to have been so.

Because of this general fondness for part-singing, an educated
person was expected to read a part at sight and join in the music-
making of any family he happened to be visiting.   The expectation
is amusingly illustrated by the well-known opening of Morley's
Plaine and Easie Introduction to Practicall Musicke (1597).   It describes
how a gentleman went out to supper one evening with his friend,
Sophobulus.

Among the rest of the guests, by chance, master *Aphron* came
thither also, who falling to discourse of Musicke, was in an argument
so quickly taken up and hotly pursued by *Eudoxus* and *Calergus*, two
kinsmen of *Sophobulus*, as in his owne arte he was overthrowne.   But
he still sticking to his opinion, the gentlemen requested mee to examine
his reasons and confute them.   But I refusing and pretending ignorance,
the whole companie condemned mee of discurtesie, being fully perswaded
that I had been as skilful in that art, as they tooke mee to be learned in
others.   But supper being ended, and Musicke bookes, according to the
custome being brought to the table : the mistresse of the house presented
mee with a part, earnestly requesting mee to sing.   But when, after
many excuses, I protested unfainedly that I could not : everie one began
to wonder.   Yea, some whispered to others, demanding how I was
brought up.[2]

---

[1] In Italy madrigals were sometimes performed by trained singers, much as
in a modern concert ; but there is no evidence that this was common in England.
[2] *Plaine and Easie Introduction*, p. 1.

Now Morley, as a music teacher, undoubtedly had something to sell, and it was in his interest to make it appear socially desirable. But he would scarcely have inferred a standard of proficiency wildly beyond contemporary realities. We are not dependent on his evidence alone. We know, for instance, that before any English madrigals were published a group of gentlemen used to meet daily at the house of Nicholas Yonge, a City merchant, to practise singing Italian madrigals. This group included several foreigners as well as Englishmen, and Yonge acted as importer for them of whatever Italian music he could gather. The Englishmen evidently enjoyed the tunefulness of the music, but found difficulty in joining in the singing, unless they knew the language. The difficulty in procuring good English songs was keenly felt, and Yonge tried to gather as many of them as he could. He eventually secured a collection of translations, and these he published in 1588 under the title *Musica Transalpina*. His dedication gives a very interesting account of the origin of his venture and of the music meetings that took place at his house.

Right honourable, since I first began to keepe house in this Citie, it hath beene no small comfort unto mee, that a great number of Gentlemen and Merchants of good accompt (as well of this realme as of forreine nations) have taken in good part such entertainment of pleasure, as my poore abilitie was able to affoord them, both by the exercise of Musicke daily used in my house, and by furnishing them with Bookes of that kinde yeerely sent me out of Italy and other places, which beeing for the most part Italian Songs, are for sweetness of Aire, verie well liked of all, but most in account with them that understand that language. As for the rest, they doe either not sing them at all, or at the least with little delight. And albeit there be some English songs lately set forth by a great Maister of Musicke, which for skill and sweetness may content the most curious : yet because they are not many in number, men delighted with varietie, have wished more of the same sort. For which cause chiefly I endeavoured to get into my hands all such English Songs as were praise worthie, and amongst others, I had the hap to find in the hands of some of my good friends, certaine Italian Madrigales translated most of them fiue yeeres agoe by a Gentleman for his private delight, (as not long before certaine Napolitans had been englished by a very honourable personage, and now a Councellour of estate, whereof I have seene some, but never possessed any). And finding the same to be singulerly well liked, not onely of those for whose cause I gathered them, but of many skilfull Gentlemen and other great Musiciens, who affirmed the accent of the words to be well mainteined, the descant not hindred (though some fewe notes altered), and in everie place the due decorum kept : I was so bolde (beeing well acquainted with the Gentleman) as to entreate the rest, who willingly gave me such as he had (for of some he kept no Copies), and also some other more lately done at the request of his particular friends.   Now when the same were seene to arise to a iust number, sufficient to furnish a great set of Books, divers of my friends aforesaid, required with great instance to have them printed, whereunto I was as willing as the rest, but could never obtaine the Gentlemans consent, though I sought it by many great meanes. . . . Wherefore I kept them (or the most of them) for a long time by mee, not presuming to put my sickle in an other mans corne, till such time as I heard, that the same beeing dispersed into many mens hands, were by some persons altogether unknowen to the owner, like to be published in print.   Which made mee aduenture to set this worke in hande, he beeing neither privie nor present, nor so near this as by any reasonable meanes I could giue him notice.

It is clear, then, that people like Yonge and his friends had a strong love of singing, and were casting round for material before the London printers had realised the market waiting for them.

Yonge's circle met specifically for the enjoyment of music, but many comfortable citizens preferred family music.   A French schoolmaster describes an evening in such a household, and the other dialogues in his book make it clear that he is trying to depict a normal day in an average home.   The family is entertaining a guest, and after supper the host says :

Roland, shall we have a song ?
ROLAND : Yea sir : where bee your bookes of musick ? for they bee the best corrected.
FATHER : They bee in my chest : Katherin take the key of my closet, you shall find them in a little til at the left hand.

(Katherine fetches the songs)

behold, ther bee faire songes at fouer partes.
ROLAND : Who shall singe with me ?
FATHER : You shall have companie enough : David shall make the base : John the tenor : and James the treble.   Begine : James, take your tune : go to : for what do you tarie ?
JAMES : I have but a rest.
FATHER : Roland, drink afore you begine, you will sing with a better corage.
ROLAND : It is wel said : geve me some white wine : that will cause me to sing clearer. . . .   I should not be a singing man except I could drink well . . . and as I perceave, you cannot tell the songe which beginneth I had rather go without hosen than forbeare drinkyng.
GUEST : I praye thee let us have it.
ROLAND : With all my harte.

GUEST : Truelie he is a merie fellowe. . . .

FATHER : . . . you are not merie : this musick doth not make you merie.

GUEST : Yes forsooth : truelie I take a great delight in it.

ANOTHER GUEST : There is a good song : I do marvell who hath made it.

FATHER : It is the maister of the children of the Queenes Chapel.

GUEST : What is his name ?

FATHER : Maister Edwards.

GUEST : I heard saie that he was dead.

ANOTHER GUEST : It is alreadi a good while ago : ther are at the least five yeers and a half.

FATHER : Truelie it is a pitie : he was a man of a good wit, and a good poete : and a great player of playes.[1]

No songs by Richard Edwards are known to have been printed,[2] and the reference to correcting copies seems to imply that the family had compiled its own part-books. The volume just quoted was published in 1573, fifteen years before the first printed collection of English contrapuntal music was issued. Part-singing was obviously widespread, and there was a demand for part-songs that was satisfied only by the large production of English madrigals round the turn of the century.

The desire of the middle classes for musical education found expression even in an educational system designed mainly for the study of the classics. It is true that the Reformation threatened the medieval song-schools, in which boys had learned to intone the services of the cathedrals and collegiate churches. But an attempt was made to save them. The Queen's Injunctions of 1559 command that

no alteration must be made in the payments of singers, but that it be permitted at the beginning of prayers, morning or evening, to sing a hymn or such like song, in the best melody or music, as long as the words be distinguishable.[3]

Music had long formed part of the Quadrivium, though it too often meant a rather dull theoretical instruction. Many Renaissance schoolmasters seem to have made it more practical and more closely related to contemporary taste. Mulcaster, the famous headmaster of the Merchant Taylors' School, regarded it as one of the four important branches of elementary training.

[1] C. Holyband, *The French Schoole-maister* (1573), reproduced in M. St. Clare Byrne, *The Elizabethan Home*, pp. 51–4.

[2] See pp. 55–6.

[3] Foster Watson, *The English Grammar Schools to 1660*, p. 206.

This therefore shall suffice now, that the children are to be trained up in the Elementarie schoole, for the helping forward of the abilities of the mind, in these fower things, as commaunded us by choice and commended by custome.   Reading, to receive that which is bequeathed us by other, and to serve our memorie with that which is best for us. Writing to do the like thereby for others, which other have done for us, by writing those thinges which we daily use : but most of al to do most for ourselves : Drawing to be a directour to sense, a delite to sight, and an ornament to his objectes.   Musick by the instrument, besides the skill which must still encrease, in forme of exercise to get the use of our small ioyntes, before they be knitte, to have them the nimbler, and to put Musicianes in minde, that they be no brawlers, least by some swash of a sword, they chaunce to lease a iointe, an irrecoverable iewell unadvisedly cast away.   Musick by the voice, besides her cunning also, by the way of phisick, to sprede the voice instrumentes within the bodie, while they be yet but young.   As both the kindes of Musick for much profit, and more pleasure, which is not voide of profit in her continuing kinde.[1]

At his own school Mulcaster taught the music himself.   Sir James Whitelocke, the judge, who left the school in 1588, says in his *Liber Familicus* :

I was brought up at school under Mr Mulcaster in the famous school of the Merchant Taylors in London, where I continued until I was well instructed in the Hebrew, Greek, and Latin tongues.   His care was also to increase my skill in music, in which I was brought up by daily exercise in it, as well in singing as in playing upon instruments : and yearly he presented some plays to the Court, in which his scholars only were actors, and I one among them ; and by that means he taught them good behaviour and audacity.[2]

Other schools taught music as a regular part of the curriculum. Westminster School, from about 1560 onwards, devoted an hour a week to it, the Choirmaster being in charge, and in addition the boys sang in the morning service.   Rivington Grammar School arranged that ' some hour of the day boys are to learn to sing and to write '.   Dulwich School Statutes of 1626 stipulate that

the music masters of the said College for the time shall teach and instruct in song and music freely all persons who are in the said college at the master or warden's appointment and for any other scholars which desire to learn song or music they shall receive such rewards as the master or warden for the time being shall appoint, the benefits or any other accruing

---

[1] *Positions*, ed. Quick, p. 39.
[2] Camden Soc. Pub., LXX, 12.

to the two said music masters shall be equally divided between them, the charge of strings, pens, ink and paper first deducted.[1]

The foundation deeds of Christ's Hospital (1552) provide for a teacher of ' prick-song ' at the annual fee of £2 13s. 4d. (it was only a part-time appointment), and in 1587 John Howes justifies the inclusion of music in the curriculum, saying :

> I also thinck it convenient that the children should learne to singe, to play uppon all sorts of instruments, as to sounde the trumpett, the cornett, the recorder or the flute, to play uppon shagbotts, shalmes, and all other instruments that are to be plaid uppon, either with winde or finger, bycause nature yelds her severall gifts and there is an aptness of conceavinge in some more than in other some, and yett every child apt to learne the one or the other, those qualities cannot be greatly chargeable bycause they are the gifts of God in nature, and they are qualities that every honest minde taketh great pleasure and delight in, and no doubt if the children be well taught, plyde, and followed it wil be a redy meane to preferre a number of them haveing theis quallities.[2]

The last sentence reminds us that Christ's Hospital tried to place its children as apprentices and servants. That music should be a recommendation in a domestic worker may surprise us ; but the Elizabethan apprentice or servant lived as a member of the family. Nor was the industrial worker much different. Factories were unknown. Cottage industry was common, and in larger enterprises master and employees worked together. Each apprentice hoped one day to be a journeyman, and each journeyman a master, working for himself in his own house or workshop. Servants and apprentices, therefore, were admitted to familiarity strange in the opinion of later times. If they had some of the restrictions of children, they had also some of the privileges. A musical family would value a servant who could join in the music-making. Among the nobility there was great competition for boys with good treble voices, and ability to accompany themselves on the lute was an added recommendation. Such boys were prized, and proprietary rights to their services were respected by other potential employers. Thus we find Sir Percival Hart writing to Sir Robert Cecil to tell him of a boy formerly in the latter's service : it would not do to engage him without Cecil's consent.

> Last night [he writes] there came to my house from Gravesend and, as I learn, from him, out of the Low Countries, one Henry Philipps,

---

[1] Foster Watson, op. cit., pp. 214–15.
[2] ib., p. 214.

who hearing what disposition I bear to music, tendered his service to me, which I was willing to entertain, as well in regard of his skill as for the satisfying of my own desire unto music.   But afterwards, learning that he lately apertained to your Honour, I have respited the receiving of him to my service till I may understand how it stands with your good liking.

Lullingham in Kent, 14 December, 1598.[1]

A likely boy might be given to a new patron as a token of friendship, or bequeathed like other property.   In a letter dated 24 February 1595–6, Lord Burgh offers Sir Robert Cecil the choice of any one of four boys he may select, adding : ' The four, with all his instruments, were all by my worthy companion bequeathed me ; choose freely as where your commandments have interest.' [2] To catch the notice of such patrons as Cecil was to ensure a good start in some walk of life when the voice broke.   But even a boy not quite so fortunate as this might find a middle-class family glad to have him for his voice, and to be able to play an instrument would be a qualification not lightly weighed.   While the grandee wanted somebody to sing to him in his hours of privacy, the middle-class household would rather seek somebody who could join in the family consort or part-singing.   Pepys has recorded his satisfaction at having a body of servants able to bear their parts with instruments, and several times he pictures family and servants joining in a consort.

The Elizabethans were firmly convinced that

> Such servants are often most painful and good,
> That sing at their labour, as birds in a wood.[3]

Of course, singing at work depends partly on the kind of work one has to do.   Monotonous repetition tasks in a noisy factory do not encourage singing ; and we should be astonished to hear a bank-clerk burst into melody.   Most Elizabethans, though they worked long hours, often under hard conditions, enjoyed varied tasks that required skill and often craftsmanship and that allowed individuality.   The lack of mechanical contrivances also meant there was a good deal of sheer hard physical effort required, and rhythmical song often made this less onerous.   In just such circumstances were many fine sea shanties born.

The proximity of masters and servants, the mingling of classes

---

[1] *MSS. at Hatfield House*, Hist. MSS. Comm., VIII, 498.
[2] ib., VI, 68.
[3] Tusser, *A Hundreth good Points of Husbandrie* (1557), ed. Dorothy Hartley, p. 168.

in the daily duties of life, kept different levels of taste and education
in contact and created a vast store of ' neat and spruce ayres ' sung
and whistled by all manner of people.   The quality of genuine
popular music that has come down from that period is amazingly
high.   It argues a fine tradition constantly enriched.   A brief study
of it shows that the vast output of art music in the sixteenth century
was a natural culmination of a deep-set habit.   People of all classes
sang readily to amuse themselves and sweeten their labours.

And hence it is that manual labourers, and Mechanical Artificers of
all sorts keepe such a chaunting and singing in their shoppes, the tailor
on his bulk, the shomaker at his last, the mason at his wall, the shipboy
at his oar, the tinker at his pan, and the tiler on the housetop.[1]

Street hawkers had their characteristic cries, and pleasant snatches
of tune most of them were.   The watchman called the hours of
the night with a tuneful phrase.   Carmen's horses responded to
a well-known whistle.   Milkmaids coaxed milk from the cow
with rhythmical ditties.   We feel that Deloney is not greatly
exaggerating the standards of cobblers when he makes them resolve
that

what Iourney-man so-euer he be hereafter, that cannot handle his Sword
and Buckler, his long sword or a Quarterstaffe, sound the Trumpet,
or play upon the Flute, and bear his part in a three mans song, and
readily reckon up his tools in Rime . . . shall forfeit and pay a pottle
of Wine.[2]

There was, in fact, a tremendous store of really popular music ;
it was a genuine national heritage.   Sophisticated people might
despise the words many humble labourers sang, but the tunes
were everybody's, as common to all the inhabitants of the island
as the English language itself.   When the most learned composers
played the virginals or the lute for aristocratic audiences they
did not disdain to decorate and comment on the tunes of the streets.
If there is anything distinctively English in their own compositions,
it is due to their absorption of a long tradition of popular discrim-
ination.

Though there was no commercial organization of music similar
to the modern concert system, Elizabethans did not lack professional
performers to assist their own efforts.   The retainers of great
personages had their humbler counterparts.   Each town of importance had its official waits.   The custom had originated in the
middle ages with the keeping of a watchman to sing out the hours

[1] John Case, *Praise of Musicke* (1588), p. 44.
[2] Deloney's *Works*, ed. Mann, p. 89.

of the night.   A horn or trumpet call drew attention to his message. His duties were widened to include attendance on other civic occasions.   Gradually other instrumentalists were added, and a small band of waits attended the mayor at important functions. Leicester had its trumpeter in 1314, and records of official waits have been found at Exeter in 1396–7, at Norwich in 1408, at Salisbury in 1409, at Coventry in 1423, at Beverley in 1423–4, at Hull in 1429–30, and at Southampton in 1433.   These records, though the earliest extant, do not indicate the real antiquity of the profession, for at Norwich ' William de Devenschyre le Wayte ' is mentioned as early as 1288.   By the sixteenth century the waits' duties had increased to attendance on the mayor on the day of his election, accompanying him to civic church services, proclaiming accessions, riding the bounds once a year and performing at the reception of celebrities.   Will Kemp praises the Norwich waits, who assisted in the civic welcome at the end of his morris dance from London :

Such Waytes (under Benedicite be it spoken) few Cities in our Realme haue the like, none better.   Who, besides their excellency in wind instruments, their rare cunning on the Vyoll, and Violin : theyr voices be admirable, euerie one of them able to serve in any Cathedrall Church in Christendoome for Quiristers.[1]

In some towns open-air concerts became part of the waits' occupation.   At Norwich, for example, they were permitted to play on the leads of the Guildhall on Sunday and other Holy Nights between 7 and 8, though first plague and then improper conduct among the crowd led to the temporary withdrawal of the permission. To supplement their fees they sometimes practised other trades, and many taught music.   The local country mansions found them useful in providing occasional concerts and playing at special festivities.[2]

Apart from the official waits, there were numerous other bands of professionals always available for private merrymaking.   These ' noises ' of fiddlers frequented taverns, playing popular songs and dances for a small fee.   Gosson complains in 1579 that

London is so full of vnprofitable Pipers and Fidlers, that a man can no soner enter a tauerne, but two or three caste of them hang at his heeles, to giue him a daunce before he departe.[3]

---

[1] *Kemps nine daies wonder* (1600), p. 24.

[2] The Belvoïr Castle accounts record visits of the waits of Newark in 1590, those of Doncaster in 1591, and those of Pontefract in 1593.   (*MSS. at Belvoir Castle*, IV, 399, 407.)

[3] *An Apologie of the Schoole of Abuse*, ed. Arber, p. 70.

It was a regular part of the social relaxation to be found in the companionable atmosphere of the inn. A traveller had no need to feel lonely, for

while he eates, if he have company especially, he shall be offered musick, which he may freely take or refuse, and if he be solitary, the Musitians will give him the good day with Musicke in the morning.[1]

Deloney describes how a widow and an old man visit an inn.

They had not sitten long, but in comes a noise of Musitians in tawny coates, who (putting off their caps) asked if they would haue any musicke. The Widow answered no, they were merry enough.

Tut, (quoth the old man) let vs heare goode fellowes what you can doe, and play mee *The beginning of the World*.[2]

Theatre players must have been more highly regarded than ordinary fiddlers : they 'scorned to come to a Taverne under twentie shillings salary for two hours'.[3] 'Fiddler' became something of a term of contempt ; yet no merrymaking would have been complete without the poor itinerant fiddler. Better-class patrons could engage them to help a love affair : Valentine has a noise of musicians to serenade Silvia in *Two Gentlemen of Verona*. At festive times the houses of the wealthy stood open to them, and they received the 'usuall Christmas entertainment of Musitians, a black Iack of Beere, and a Christmas Pye'.[4]

There were, too, innumerable fêtes and dances at which fiddlers were welcome. The Englishman of the sixteenth century was a countryman at heart, as surely as the modern Englishman is a townsman. The Londoner needed only to take a short walk and he was out in the open fields. Psychologically he was little different from the inhabitant of a country town, and he maintained all the seasonal celebrations. May-day and harvest time had their songs and dances and Christmas its Lords of Misrule. The Queen herself went maying at Highgate in 1601, and at Lewisham in 1602. Freedom from work at any part of the year meant for the countryman an opportunity to dance on the village green.

Sunday he esteemes a day to make merry in, and thinkes a Bagpipe as essentiall to it as Evening-Prayer where he walkes very solemnly after the service with his hands coupled behinde him and censures the dauncing of his parish.[5]

---

[1] *Fynes Morysons Itinerary* (1617), Pt. IV.
[2] op. cit., p. 10.
[3] *The Actors Remonstrance* (1643).
[4] *Return from Parnassus* (1606), fol. H2.
[5] Earle, *Microcosmographie* (1628), ed. G. Murphy, p. 36.

The townsman rejoiced in the same pastimes.

The youths of this city [says Stow of London], also have used on holy days after evening prayer, at their masters' doors, to exercise their wasters and bucklers ; and the maidens, one of them playing on a timbrel, in sight of their masters and dames, to dance for garlands hung athwart the street.[1]

Disturbances at these gatherings led to their temporary suspension about the time Stow wrote, but they are sanctioned for Sundays in James I's Book of Sports, and Baxter, looking back on his youth, recalls how, in the middle of the seventeenth century,

We could not, on the Lord's Day, either read a chapter, or pray, or sing a psalm, or catechise, or instruct a servant, but with the noise of pipe and tabor continually in our ears.[2]

Dancing was, indeed, a national passion which even Puritanism did not eradicate. Queen Elizabeth was an enthusiastic dancer, and the Spanish ambassador sarcastically reported that in the Twelfth Night revels of 1599 ' the head of the Church of England and Ireland was to be seen in her old age dancing three or four galliards '.[3] The courtier prided himself on his agility and grace in the pavan and galliard, and the countryman was no less attached to his humbler measures.

The amusements of all classes were thus supplied with music. For our present purpose it is more pertinent to notice that for the great mass of the people music served also many of the purposes of modern reading matter. Only a fraction of the population could read, and even to them reading was scarcely the constant employment of spare time, as it is to many to-day. The illiterate, however, possessed a vast oral literature, and most of it was sung. The popular journalism of the day was set to popular tunes of the kind we have just been discussing. Pamphlets did the work of higher journalism only. Publishers had already hit on the idea of reaching the ordinary public by means of roughly produced sheets covered with black-letter type. This crude literature was hawked round fairs and places of resort by despised ballad-sellers. The vigour of the writing and the sensationalism of the contents won a great response among the illiterate, despite the scorn of educated people. But the printers did not rely on country clowns' reading the ballads. The seller usually

[1] *Survey*, Everyman ed., p. 87.
[2] *Divine Appointment*, quoted by P. Scholes, *The Puritans and Music*, p. 304.
[3] *Calendar of Letters and Papers in the Archives of Simancas*, IV, 650.

carried a crowd or fiddle and sang the verses to a well-known tune, which they had been designed to fit.   One copy with the tune marked on the top would supply a large number of people with a song and an account of a contemporary sensation at the same time, if they could procure someone to decipher the text in the first instance.   A good ballad-seller could reel off ' forty yards of ballad ' [1] and sing ' several tunes faster than you'll tell money '.[2] He studied his audience and had something for everybody.

He hath songs for man or woman of all sizes ; no milliner can so fit his customers with gloves : he has the prettiest love-songs for maids ; so without bawdry, which is strange ; with such delicate burdens of *dildos* and *fadings, jump her and thump her* ; and where some stretch-mouth'd rascal would, as it were, mean mischief, and break a foul gap into the matter, he makes the maid to answer, *Whoop, do me no harm, good man* ; puts him off, slights him, with *Whoop, do me no harm, good man.*[2]

It was a genuine form of early popular journalism, with all the vigour and all the vices inseparable ever since from that public utility.   Since it was oral, rime assisted the memory, and rime almost inevitably involved a tune, for only with a tune was poetic form observable by the illiterate.   The rest of their literature, legend, and anecdote in prose, was appreciated for its dramatic, narrative, and humorous qualities, but poetic form at such a level of civilization depends on the regular rhythm of a tune or dance. This is only another way of saying that folk-song was the poetry of the mass of the people.   Folk-songs were not only being widely sung but were all the time being created, not only then but long afterwards.   The printed ballads probably penetrated the rural areas immediately round towns.   Elsewhere an older form of art was the only literature of the people.   Now the folk-singer cannot separate in his mind the words and the tune of his song.   The versification is part of the form of the tune ; on the other hand, the sentiment of the words, on which he chiefly concentrates his attention in singing, produces a hundred nuances in the performance. Take away the tune and the singer will not be certain that his text has any poetic form at all.   The Chadwicks quote an amusing experience of a Russian collector.   He got a folk-singer to recite a song without its music, but the result was always prose.   Only when singing did the man make little adaptations to convert it into metre.[3]

[1] Jonson, *Pleasure Reconciled to Virtue.*   [2] *Winter's Tale,* IV, iii.
[3] *The Growth of Literature,* II, 21–2.

To call the reader's attention to this peculiarity of folk-art will sufficiently emphasize an important point to be kept in mind in any investigation of Elizabethan poetry. The study of past literature must be accompanied by a realization of the ways in which the experience of its writers and the expectations of its readers differed from ours. We are concerned here with the part music played in creating that experience and that expectation. The Elizabethan poet could not avoid contact with music. We have tried to sketch the manner in which the lives of all classes were filled with music. Interest in it was not the concern of specialists. Social life was so conducted that everybody had a chance not only of hearing music but of taking part in it by singing, playing, or dancing. Active rather than passive knowledge of it is perhaps the most significant characteristic compared with modern modes of musical appreciation. Even whistling at work gives a rather different musical outlook from sitting comfortably in the Albert Hall while other people play, and dancers notoriously value music in a way foreign to music critics in arm-chairs ; indeed, it is not easy to account for the popularity of modern dance-bands in any other way. The mere range of technical terms in common use in Elizabethan times is astonishing to a modern reader. Puns on them are very common in the Elizabethan drama, and we must conclude that the audiences saw the point of them, else the dramatist would gain little and actors would complain they could not raise a laugh with their parts. Such a music-laden atmosphere must be taken into account in studying Elizabethan poetry. But it is even more important to remember how closely associated with music was the literature of the ordinary people. Poetry to them meant song almost exclusively. The conditions of folk-art are unconscious but most potent determinants of the character of all Elizabethan literature. It was no more possible for a writer to escape their influence than for a modern writer to be uninfluenced by broadcasting and the cinema.

It is clear, then, that the relations between literature and music in the sixteenth century are one aspect of a certain stage in the development of civilization. The feudal society of the middle ages had not entirely been transformed into a modern economy ; agriculture was still the staple industry of the country, and industrial organization was still very simple. Conditions were favourable for folk arts and crafts, and communication between different levels of artistic taste was assisted by the simplicity of the social structure. There was constant interchange between folk tradition and the art of the educated classes. The folk-singer's mental habits were therefore an important heritage, often unconscious, of all readers and writers of poetry. They were reinforced, as will presently be seen, by the fact that art-poetry itself had not long emerged from similar association with music, and still bore some traces of its former alliance. Printing was only a century old when Shakespeare conceived his plays. The difficulty of procuring manuscripts before printing became general involved a greater reliance on oral transmission than we find it easy to remember ; and there were many social conditions tending to perpetuate oral transmission right down to the seventeenth century. The emancipation of poetry from music is largely due to a development of the practice of reading rather than listening to poetry. Certain kinds of poetry were expected to be sung right down to the seventeenth century, even in cultured circles, and the mass of the people knew no other sort of poetry than song.

CHAPTER II

THE SINGING OF POETRY

ELIZABETHANS were quite aware that primitive poetry was sung. Explorers had told them of tribes with oral but not written poetry. Sidney, in defending the proposition that poetry is the oldest kind of learning, mentions that

> Even among the most barbarous and simple Indians where no writing is, yet haue they their Poets, who make and sing songs, which they call *Areytos*, both of theyr Auncestors deedes and praises of theyr Gods : a sufficient probabilitie that if euer learning come among them, it must be by hauing theyr hard, dull wits softned and sharpened with the sweete delights of Poetrie.[1]

Puttenham adduces the evidence of

> marchants and trauellers, who by late nauigations haue surveyed the whole world, and discouered large countries and strange peoples wild and sauage, affirming that the American, the Perusine, and the very Canniball do sing and also say their highest and holiest matters in certaine riming versicles, and not in prose, which proues also that our maner of vulgar Poesie is more ancient than the artificiall of the Greeks and Latines, ours comming by instinct of nature, which was before Art or obseruation, and vsed with the sauage and vnciuill, who were before all science or ciuilitie, euen as the naked by prioritie of time is before the clothed, and the ignorant before the learned.[2]

Even nearer home on the Continent travellers had probably found nations whose literatures were transmitted orally. The Chadwicks have pointed out that Russia and Yugo-Slavia in quite recent times have had no other native 'literature than prose sagas and long poems, the sagas being told and the poems sung from memory. Moreover, the Elizabethans knew that the Greeks had sung their poetry until historical times ; and this knowledge was to have consequences to which we shall have to refer several times in the course of the present study. The Homeric epics were originally sung to the harp by rhapsodists, though later recitation took the place of singing, the strong accents being marked by the fall of a staff.[3] Public recitations continued to be a feature of Roman literary life, despite the better organization of Roman book pro-

[1] Gregory Smith, *Elizabethan Critical Essays*, I, 153.
[2] ib., II, 10–11.
[3] R. C. Jebb, *Homer : an Introduction to the Iliad and the Odyssey*, p. 77.

duction.[1] The Greek lyric all through classical times remained
a genuine lyric—that is to say, it was literally sung to the lyre ;
and the ode was a choral composition. Writing among the Greeks
never entirely lost sight of the intention of its inventors ; it remained to some extent an aid to memory, not a substitute for the
disputations of the schools, the oratory of politicians, the discussions
of the forum, and the songs of poets. The read has so much
displaced the spoken or sung word to-day that we have to make
a conscious effort to remember the smallness of the Greek city
states, which made oral communication practicable.

The earliest English poetry was produced in much more
primitive conditions than those of Greece in classical times. We
need not consider the Celtic inhabitants of these islands, since they
have left no significant trace on the traditions of later literature,
their very language having been driven into the mountain recesses
of Wales and Scotland. They do not seem to have possessed a
written literature until they were conquered by the Romans, and,
as they were isolated from the Continent, they seem to have
relapsed into oral literature, their bards continuing to be important
members of the community until comparatively modern times.[2]
The Anglo-Saxons, from whom our language and earliest recorded
literature are derived, shared the general traditions of the Germanic
tribes. They had a method of writing, but there is no evidence
that the runic alphabet was ever used for literary purposes. Indeed,
it seems particularly unsuited for work of any length, and the
forms of the letters seem intended for carving on wood and stone.
But lays sung to the harp were of great antiquity among the
Germanic peoples. Tacitus says that songs were their only historical records,[3] and that Arminius, one of the Germans who
conquered a Roman army, was afterwards celebrated in song.[4]
One of the chief uses of poetry for some centuries was the preser-
vation of the deeds of heroes. Gensimund is described by Athalaric
as ' cantabilis ', meaning worthy of commemoration in verse ;
and some of the poems still extant would seem to owe a great
deal to the earlier lays sung about contemporary heroes. Thus
Paulus Diaconus tells us that the Gothic warrior Alboin survived

---

[1] Suetonius says that Virgil's *Georgics* and parts of the *Aeneid* were read before
Augustus.

[2] E. David, *Études Historiques sur la Poésie et la Musique dans la Cambraie.*

[3] [Carmina] ' quod unum apud illos memoriae et annalium genus est '
(*Germania*, 2).

[4] ' canitur adhuc barbaros apud gentes ' (*Annales*, II, 88).

in the songs of several Germanic tribes on account of his generosity :[1] he actually seems to have figured in Langobard epic and
is found in the English *Widsith*. Long after the Anglo-Saxons
had settled in England the Germanic peoples were still singing
popular lays about their ancestors.[2] There is no doubt that many
of the songs were of great antiquity and of obscure origin,[3] and
the Old English heroic poems reflect the acquaintance of our
ancestors with their earlier versions before separation from the
other Germanic tribes. Eulogies of heroes and funeral and wedding
songs, of all of which traces persist in England, would be among
the kinds of poetry sung. A good deal of the composition was
perhaps suggested by the circumstances of the moment : Gelimer,
the last king of the Vandals, begged the Herulian chief, who was
besieging him, to send him a harp, a loaf, and a sponge, that he
might bewail his misfortunes to the accompaniment of a mournful
tune played by a minstrel.[4] It is at least certain that a large repertoire of songs was being composed and sung among the Germanic
tribes long before any was written down, and when those educated
in the Roman tradition despised the bawling and strumming of
people they considered barbarians. Both Venantius Fortunatus
and Sidonius Apollinaris complain that the continuous sounds of
voice and harp prevent their creating Latin verse.[5] The usual

[1] ' Alboin vero ita praeclarum longe lateque nomen percrebuit, ut hactenus
etiam tam apud Baioariorum gentem quamque et Saxonem, sed, et alios eiusdem
linguae homines eius liberalitas et gloria bellorumque felicitas et virtus in
eorum carminibus celebretur ' (*Monumenta Germaniae Historica, Scriptores Rerum
Langobardicarum et Italicarum, Saec. VI-IX,* p. 70).
[2] Poeta Saxa : ' est quoque iam notum ; vulgaria carminia magnis laudibus
eius avos et proavos celebrant. Pippinos, Karolos, Hludiwicos, et Theodoricos,
et Carlomannos Hlothariosque canunt ' (*Monumenta Germaniae Historica,* I, 268).
[3] Jordanes, *de origine Getarum* (*Mon. Germ. Hist.*), c. 4 : ' in priscis eorum
carminibus pene storicu ritu in commune recolitur '.
[4] *De Bello Vandalico* (*Mon. Germ. Hist.*), II, 6.
[5] Venantius Fortunatus, *Prefatio* to Poems (*Mon. Germ. Hist. Auct.*, IV, 2) :
' Ubi me tantundem valebat raucum gemere quod cantare apud quos nihil
disparat aut stridor anseris aut canor oloris, sola saepe bombicans barbaros leudos
arpa relidens.'
Sidonius Apollinaris, *Carmina,* Bk. XII, ll. 1-11 :

> Quid me, etsi valeam, parare carmen
> Fescenninicolae iubes Diones
> inter crinigeras situm catervas
> et Germanica verba sustinentem,
> laudantem tetrico subinde vultu
> quod Burgundio cantat esculentus
> infundens acido comam butyro ?

accompaniment of Germanic poetry was the harp, just as the Roman instrument was the lyre and that of the Celts the crwth.[1] A eulogy is declared by Cassiodorus to be intended for performance by a 'citharoedus'—i.e. a player on the 'cithara' or harp.[2]

Old English heroic poetry refers to a time when poetry was sung in the king's hall after banquets. In Heorot, when Beowulf was entertained by Hrothgar

> þaer waes hearpan sweȝ

swutol sanȝ scopes, (ll. 89–90).

Whether *Beowulf* itself were ever sung to the harp is doubtful. In its present state it bears the marks of Christian adaptation. The conversion of England and the adoption of the Roman alphabet made possible a written literature. The Old English poetry we now possess may have been worked over by monkish scribes and deposited in monastery libraries. What is certain is that if heroic poetry in its present form ever reached a lay audience it must have done so by the old method of recitation to the harp, for there is no evidence that reading ever became widespread among the laity. After the Danish invasions literacy declined even among the clergy, and Alfred's educational plans were intended to touch only a small section of the secular population.[3] Singing to the harp certainly continued throughout the Saxon period. Bede describes how Caedmon used to take part in social gatherings where the harp was passed round and each member of the company entertained the rest with a poem,[4] and Bede himself is said by Cuthbert to have been 'skilled in our songs' ('erat doctus in nostris carminibus').[5] Alfred loved the old songs, and memorized them and had them taught in his schools.[6] He is to be compared with Charlemagne, who had old Germanic

---

> vis dicam tibi quid poema frangat?
> ex hoc barbaricis abacta plectris
> spernit senipedem stilum Thalia
> ex quo senipedes videt patronos.

[1] V. Fortunatus, *Carmina*, VII, 8, ll. 63–4 :

> Romanus lyra, plaudat tibi barbarus harpa,
> Graecus Achilliaca, crotta Britanna canat.

[2] *Variarum Epistolarum Lib. II*, 40, 41.
[3] Preface to *Cura Pastoralis*.   [4] Ecclesiastical History, 4. 24.
[5] Migne, *Patrologia Latina*, 90. 40.
[6] Asser, Life of Alfred (*Mon. Hist. Brit.*), 473, 486.

lays sung to him at table and written out for the benefit of posterity.[1] That this was necessary is a clear sign that the old Germanic songs were still transmitted orally to the accompaniment of the harp. Dunstan (924–88) often made ten-stringed psalteries, and used to entertain Edmund, Alfred's grandson, with the harp and timpan. The timpan was an Irish stringed instrument; the English had ample opportunity of hearing Celtic music. Northumbrian students were sent to the Irish schools at Iona, Lismore, and Clonard; and Oswald, Oswy, and Aldfrith were all educated at Iona. Now music was very widely cultivated in Wales, and Giraldus Cambrensis declared the Irish the best musicians in the world.[2]   Contact with Celtic bards must have stimulated English minstrelsy, though we have no reason to suppose it needed stimulation.   Even if versions of heathen poetry now found in manuscripts were read, the great mass of English poetry must still have circulated by oral transmission. Epic probably came to be declaimed rather than sung : the Old English expression is ' singan ond secgan '—to sing and say.   This is a development parallel to that of the Homeric epics.   The stresses would continue to be marked by the strum of the harp, and the laws of music would still govern the composition, except for the loss of melody.   The vitality of the alliterative tradition is proved by its re-emergence in the fourteenth century, after being driven underground for three centuries by French versification, and it has left sufficient impression on our popular ballads to suggest that it had a long history on the lips of the people.

The subjugation of England by William the Conqueror, at the end of the eleventh century, brought the Norman language to England and strengthened English ties with the Continent.   A new literature settled beside the remnants of English tradition.   The Normans had their minstrels, who sang French poems.   Taillefer, William's minstrel, is said to have encouraged the troops at the battle of Hastings, by singing a song of Roland.   The *chansons de geste*, of which the Song of Roland is one, were always sung, and no doubt they made their way to England with the Normans. The earliest English verse after the Conquest bears obvious signs of French influence.   Unfortunately we do not possess any of the music to which it was sung.   Probably, as in the *chanson de geste*, a little snatch of melody served for a single line and was repeated throughout the composition.   This sounds terribly tedious to us, but the attention of the audience was no doubt concentrated on

---

[1] Eginhard, *Vita Karoli*, c. 24.
[2] *Opera (Rerum Britannicarum Medii Aevi Scriptores)*, V, 153.

the story. Many of the Middle English poems are divided into
'fits', which may mean that the harper rested after each section,
or that a different snatch of melody was used for each 'fit'.
Harping was still popular. Bishop Grossteste is said to have been
much addicted to hearing minstrels playing the harp.

> He loued moche to here þe harpe,
> For mannys wytte hyt makyþ sharpe ;
> Next hys chaumbre, besyde his stody,
> Hys harpers chaumbre was fast þerby.
> Many tymes, be ny3tys and dayys,
> He had solace of notes and layys.
> One asked hym onys, resun why
> He hadde delyte yn minstralsy :
> He answerede hym on þys manere,
> Why he helde þe harper so dere,
> 'þe vertu of þe harpe, þurgh skylle and ry3t,
> Wyl destroye þe fendes my3t.' [1]

Robert of Brunne, who reported the above, declared that he wrote
his *Handlynge Sinne* for companies of men at the ale-bench. The
custom of listening to songs and tales over the mead had earlier
been described in Bede's story of Caedmon, and it was apparently
still widespread.

> For many ben of swyche manere,
> þat talys and rymys wyl bleþly here ;
> Yn gamys, & festys & at þe ale,
> Loue men to lestene troteuale. [2]

To use this love of popular song for more edifying purposes, as
Robert of Brunne proposes to do, is a very old idea. Aldhelm
is said to have disguised himself as a minstrel and sung pious words
to popular tunes to attract people as they returned from Mass,
and one of his moralizations was still a popular song in the twelfth
century. [3] The very method of inculcating Christian sentiments
reveals the existence of a body of popular song accompanied by
the harp. But narrative verse of all kinds was still sung to the
harp or *vielle* during the greater part of the middle ages. Many
of the extant poems begin with a reference to the audience—
'Listen, lordlings', or some such phrase, an echo of the Anglo-
Saxon 'Hwaet', the stereotyped exclamation that attracted the
attention of the audience at the beginning of a heroic recital.
Minstrels sang such poems in the hall after supper. The adoption
of the French word *geste* allows us to suppose that the conditions

---

[1] Robert of Brunne, *Handlynge Sinne*, ll. 4743–4754.
[2] op. cit., ll. 43–8.
[3] William of Malmesbury, *De Gesta Pontificum Anglorum* (Rolls Series), 336.

under which the French *chansons de geste* were disseminated in their native land were reproduced in England, and that English verse modelled on French originals was sung to the *vielle* or to the harp. Recitation, which was perhaps the Old English method of performing heroic poetry, may still have been practised ; but many references suggest that much narrative poetry was actually sung, after the fashion of French verse.   The author of *King Horn* thus asks attention for his *song* :

> Alle beon he bliþe
> Þat to my song liþe :
> A sang ihc schal ȝou singe
> Of Murry þe kinge.[1]

In the romance of *Emaré* a character says :

> y haue herd Menstrelles syng yn sawe.[2]

Chaucer says of his Friar that

> . . . in his harpyng, whan that he hadde songe,
> His eyen twynkled in his heed aryght.[3]

The question of what was intended for singing is complicated by undoubted references to the reading of romances.   Generally this refers not to private reading, after the modern manner, but to reading aloud to a company.   Thus in *Havelok* among the entertainments at the coronation was

> Romanz-reding on þe bok.[4]

It was also customary to read aloud at table, and in the monasteries definite times were set apart for it.   The *Ancren Riwle* requests that ' Ye ancren owen þis lutle laste stucchen reden to our wummum eueriche wike eues, uort þet heo hit kunnen.' [5]   But a work thus written down for educated readers might also be sung to popular audiences.   The French Life of St. Alexis is an example.   The first version extant is certainly for a clerical audience ; but the second has been adapted by minstrels, and it later became a general favourite in their repertory.   Gaston Paris has summed up the history of the poem thus :

Sortie de l'austère église romane où les fidèles, après l'office, l'écoutaient avec un recueillement religieux, notre *amiable chançon* est allée courir, avec le jongleur du xiie siècle, les châteaux et les places publiques ; elle entre, au xiiie siècle, par la main de quelque écrivain habile, dans une librairie de cloître ou de manoir, en attendant qu'une

---

[1] ll. 1–4.   [2] l. 319.   [3] Prologue, ll. 266–7.
[4] l. 2327.   [5] Ed. Morton, p. 428.

nouvelle métamorphose vienne attester, au xive siècle, la faveur dont elle jouit encore.[1]

As we know only the manuscript versions of Middle English poems, we are tempted to over-emphasize the importance of reading in their diffusion.   This typical case should warn us that even religious poems often spent parts of their career in the minstrel's memory as well as in the monk's manuscript ; and the warning applies more forcibly to secular work.   The numerous references to singing by minstrels are therefore of more weight than would at first sight appear, since they have survived the passing of the poems through the hands of scholars and clerics, who would naturally regard them as documents and tend to obliterate the rest of their history.   Mr. Sisam has put the case judiciously :

> Up to Chaucer's day, the greater the popularity of an English poem the less important becomes the manuscript as a means of early transmission . . .   To determine the relative popularity of the longer tales in verse we need, not so much a catalogue of extant manuscripts, as a census, that cannot now be taken, of the repertoires of the entertainers.[2]

Of course, there was a spoken literature alongside the sung romances.   Besides sung poetry, most primitive peoples have sagas or legends in prose.   In time romances were put into prose to speed up the action.   The French *Aucassin et Nicolette* is an interesting transition example.   Here sections of prose and verse alternate, the verse being supplied with fragments of tune and headed ' Or se cante '.   The style of the verse is not lyrical but of the old *chanson de geste* type, and the same melody is repeated for each line.   This *cante-fable* probably represents the way romances came to be told instead of sung.   No English romance entirely in prose dates further back than 1400, and by that time manuscripts were in commoner circulation.   But the extant works are probably slightly later than the first attempts to tell romances in prose, though this seems to have been a late medieval development.   From it would afterwards result the speaking of verse too.   Chaucer distinguishes between minstrels and ' gestours '.

> Do come, he seyde, my minstrales,
> And gestours, for to tellen teles.[3]

> Of alle maner of minstrales,
> And gestiours, that tellen tales,
> Bothe of weping and of game.[4]

---

[1] *La vie d'Alexis*, ed. L. Pannier and G. Paris, p. 265.
[2] *Fourteenth Century Verse and Prose*, pp. xxxii, xxxiv.
[3] *Sir Thopas*, l. 134.   [4] *Hous of Fame*, III, 1197.

The distinction would appear to be between those who sing and those who recount in prose or verse. Gower calls the latter ' disours ' :

> And every menstral hadde pleid,
> And every disour hadde seid.[1]

Fabulator, fableor, conteor, and *segger* are other terms that appear even earlier for tellers of tales, whether in prose or verse. Such men were still to be heard telling prose tales in England at the beginning of the sixteenth century. Erasmus compares them with the Italian *improvisatori.*

> Apud Anglos est simile genus hominum, quales apud Italos sunt circulatores, de quibus modo dictum est ; qui irrumpunt in convivia magnatum, aut in cauponas vinarias ; et argumentum aliquod, quod edidicerunt, recitant ; puta mortem omnibus dominari, aut laudem matrimonii. Sed quoniam ea lingua monosyllabis fere constat, quemadmodum Germanica ; atque illi studio vitant cantum, nobis latrare videntur verius quam loqui.[2]

It is probable, too, that recitation of verse to an instrument was common throughout the middle ages. Old English epic was so performed, and the English tradition perhaps remained, alongside the French practice of singing verse. Such recitation would still be subject to some of the rules of music. Practice was not uniform, however, and we cannot assign even approximate dates for a general abandonment of music in narrative poetry. It was still the custom in the reign of Elizabeth for companies to be entertained by singing to the harp tales of King Arthur and other heroes, as Puttenham attests.[3] Folk-song collectors know that narrative poems were sung among the illiterate into modern times. In discussing medieval practice we are considering a gradual development in the customs of polite society as shown by the written specimens extant, though these are probably a mere fragment of the literature then produced. As reading became more general, singing of narrative verse sank down to the illiterate sections of the population. The medieval lay reading public was never very large. In the sixteenth century Sidney could still declare he was moved to tears when he heard the old song of Percy and Douglas sung by a blind harper. The popular singer handed on the old material. Medieval romance has passed into the tradition of folk-song and remained a sung form all the time.

Lyric poetry retained its music much longer than narrative

---

[1] *Confessio Amantis,* VII, 2424.   [2] *Opera,* V, col. 958.
[3] Gregory Smith, op. cit., II, 43–4.

verse. The modern lyric owes its inception to the troubadours of Provence. Social and cultural conditions in the south of France, and perhaps contact with the Moors, gave birth to a new art form quite unlike anything derived from Germanic tradition. The novelty of its sentiments was equalled by the greater variety of its form, in which music had a great share, for it gave a new scope for melodic invention. It was always sung. The text was called the *motz* and the melody the *son* or *note*, and usually the same person composed both. Originality of tune was as important as originality of text, except in the *sirventé*, where the poet replied to another poem, maintaining the same verse pattern and borrowing the tune. The music was, of course, entirely monodic, harmony not yet being perfected, but the melody, composed according to the current metrical rules, was doubled on a *vielle*, an ancestor of the violin. The underlay was usually syllabic.

Either directly or through northern French, Englishmen had ample opportunity for learning the technique of the troubadours, and after about 1150 its impress is apparent in the metrical forms of the English lyric. It is probable that rime-schemes borrowed from troubadour sources often reveal English poets writing to troubadour melodies. Tunes would travel much more easily than manuscripts. The melody remained as important to the English imitators of the troubadours as to the original poets. *Puys* or contests of song were a feature of French courtly life, and at a *puy* organized in London it is explicitly stated that the music must be taken into account in judging entries.

E qe il ieit a les chauncouns juger eslu ii ou iii qi se conoisent en chaunt et en musike, pur les notes et les poinz del chaunt trier et examiner, auxi bien com la nature de la reson enditee. Kar saunz le chaunt ne doit on nie appeler une resoun endite chauncoun, ne chauncoun reale corounee ne doit estre saunz doucour de melodies chaunte.[1]

Chaucer's squire exemplifies the active use of song in the chivalric tradition, and the expectation that a well-bred young man would be able to compose songs in honour of his lady. He was a lively young gentleman :

> Singinge he was, or floytinge al the day.

But his addiction to singing and whistling was not mere ebullience ; he knew the rules for composing courtly songs :

> He coude songes make, and wel endyte.

---

[1] Chaytor, *The Troubadours and England*, p. 29.

The importance of songs in the technique of courtly love is stressed
by *The Romaunt of the Rose*.   Just as Victorian young ladies used
to play the pianoforte to impress their suitors, the medieval young
squire might attract his lady's notice by ability to sing or dance.
A tolerable performance was all that was desired of either.

> And if thy voice be fair and clere,
> Thou shalt maken no gret daungere
> Whan to singe they goodly preye ;
> It is thy worship for to obeye.
> Also to you it longith ay
> To harpe and giterne, daunce and play ;
> For if he can wel foote and daunce,
> It may him greetly do avaunce.
> Among eek, for thy lady sake,
> Songes and complayntes that thou make ;
> For that wol meve hem in hir herte,
> Whan they reden of thy smerte.[1]

Chaucer himself shows a considerable emancipation of the
poet from music.   He began by working over French manuscripts
for a courtly circle, and his great works were not set to music but
intended to be read.   Though fond of music, he was not a composer,
as far as is known ; he was therefore much more narrowly a man
of letters than the troubadours and their successors.   Yet he does
not rule out the possibility of even lengthy works being sung.
Troilus and Criseyde concludes with a reference to its being either
read or sung.

> And red wher-so thou be, *or elles songe*,
> That thou be understonde I god beseche.[2]

His lyrics were intended to be sung.   The roundel of the birds
in *The Parlement of Foules* is set to a French tune, Chaucer stating
' The Note, I trowe, maked was in France ', and some early texts
give as the original ' Qui bien aime a tard oublie.'   There were
actually several French songs beginning with these words.   One
is a ' lay de plour ' by Guillaume de Machaut, but it is in a different
metre and cannot have been the one in Chaucer's mind.   *The
Canterbury Tales*, of course, cannot have been sung, except perhaps
the mock romance of *Sir Thopas*.   A literary audience is assumed
for work such as Chaucer's, as for the very polished art of *Sir
Gawayn and the Green Knight* and *Pearl*.   While lower levels of
society no doubt still sang their romances, a reading public was
developing in the higher ranks.   The lyric, however, was still an
elegant social form of art and still sung.   Gower declares that

---

[1] Chaucer's translation, ll. 2317 ff.   [2] V, 1797-8.

' the Londe fulfilled is over all ' with Chaucer's ' ditees and Songes ' ;
and this implies that they were actually sung a good deal, for such
a widespread knowledge of them could hardly come from diffusion
of manuscript copies.[1]

Chaucer's Continental contemporaries, who, like him, developed
the tradition of the troubadours in a more purely literary direction,
reveal the same transitional stage as regards the association of
music and poetry. De Machaut was himself a great composer
and set his own works to music. His art is very different from
that of the troubadours, and he was as much an innovator in music
as in poetry. He expected his poems not merely to be read but
to be sung to his own settings. Dante was trained as a musician,
according to Boccaccio. There is no evidence that he ever tried
to set any of his works to music himself ; yet his critical treatise,
De Vulgari Eloquentia, explicitly links poetry with music. Vernacular poetry, he contends, is nothing else but ' a rhetorical composition set to music '. ' Whatever we write in verse is a Canzone '
(that is, a song). The form technically known as the Canzone is
the noblest kind of poetry, for it does not require dance movements, as the Ballata does, for its complete effect, and it is less
popular in style than the sonnet ; but all kinds of lyric poetry
are intended for music. Neither poetry nor music alone can be
called a Canzone : ' no music alone is ever called a Canzone,
but a Sound, a Tone, or a Note, or Melody.' ' And therefore
a Canzone appears to be nothing else but the completed action
of one writing words set to music.'

Eustache Deschamps is more completely literary in his outlook
than Dante. His Art de Dictier (1392) recognizes the close affinity
of the two arts, but insists that each has an interest of its own.
He divides music into natural and artificial. Natural music is
that of the speaking voice, of which poetry takes advantage ;
artificial music that of fixed intervals of pitch sounded by voice
or instruments.

Et ja soit ce que ceste musique naturele se face de volunté amoureuse
a la louenge des dames, et en autres manieres, selon les materes et le
sentement de ceuls qui en ceste musique s'appliquent, et que les faiseurs
d'icelle ne saichent pas communement la musique artificiele ne donner
chant par art de notes a ce qu'ilz font, toutesvoies est appellée musique
ceste science naturele, pour ce que les diz et chançons par eulx faiz ou
les livres metrifiez se lisent de bouche, et proferent par voix non pas
chantable, tant que les douces paroles ainsis faictes et recordées par une

---

[1] Gower's lines are quoted by Burney, History of Music, I, 665.

voix plaisent aux escoutans qui les oyent, si qui au *Puy d'amours* anciennement et encores est acoustumez en pluseurs villes et citez des pais et royaumes du monde.[1]

The earlier *puys*, as we have seen, judged verse and music together. Now apparently poems were read before the judges and not necessarily sung at all. The implication, that poetry was now written according to rhetorical and metrical rules and not in expectation of musical setting, is supported by the contemporary treatises on versification, which term poetry ' la seconde rhétorique ' or ' l'art de dictier '. Yet the traditional union of the two arts survives in the feeling that each is improved by association with the other.

Et est de ces deux ainsis comme un mariage en conjunction de science, par les chans qui sont plus anobliz et mieulx seans par la parole et faconde des ditz qu'elle ne seroit seule de soy. Et semblement les chançons natureles sont delectables et embellies par la melodie et les teneurs, trebles et contreteneurs du chant de la musique artificiele. Et neantmoins est chascune de ces deux plaisant a ouir par soy ; et se puet l'une chanter par voix et par art, sanz paroles ; et aussis les diz des chançons se puent souventefoiz recorder en pluseurs lieux ou ilz sont moult voulentiers ois, ou le chant de la musique artificiele n'aroit pas tousjours lieu, comme entre seigneurs et dames estans a leur privé et secretement, ou la musique naturele se puet dire et recorder par un homme seul, de bouche, ou lire aucun livre de ces choses plaisans devant un malade, et autres cas semblables ou le chant musicant n'aroit point lieu pour la haulteur d'icellui, et la triplicite des voix pour les teneurs et contreteneurs neccessaires a ycellui chant proferer par deux ou trois personnes pour la perfection dudit chant.[2]

Reading was still regarded as something of a makeshift ; but the mention of part-music provides one reason why the poet no longer composed his own musical settings, as in the days of the troubadours. Music was becoming far too complicated for amateurs. The simple airs of the troubadours needed little more than the technical equipment of a folk-song composer. But counterpoint demanded more than a natural and cultivated gift for melody. Moreover, reading was becoming more widespread ; the supply of manuscripts was increasing, helped by the growth of universities and the rise of the *bourgeoisie*. Right through the middle ages, however, actual possession of a manuscript betokened a certain amount of prosperity : students were usually glad enough to be allowed to inspect one. Chaucer's poor scholar had little prospect of ever attaining his fondest ambition, twenty books of

---

[1] *Œuvres (Soc. des anc. textes franç.)*, VII, 270.   [2] ib., pp. 271-2.

his own. Manuscripts of longer works were generally commissioned
by wealthy patrons or institutions. Edward III paid as much as
£66 13s. 4d. for a book of romance.[1] It was probably illuminated
and finely bound ; but, considering the value of money then, it
was not exactly a bargain. This gives some idea of the scarcity
of texts. It is not surprising that artistic poetry was cultivated
only by a very limited class. Oral literature had to suffice for the
majority of the population. Hence popular literature suffered less
break in continuity than learned during the anarchy of the fifteenth
century ; it had deeper roots, and it did not depend on perishable
parchment.

At the end of the middle ages, then, folk-literature was still
being sung, but courtly music and poetry had become the provinces
of experts in each art, though the lyric remained a form expected
to receive musical treatment. The sixteenth century produced
little change until printing had become common enough to effect
a considerable enlargement of the reading public for poetry. The
lyrics of Henry VIII and his contemporaries were intended for
performance in the court circle. Henry set his own poems to
music. Wyatt and Skelton had their lyrics set by court composers
of whom more will be said in later chapters. Wyatt always
speaks of his lyrics as songs.

> The songes I sing do mone ;
> Sins you will needs that I shall sing : &c.

And it was no conventional phrase, for he delighted in playing
the lute and probably sang his poems over to himself as he composed
them. He several times makes explicit mention of the lute with
which he accompanied his singing.

> Blame not my lute for he must sound,
> Of thes and that as lyketh me,
> For lak of wit the lute is bownd
> To give suche tunes as plesithe me ;
> Tho my songes be sumwhat strange,
> And spekes suche words as toche thy change
> Blame not my lute.[2]

> My lute awake ! perfourme the last
> Labor that thou and I shall wast,
> And end that I have now begon ;
> For when this song is song and past,
> My lute be still, for I have done.[3]

---

[1] Jusserand, *English Wayfaring Life*, p. 198.
[2] *Poems*, ed. A. K. Foxwell, I, 303.   [3] ib., II, 117.

Skelton's lyrics are termed by Pynson, their first printer, ' Balettys and Dyties ', names that suggest texts of songs, as opposed to the complete settings with music. There are manuscript collections of early Tudor lyrics without music, from which it can be inferred that their poetical qualities were admired by a restricted court circle ; but the incentive to lyric composition was primarily the prospect of musical performance. Behind literary fashion were the court's interest in songs and the demand of the musical establishment for texts to sing.

Later lyrics, too, were generally intended in the first place for a restricted audience. Printers often realized their attraction for a wider public, just as they saw a market for plays, which were released for legitimate publication only when no longer required in the theatre. Printed editions supply a more or less accidental selection of Elizabethan lyrics ; in fact, just those that happened to fall into printers' hands. Amateurs of high rank intended their poems primarily to circulate among their friends, and manuscript copies of them were usually well known long before any enterprising printer laid hands on them. Puttenham complains that this exclusiveness makes it difficult to gain a complete view of poetic activity.[1] Many of the lyrics so circulated had been set to music by composers of the poets' acquaintance. Authors of lesser rank sometimes used their lyrics to fill out novels, for songs were a regular feature of the contemporary romance, or might even publish their verses separately ; but they too had often written their lyrics for musical performance, either privately or in plays and other entertainments. In the seventeenth century, when reluctance to publish was no longer a gentlemanly pose, it became the practice to put the composer's name at the head of any lyric set to music before a book of poems was printed.

One of the chief sources of Elizabethan lyrics is the miscellanies modelled on Richard Tottel's 1557 collection of poems by Wyatt, Surrey, and other poets of Henry VIII's reign. An early miscellany, *The Paradise of daynty devises* (1576), practically admits that its contents were mainly intended for music by their authors and advises its readers to find tunes for the

ditties . . . [which] are both pithy and pleasant, as well for the invention as meter, and wyll yeelde a farre greater delight, being as they are so aptly made to be set to any song in .5. partes, or song to instrument.

The other miscellanies sometimes borrow from musical settings.

[1] Gregory Smith, op. cit., II, 22.

The Passionate Pilgrim contains a separate section designated ' Sonnets to sundrie notes of Musicke ', one of the poems being ' My flocks feed not ', which had been published two years previously in Weelkes' 1597 *Madrigals*. *Englands Helicon* contains excerpts from the musical volumes of Byrd, Dowland, and Morley. *A Handeful of pleasant delites* is a collection of ballads, for each of which a tune is specified.

Many of the best lyrics of the period have survived because they were published by the composers of the musical settings. Few of the poems in the volumes of madrigals and airs can be assigned to definite authors, but it need not be assumed that the musicians themselves wrote the texts. Campion was probably an exception. Most of the other composers set words by their friends and patrons. No doubt the settings were performed at social gatherings. The texts of Orlando Gibbons's madrigals were chosen by ' my Honoured friend ' Sir Christopher Hatton. They

were most of them composed in your owne house, and doe therefore properly belong unto you, as Lord of the Soile ; the language they speake you provided them, I onely furnished them with Tongues to utter the same.[1]

The lutanist Robert Jones says that his airs were composed at the request of various gentlemen, who asked him to fit verses to music for their private recreation. The verses would never have reached a public wider than the circle of the author's acquaintances, had not Jones sought permission to publish them along with his music : being a professional musician, he had not the poets' modesty about courting popular favour.

I confesse I was not vnwilling to embrace the conceits of such gentle-men as were earnest to haue me apparel these ditties for them ; which though intended for their priuate recreation, neuer meaning they should come into the light, were yet content vpon intreaty to make the in-couragements of this my first aduenture, whereupon I was almost glad to make my small skill knowne to the world ; presuming that if my cunning failed me in the Musicke : yet the words might speake for them selues, howsoeuer it pleaseth them to account better of that, then of those. Of purpose (as it should seeme) to make me belieue I can do something ; my only hope is, that seeing neither my cold ayres, nor their idle ditties (as they will needes haue me call them) haue hitherto beene sounded in the eares of manie : they may chance to finde such entertainment, as commonlie newes doth in the world.[2]

---

[1] Dedication of *The First Set of Madrigals and Motetts* (1612).
[2] To the Reader, *The First Booke of Songes and Ayres* (1600).

In the Preface to his *Second Booke of Songs and Ayres* (1601) Jones admits that he has taken for granted the permission of the poets to publish his texts, but again implies that the settings were intended primarily for the private delectation of the authors of the lyrics, who had asked him to set the verses to music, or consented to his doing so.

> If the Ditties dislike, 'tis my fault that was so bold to publish the priuate contentments of diuers Gentlemen without their consents, though (I hope) not against their wils : wherein if thou find anie thing to meete with thy desire, thanke me ; for they were neuer meant thee.

Philip Rosseter, in publishing a volume of Campion's airs, explains that they were

> made at his vacant houres, and priuately emparted to his friends, whereby they grew both publicke, and (as coine crackt in exchange) corrupted ; some of them both words and notes vnrespectiuely challenged by others.[1]

The corruption may have come from the circulation of faulty copies ; it may equally have arisen from their being inaccurately remembered by the composer's acquaintances. There can be little doubt that the great majority of Elizabethan lyrics, except those written to be sung in the theatre, had histories similar to those of Jones's and Campion's airs—that is to say, they were written to be set to music and presented as airs or madrigals to particular audiences. The lyrics in the drama, which are among the best of the time, would, of course, be prepared for specific members of the company to sing. In short, lyrics were intended to be sung, not read, and passed straight from poet to composer. As well as demonstrating the poets' mastery of current literary technique, they met the social demand for vocal music ; they fulfilled a purpose in entertainment, public or private, formal or informal.

A great conservative force keeping music and poetry together was the increasing interest in Greek practice. The knowledge that Greek lyrics had been sung strengthened the bonds between the two arts forged by tradition and social circumstances. To associate poetry and music in the definition of the lyric became a commonplace. Ronsard, whose influence on English poetry was considerable, deliberately aimed at restoring the lyre to verse. An early biographer records his frequent assertion that poetry without music was lacking in grace, while music was no better unless

[1] Dedication to *A Booke of Ayres* (1601).

inspired by good verse. For this reason he liked to hear his own verse sung.

La musique lui estoit à singulier plaisir, et principalement amoit à chanter et a ouyr chanter ses vers, appelant la musique sœur puisnée de la Posie, et les Poetes et Musiciens enfans sacrez des Muses, que sans la Musique la Poesie estoit presque sans grace, comme la Musique sans la Melodie des Vers, inanimée et sans vie.[1]

That the biographer is faithfully reporting Ronsard's views is proved by Ronsard's own instructions to a young poet. He tells him that he must make his verse suitable for music, which is the chief end of poetry, and adds a piece of technical advice about how this can be done.

Après, à l'imitation de quelqu'un de ce temps, tu feras tes vers masculins et fæminins tant qu'il sera possible, pour estre plus propre à la Musique et accords des instrumens, en faveur desquels il semble que la Poesie soit née ; car la Poesie sans les instrumens ou sans la grace d'une seule ou plusieurs voix, n'est nullement aggréable, non plus que les instrumens sans estre animez de la melodie d'une plaisante voix.[2]

This was more than theory : Ronsard tried to carry it into practice. Some of the most eminent French composers contributed settings to the 1552 edition of his *Amours*.

Sidney, a disciple of Ronsard and the Pléiade, follows him in picturing the poet as preparing his lines for music.

Hee cometh to you with words set in delightful proportion, either accompanied with or prepared for the well inchaunting skill of Musicke.[3]

Among the virtues of poetry Sidney reckons ' the just prayse it hath, by beeing the only fit speech for Musick (Musick, I say, the most divine striker of the senses) '.[4] Puttenham is less general, ascribing a musical intention specifically to lyric poets.

Others who more delighted to write songs or ballads of pleasure, to be song with the voice, and to the harpe, lute, or citheron, and such other musical instruments, they were called melodious Poets (*melici*), or by a more common name, Lirique Poets : of which sort was Pindarus, Anacreon, and Callimachus, with others among the Greeks, Horace, and Catullus among the Latines.[5]

The mention of contemporary instruments for accompanying airs shows that this is more than an exhibition of antiquarian know-

---

[1] Claude Binet, in *Œuvres de Ronsard* (1609), p. 1164.
[2] *Abrégé de l'art Poétique.* [3] Gregory Smith, op. cit., I, 172.
[4] ib., I, 182. [5] ib., II, 26.

ledge. Campion, too, defines lyric verses as those ' apt to be soong to an instrument, if they were adorned with convenient notes '.[1]

From Greek practice sprang not only a re-affirmation of the need for music to complete the lyric's effect, but also the famous parallel between music and poetry that was to influence criticism down to the eighteenth century. The two arts were ' the sister and the brother ' ;

> One god is god of both, as poets feign.[2]

To Milton they were

> Sphere-born harmonious sisters, Voice and Verse.[3]

At the end of the seventeenth century Purcell could still repeat the family metaphor as an agreed critical doctrine, although poetry had by then drawn nearer to ordinary speech and away from music. In the sixteenth century the close relationship between the two arts was something more than a mere rhetorical survival of the past. A poet expected his lyrics to be set to music and heard rather than read.

---

[1] Gregory Smith, op. cit., II, 346.   [2] *The Passionate Pilgrim*, Sonnet VI.
[3] *At a Solemn Music.*

CHAPTER III

THE LITERARY AND MUSICAL PROFESSIONS

SONG entails the co-operation of poet and musician, and its nature at any particular time will depend partly on the conventions governing the two arts in that period, partly on the characters of individual artists, and partly on the personal relationships of poets and composers. In modern conditions it is a matter of chance whether a poet cares anything for music. Musicians, too, are satisfied if they can master a very exacting technique in their own art ; they may devote themselves entirely to instrumental work. Only rarely do poet and composer deliberately consult together. Songs are usually born of a composer's reading. The text has seldom been prepared specifically for music. Specialization has become so general that even practitioners of related arts may move in different spheres and be almost completely ignorant of each other's problems.

In the first chapter it was suggested that an Elizabethan poet could scarcely be indifferent to music, since it was a normal part of his environment. The creative members of the educated classes were so few and so much centred round the Court and round London that it was easy for them to maintain personal contacts ; and besides, as the last chapter tried to suggest, music and poetry had special reasons for close association. Their roots in a common tradition drew them together. The singing of many kinds of poetry had but recently been replaced by reading among the educated, and the lyric was still expected to be sung. This was a phase in the development of society, of the conditions in which art was created and presented to its public. To understand it a rather fuller investigation must be made into the situations of the literary and musical professions and into the position of the amateur in each art.

The earliest English poetry, as we have seen, was sung or recited to the harp. Poetry was almost a branch of music, and this primitive union was long to persist. The author of a poem would himself give the first performance. Many of the early Germanic warriors no doubt celebrated their own deeds. Kings were often skilled harpists. Hrothgar entertained the company at Heorot with his harping.[1] Gunnar is alleged to have been able to play the harp with his toes.[2] Once a song met the approval of the poet's

---

[1] *Beowulf*, l. 2197.　　　　[2] *Volsunga Saga*, c. 37.

audience it would become common property, passing into the general stream of Germanic tradition.

Alongside the noble amateur, however, there existed from quite early times the professional minstrel or *scop*. The elaborate vocabulary of Old English poetry presupposes a long tradition of artistic effort, no doubt largely built up by the official minstrels. Harping and poetry were combined in their functions. Composers of eulogies are usually termed *citharoedi*, harpers, by the Latin writers who had dealings with Germanic monarchs.[1] The *scop* was the king's personal attendant and was often richly rewarded for his services. The minstrel who tells the Finn episode in *Beowulf* is called 'Hrothgares scop'. But some minstrels wandered from place to place, increasing their stocks of narrative and winning reward from several kings. *Widsith* is an exceedingly interesting account of the travels of such a minstrel. On occasion he took part in duets.

When Schilling and I with clear voice raised the song before our victorious lord—loud to the harp the words sounded in harmony— then many men proud in mind, of full knowledge, said they had never heard a better song.[2]

This serves to emphasize the importance of the musical functions of the *scop*. In glosses *scop* is often given as the equivalent of *poeta*, but the harp is always mentioned in the recitals of heroic verse. Jordanes describes a courtly assemblage listening to a recital about the deeds of its ancestors sung to the harp ; a very typical specimen, no doubt, of Germanic heroic verse in general, for celebration of historical and legendary figures of the past occupies much of the extant Germanic poetry.[3]

The noble amateur and the courtly professional, Hrothgar and Widsith, are types that persist throughout the middle ages. From the eighth century at least appear references to humbler professionals who also had a long succession, the *mimes* or *histriones*, who won applause by comic and often questionable entertainment. Sir E. K. Chambers argues that these more frivolous minstrels were descended from the Roman theatrical mimes.[4] It is quite likely

[1] 'Cum rex Francorum convivii nostri fama pellectus a nobis *citharoedum* magnis precibus expetisset' (Cassiodorus, *Var. Epist.*, II, 40). '*Citharoedum* etiam arte sua doctum pariter destinavimus expetitum, qui ore manibusque consona voce cantando gloriam vestrae potestatis oblectet' (ib., II, 41).

[2] Trans. Gordon, *Anglo-Saxon Poetry* (Everyman Library), p. 78.

[3] 'Etiam cantu maiorum facta modulationibus citharisque canebat' (*De origine Getarum, Mon. Germ. Hist.*, V, 45).

[4] *The Mediaeval Stage*, Chap. II.

that the Germanic tribes became infected with the amusements of
the decadent empire they conquered ; but pantomime and risqué
songs appeal to all races at all periods, and even the serious early
Germans can hardly have endured lofty heroic verse all the time.
However we regard the origins of the two types, both are equally
entitled to inclusion in the minstrel profession, which was a very
complex one during the whole middle ages and covered every kind
of entertainer between these two extremes. The Council of
Clovesho (747), issuing one of the many ecclesiastical condemnations
of minstrels, describes them as poets, harpists, musicians, and satirical
jesters ; [1] and all these activities belonged to minstrelsy. It is not
possible to divide the profession very rigidly into classes. There
were some who lived on the generosity of noble patrons, and others
who wandered from place to place, frequenting taverns and fairs
and picking up what they could from any crowd willing to spare
them a few minutes. But the same men might appeal to both
sorts of patron. Court minstrels often travelled abroad, and those
of nobles were lent to other households. Wandering minstrels
were often welcomed with open arms into abbeys and castles that
maintained their own professionals. Nor did particular minstrels
restrict themselves to one kind of work. Some could entertain
their masters with romances and lyrics at one time and with
tumbling and parlour tricks at another. Some worked in groups
and some were solitary. A number could compose their own
songs, but they also carried the songs of others in their memories.
Piers Plowman, in disclaiming the powers of a minstrel, gives a
pretty comprehensive list of the professional entertainer's stock-in-
trade.

> Ich can nat tabre ne trompe· ne telle faire gestes,
> Farten, ne fithelen· at festes, ne harpen,
> Iapen ne Iogelen· ne gentelliche pipe,
> Nother sailen ne sautrien· ne singe with the giterne.[2]

A good minstrel would pride himself on the variety of his gifts :
his aim was to adapt himself to any company and provide any sort
of amusement. Even the highest class of minstrel, attached to
cultured nobles, had a varied repertoire. Daurel, in the romance of
Daurel et Beton, is represented as a courtly minstrel, the confidant of
his master, who gave him the castle of Montclair. He played the

---

[1] '. . . ut monasteria . . . non sint ludicrarum artium receptacula, hoc est
poetarum, citharistum, musicorum, scurrorum' (Haddan and Stubbs, *Councils
and Ecclesiastical Documents*, III, 133).

[2] *Piers Plowman*, C, Passus XVI, 205–8.

vielle and the harp, sang *chansons de geste* and *lais d'amour*, composing his own songs. Yet both he and his wife were acrobats and performed as such on occasion. Poet, musician, mime, acrobat—all were included in the role of a good minstrel.

With the progress in musical technique a bewildering variety of instruments had to be mastered by minstrels. Lydgate, at the beginning of the fifteenth century, pictures

> . . . al maner Mynstralcye,
> That any man kan specifye.
> Ffor there were Rotys of Almayne,
> And eke of Arragon and Spayne :
> Songes, Stampes, and eke Daunces :
> Divers plente of plesaunces :
> And many unkouth notys new
> Of swiche folke as lovid treue.
> And instrumentys that did excelle,
> Many moo than I kan telle,
> Harpys, Fythales, and eke Rotys
> Well according to her notys,
> Lutys, Ribibles and Geternes,
> More for estatys, than tavernes :
> Orgaynes, Cytolis, Monacordys.
> There were Trumpes, and Trumpettes,
> Lowde Shallmys, and Doucettes.[1]

It is interesting that poems should be included among the musical forms these instrumentalists handled—'notes' (airs) about true lovers. This is in accord with what was said in the last chapter about the singing of poetry during the middle ages. Thomas de Cabham (d. 1313) similarly includes poetry with music. He is trying to distinguish minstrels that the Church may tolerate from those that carry moral infection with them. He divides all minstrels into three main classes. The first are those that contort themselves into strange postures ; the second those who wander about spreading satires and libels against those not present to refute them. The third class consists of musicians who carry instruments.[2] They in turn are of two kinds. There are those who sing lascivious ditties in taverns and places of resort : they can no more be tolerated than the non-musicians. The second kind is more honourable ; it consists of singers of heroic verse and the lives of saints.[3] Thus both convivial and serious poetry are assigned to the

---

[1] Quoted from Percy's *Reliques*, notes to Essay on Ancient Minstrels.

[2] 'Est etiam tertium genus histrionum qui habent instrumenta musica ad delectandum homines.' Reproduced in Chambers, op. cit., II, 262.

[3] 'Qui cantant gesta principum et vitas sanctorum.'

musical repertoire of the minstrel. *Chansons de geste, vies de saints, lais*, and drinking songs are all counted as songs. Poetry of all kinds is sung to instrumental accompaniment, and the minstrel is the normal agent for its dissemination.

In the early middle ages it is probable that the poems sung by minstrels were largely their own composition. This does not mean that they disdained to borrow material from their rivals or to avail themselves of common and traditional property. But, as far as details of presentation went, each minstrel tried to impose his own characteristics on his work. The *chansons de geste* and the lives of saints are undoubtedly the work of minstrels for the most part. A French minstrel, Garnier, who specialized in ecclesiastical poetry, saw St. Thomas à Becket passing through Normandy at the head of the king's army, and composed a life of him. News of Becket's death, which stirred all Christendom, inspired Garnier to revise the Life and cross to England, where he earned many honest pennies by singing his work to pilgrims on their way to Canterbury. Many minstrels thus composed their works with an eye on a possible audience, and in time recast them in the light of experience gathered from the reactions of different hearers. Most of the medieval English poems are rather late redactions of French material and do not show minstrel authorship as clearly as the French *chansons de geste* and lives of saints ; but such romances as *The Lay of Havelok* (before 1275), *Sir Tristrem* (late thirteenth century) and *Sir Cleges* (early fifteenth century), all of which were certainly recited by minstrels, may have been the original work of the people who first recited them. In France Colin Muset and Rutebeuf were minstrels by profession and carried their own poems in their memories to sing to the *vielle*.

In the eleventh century, however, appears the word *troubadour* or *trouvère*, expressing a more discriminating kind of authorship. Among the Provençal troubadours were numbered two kings and several nobles of high rank. Such men naturally did not attempt the full variety of the minstrel's tricks. They composed courtly verse for their own circles. Whereas the *jongleur*, as the professional came to be called, concentrated on narrative, the *trouvère* preferred lyric. His music was more *recherché* than the simple reiterated strain of the *jongleur*. Often he employed professionals to sing his works, or at least one to accompany him on the *vielle*. Because his livelihood did not depend on the favour of his audience, many historians have assumed that he was a composer, uninterested in the diffusion of his works, while the *jongleur* hawked round the work of others. No such rigid distinction can be maintained. Many of the original troubadours sang their own works, and some were not ashamed to accept gifts of horses and trappings as they progressed from castle to castle, like any minstrel. All that can be said is that the *trouvère* could neglect all but the small and refined society that upheld the code of medieval chivalry ; and this economic freedom encouraged a new and highly sophisticated lyric art. The *jongleur* could not compete with these educated nobles and their protégées except by copying them or, where possible, even filching lyrics from them. For popular audiences his old narrative verse sufficed : for higher circles he had to learn something new. Thus the ordinary minstrel came more and more to rely on unoriginal material. Petrarch speaks disparagingly of men who had no works of their own but gained reward by reciting the works of others in the halls of nobles.[1]

The *trouvère*, although he left to professional entertainers the acrobatics and miming so dear to noble and simple alike, continued to be both poet and musician. Indeed, it is surprising how long this tradition persisted. The development of harmony in the thirteenth and fourteenth centuries made it more difficult for an amateur to set his own verses to music ; but specialization was so contrary to tradition that many of the innovators in music continued to be poets as well. The *ars nova* of the fourteenth century was largely the creation of amateurs who were important literary and musical figures at the same time. A manual of rhetoric thus describes the two leaders of the movement :

Après vint Philippe de Vitry qui trouva la maniere des motès et des balades et des lais et des simples rondeaux, et en la musique trouva les iiij prolacions et les notes rouges, et la noveleté des proporcions.

Après vint maistre Guillaume de Machault le grant rethorique de nouvelle fourme, qui commencha toutes tailles nouvelles, et les parfais lays d'amours.[2]

Philippe de Vitry (1291–1361) was a churchman—prebendary of Clermont from 1323 to 1350 and Bishop of Meaux from 1350 until his death. Two letters to him from Petrarch in 1350 and 1351

---

[1] ' Sunt homines non magni ingenii, magnae vero memoriae, magnaeque diligentiae, sed maioris audaciae, qui regum ac potentum aulas frequentant, de proprio nudi, vestiti autem carminibus alienis, dumque quid ab hoc, ant ab illo exquisitius materno praesertim charactere dictum sit, ingenti expressione pronunciant, gratiam sibi nobilium, et pecunias quaerunt, et vestes et numera' (*Epistolae Rerum Senilium*,V, 3).

[2] Langlois, *Arts de Seconde Rhétorique*, p. 12.

praise him as a savant, a poet, and a musician, and he was undoubtedly a man of wide interests.   Not only did he originate new poetic forms, but he did more than any other single composer to establish binary rhythms in music on an equality with ternary, a development that freed counterpoint from the restrictions of the *ars antiqua* of the thirteenth century.   Guillaume de Machaut, a great influence on Chaucer, must also be classed as an amateur, though his ability in music and poetry may have helped his advancement in court circles.   Born in the last years of the thirteenth century, he became in 1316 secretary to John of Luxembourg, King of Bohemia, in whose service he remained until the king's death at the Battle of Crécy in 1346.   Four years later de Machaut became secretary to John the Good, King of France, and ended his life about 1377 as a canon at Rheims.

The amateur was obviously in a much stronger position than the professional for combining the two arts after the development of polyphony.   The motet, the characteristic type of secular music, was, as John of Grocheo says, intended for cultured people, that is to say, for courtly audiences.   A secretary to princes, like de Machaut, had at his disposal singers of the royal chapel and skilled instrumentalists trained in the intricacies of contrapuntal music. Only in palaces and large private establishments could elaborate music like this be produced.   A poet with access to such resources as were necessary for it could dabble in music.   But the professional had to specialize to master the greater complication of musical technique and the more strenuous demands of improved instruments.

On the other hand, the changes did cause a certain rise in the status of certain professional minstrels.   The new public of the *trouvère* lyric was not easily satisfied with the fare of wandering *jongleurs*.   The very word ' minstrel ' denotes the growing importance of professionals attached to great households.   Originally it implied any kind of retainer.   In the second half of the twelfth century it came to mean a court *jongleur* attached to a palace or castle.   During the following century all kinds of *jongleurs* assumed the title, and it acquired its modern sense.   Many of these professional entertainers in noble houses attained comparative affluence and became the confidants of their masters.   With the increased production of manuscripts, the growth of universities, and the general diffusion of literacy, the more intelligent men whose fortunes obliged them to make a living out of literature were often lucky enough to attract noble patrons and gain security for writing at leisure. Reading ceased to be the exclusive concern of churchmen ; knights commissioned handsome manuscripts, and no longer thought of poetry as something recited to the harp. History had to be written down systematically ; legendary songs about one's ancestors no longer supplied its place. Wace wrote his history of the Dukes of Normandy for King Henry II ; Gaimer his *Le storie des Engles* for Constance Fiz-Gislebert.[1] The complication of music had, in any case, made it an impossible vehicle for literature. While the lyric continued to be sung in ever more elaborate settings, narrative works would be read, the old reiterated strains of the minstrel being outmoded and the new music too intricate for the words to be heard. Popular narrative verse was still sung by the wandering minstrels, whose status gradually declined with the growth of literacy, until in the sixteenth century they were classed as vagabonds. The Elizabethan ballad-seller is lineal descendant of the wandering *jongleur*. The court minstrel had become a man of letters ; but, until the invention of printing, his potential public was too small for him to secure any independence : he flourished only under patronage. His education made him generally useful to his patrons, and he often served them in other ways than as a writer. This professional class never became numerous. By far the greater part of courtly literature was produced by amateurs, *trouvères*, who no longer sang their verses or necessarily had any skill in music, de Machaut's achievement being already something of a *tour de force*. To the old aristocratic and ecclesiastical amateurs was added a new class of *trouvère*, as the *bourgeoisie* rose in importance and an official caste emerged. Geoffrey Chaucer, son of a vintner, adherent of John of Gaunt, and customs official, is the culmination of the *trouvère* tradition.

The majority of courtly minstrels were absorbed into the production of music rather than into a literary profession. The rise of the great fifteenth-century schools of polyphonic music was partly the cause and partly the effect of the specialization of minstrels into musicians. The pre-eminence of the English at the beginning of the century may be ascribed to the development of the royal chapel ; and the later dominance of the Netherlands School is due to the generous musical establishments of the Dukes of Burgundy. The songs of de Machaut, Dunstable, and the First Netherlands School entail very proficient performers, both vocal and instrumental. Organists in great churches and directors of royal music led the

---

[1] *Roman de Rou*, ed. Andreson, I, 207 ; II, 36, 243. *Le storie des Engles*, ed. Hardy and Martin (*Rerum brit. script.*), l. 6436.

polyphonic movement of the fifteenth century; only in such positions could professionals acquire enough experience for effective composition. The less original became singers and players of instruments. As early as the fourteenth century minstrels were distinguished by the names of the instruments they habitually played. At the Whitsuntide feast of Edward I, in 1306, there are mentioned ' Janin le Lutour ', ' Gillotin le Sautrour ', ' Le Gitarer ', ' Guillaume le Harpur ' and others.[1] In the later middle ages such men must have become practically professional musicians. The name minstrel still occurs in records at the beginning of the sixteenth century, but no longer are the old unspecialized entertainers intended. In Edward IV's Black Book provision is made for

Mynstrelles, xiii, whereof one is verger, that directeth them all in festivall dayes to theyre stations, to bloweings and pipynges, to such offices as must be warned to prepare for the king and his household at metes and soupers, to be the more readie in all services; and all these sittinge in the hall togyder; whereof sume use trumpettes, sume shalmuse and small pipes, and some as strengemen, comyng to the court at five festes of the yere.[2]

These men are clearly instrumentalists with duties rather like those of the ' waits '.

Minstrels not attached to courts found in the rising *bourgeoisie* a new public. In Germany the aristocratic Minnesinger were succeeded by the more *bourgeois* Mastersinger. The formation of minstrel guilds is a sign that professional entertainers were settling down beside the *bourgeois* patrons who treated the more respectable of them as equals and allowed them greater independence than patronage in a noble household.[3] It is noteworthy that the Paris guild of 1321, the type of most of the later ones, seems to include only musicians. Such privileged bodies, claiming sole right to free performance in a town, are a step towards the organization of a musical profession. The individualist tradition of minstrelsy yielded to co-operative association. Two types of professional band that emerged were city waits and companies of performers bearing the names of noblemen. Often, of course, these companies fulfilled only nominal duties for their patrons; they gradually broke away from service of one house-

[1] *Manners and Household Expenses of England in the Thirteenth and Fifteenth Centuries* (Roxburgh Club), p. 141.
[2] *Household Ordinances*, 48, quoted Burney's *History*, I, 697 ff.
[3] An account of the medieval guilds is given by E. K. Chambers, *Mediaeval Stage*, II, 258–62.

hold, just as the acting companies later went on tour and founded the public theatres, though all the time bearing the names of their former patrons. In the Belvoir Castle accounts for 1530–1 are these payments :

> Item to the erle of Sussex mynstrelles, iij *s.* iiij *d.*
> Item to the mynstrelles of the cytye of London, iij *s.* iiij *d.*
> Item to Sir Henry Gudefordes mynstrelles, iij *s.* iiij *d.*
> Item in rewarde to my Lorde Marques Execeter mynstrelles, v *s.*
> Item to Sir Edward Nevelles mynstrelles, iij *s.* iiij *d.*

After about 1550 these would probably all have been described simply as ' musitians ', except for the London minstrels, who were clearly the waits. In the 1549 accounts are two references to minstrels playing on instruments.

> Gyvyn ther the camp at Dunglass, the ix of Julye, by th' ande of Gyles Bygges, to tow Irysshe mynstrelles that playd before my Lord, iij *s.* iiij *d.*
>
> `Gyvyn, the xix day of November, at Barwyke to tow mynstrelles that plaid before my Lord in the castell ther, iij *s.* iiij *d.*[1]

By the end of the fifteenth century, then, the minstrel profession had degenerated until it supplied only popular literature. Its other functions had passed to specialists. Buffoons and bearwards continued the cruder appeal of the mimes ; dramatic interest was more effectively provided by the companies of professional players, a natural result of several centuries of religious and folk-drama. A musical profession with specialized training had evolved from the higher functions of minstrelsy. As yet, however, there was no real literary profession, though there were isolated men of letters protected by patronage. Poetry was mainly in the hands of men who had other means of livelihood. We shall see that occasional writing for courtly audiences often fell upon the musical profession, which to this extent maintained the minstrel tradition.

Henry VIII's court shows the late medieval situation just beginning to be transformed by the Renaissance. Printing had not yet affected the literary world to any very marked degree. The public for artistic literature was still very small. Yet important literary forms were being shaped. The new poetry of Italy was making a somewhat premature appearance with Wyatt and Surrey, and the drama was emerging. These changes were largely in the hands of the successors of the medieval amateur and professional types, the *trouvère* and the minstrel.

[1] *MSS. at Belvoir Castle* (Hist. MSS. Comm.), IV., 270, 354, 358.

Henry himself bears obvious resemblance to the earlier *trouvères*.
He was both a poet and a composer, and recalls royal troubadours,
like the King of Navarre and Richard I.   The collection of his
works into handsome manuscripts, now in the British Museum,
suggests that they were intended for performance at court.   Compositions by others of the court circle rub shoulders in these manuscripts with the king's own works.   The same court audience is
implied by Skelton and Wyatt.   Skelton satirized figures recog-
nizable by the court, and several of his poems were set to music
by Cornish and other court musicians.   Wyatt perhaps sang some
of his poems to his own lute ; others were set by court musicians.
His appeal, too, was primarily to a restricted audience with which
he was in immediate contact.   His lyrics were a relaxation from
his diplomatic duties and a contribution to the social life of the
court.

If poetry was mainly in the hands of the *trouvère*, the early
drama was largely shaped by court musicians, the successors of
the medieval minstrels.   Folk-customs had been stylized into
' disguisings ' by the end of the fifteenth century, and special
pageantry for important occasions was a feature of life at court
and in the great houses.   Many nobles kept troupes of players
for miscellaneous entertainments.   The organization of such amusements had to be done either by members of the family or by
retainers.   The Northumberland Household Book (begun in 1512)
stipulates that, if the Almoner be a ' maker of interludys ', he shall
have a servant to copy the parts.   Among the educated retainers
available for production of spectacles and short dramatic interludes
the musical establishment figured very largely.   We have already
seen that the complication of sacred and secular music entailed
the retention of trained staffs.   These provided both actors and
producers and writers.   The royal directors of music had in their
command the men and boys of the Chapel Royal choir, an important potential supplement to the troupe of players employed
in the king's service.   It was natural they should begin to write
as well as produce plays.   The infant drama owed much to them,
and thus, during the first half of the sixteenth century, the professional musicians in some degree supplied the place of a literary
profession.

The men and boys of the Chapel Royal were first probably
drawn into dramatic entertainments merely to add music.   It was
only in the sixteenth century that they extended their functions
and began to act.   One of the boys' late fifteenth-century masters,

however, displayed the kind of ability that was to turn later masters into dramatists.   Gilbert Banister, who was appointed in 1478, is credited with the authorship of a *Miracle of St. Thomas*, now in the library of Corpus Christi College, Cambridge, as well as with musical compositions in the Fairfax Book, the Eton College MS. and a MS. in the Pepysian Library.   William Newark, a prominent composer, who took over the mastership in 1493, is not known to have attempted literary work, but he may have acted as producer.   In 1501 the children of the Chapel took part in an elaborate entertainment to celebrate the marriage of Prince Arthur and Katherine of Aragon.[1]   The Gentlemen of the Chapel seem to have formed a more or less regular dramatic company in the first decade of the century.   Whatever Newark had to do with their performances, his successor, William Cornish, who ruled the children from 1509 to 1523, had a much greater influence on the development of court entertainment into proper drama. As part of his primary official duties, he set songs for special occasions. In 1502 he received 13s. 4d. ' for setting of a carrall upon Cristmas day '.   He sometimes sang himself.   In December 1513 he was paid 20s. for singing ' Audivi ' at Windsor on Allhallows Day. Like Banister, he added literary work to his musical activities. A ballad against Sir William Empson, written at the request of the Earl of Kent, landed him for a while in the Fleet prison ; and during his sojourn there he wrote *A Treatise betweene Trouthe and Enfor-macon.   The Story of Troilus and Pandor*, presented at Eltham during Christmas, 1515, may have been a classical play of some kind. But Cornish realized that his resources were more adaptable to spectacular entertainments with music.   He accompanied King Henry to the Field of the Cloth of Gold, in charge of his choir-boys ; and many of his court entertainments, which were acted by the same children, were dramatic stylizations of pageantry and song similar to those he must have prepared for the ceremonial meeting of the English and French kings.   On 26 October 1502, he was paid £30 for three pageants he had devised.   His *Tryumph of Love and Beauty* was presented at court by the children during the Christmas festivities of 1514, and in August 1520 a masque was produced before the king at New Hall, Essex.   It was natural that his attention should have been engaged chiefly by the elaborate pageants of the court, for in them singers and instrumentalists would take part in any case.   His work is an important step towards the organization of the traditional ' momerie ' and ' dis-

[1] Harleian MS. 69 ;   Reyher, *Les Masques Anglais*, pp. 500–4.

guising' into the masque. Besides writing and producing, he acted. In 1510–11 he took two prominent parts in *The Golldyn Arber in the Arche Yerd of Plesyr* at Westminster, and later a part in Gibson's pageant *The Fortresse Dangerus* at Greenwich. On 6 January 1514–15 he was again in a show of Gibson's, *The Pavyllyon un the Plas Parlon*. Indeed, his versatility is amazing. We even find him looking after property repairs, and receiving payments of £100 and £36 10s. for 'paving gutters of lead for urinals and other necessaries at Greenwich'. He was clearly a general court factotum and a provider of entertainment, rather than a mere court musician. His versatility is in the tradition of medieval minstrelsy.

If the masque, by its very nature, developed at court, the interlude, from which legitimate drama more directly descends, was perfected in the circle of Sir Thomas More and in the household of Archbishop Morton, where More served his apprenticeship. Just as Cornish's entertainments were a stylization of pageantry already found at court, so the interlude was created from material already familiar to humanist households like Morton's and More's. Disputation was a recognized method of medieval learning. The minstrels, too, were fond of the cross-talk comedy that still enlivens the variety stage. No doubt informal argumentation, in character, had long been an amusement of learned households. Another ingredient in an evening's entertainment would be music. From a fusion of these elements the interlude developed very naturally. Roper tells us that, even when a properly arranged interlude was being acted, More would

sodenly sometimes steppe in among the players, and neuer studyeng for the matter, make a parte of his owne there presently among them, which made the lookers-on more sport then all the plaiers besides.[1]

None of the early interludes are very far from the informal charades we can imagine as preceding them. *The Four P's*, for instance, is only a satirical argument among four tradesmen as to the merits of their callings. It is very natural, then, that the earliest interludes should all include songs, which would have their part in an ordinary evening's entertainment. The words of the songs are not generally given ; they are not an integral part of the interlude. Often they are quite artlessly introduced : one character asks another to sing, and the dialogue is suspended during the song, resting both actors and audience. But the inclusion of the songs started a tradition,

[1] *Life of More*, ed. E. V. Hitchcock (Early English Text Society), p. 5.

and the Elizabethan drama employs music throughout its career. In the early plays it is a mere background, but gradually dramatists learned to apply it to the heightening of dramatic effect.

In such circumstances it is not surprising that the interlude, like the more lavish court spectacle, should attract the attention of musicians. The most important of the early interlude writers was a member of More's circle who held a musical appointment at court. John Heywood (1497–1578) must be reckoned a professional musician, though his status was that of *generosus*, he owned estates in Essex, Hertfordshire, and Kent, and was a member of the Mercers' Company and measurer of linen cloths in the City of London. According to Anthony à Wood, he was a graduate of Broadgates Hall, Oxford, and the woodcut in *The Spider and the Flie* represents him in an M.A. gown. His reputation, however, was not that of a scholar but that of a wit who attempted both poetry and music. According to Bale,

Johannes Heywode, ut Orpheus alter, instrumentorum studiosus, musica et poeta, habebat in sua lingua gratiam.[1]

Puttenham says that he came to be preferred by the king ' for the myrth and quicknesse of his conceite more than for any good learning was in him '. His epigrams continued to enjoy some reputation long after the tedious allegory, *The Spider and the Flie*, had been forgotten. A lute song of his can be found in the British Museum manuscript, Additional 4900. It was rather as a performer than as a composer that he won favour at court. In the quarterly returns of the royal household for Michaelmas, 1519, occurs the entry : ' Item for John Haywoode qrtor wages at xxli by the yere 100/–.' The mention of the annual salary makes it probable that this refers to the first payment. His duties are revealed by the accounts of the next year : ' Item for John Haywode synger wages 100/–.'[2] In a short time additional emolument was added. Thomas Farthing, one of the Gentlemen of the Chapel, died in December 1520, and his ten marks a year, from the issues of the manors of Torpull and Makesey, Northamptonshire, were granted to Heywood. When the combined payments figure in the list of wages for the Michaelmas quarter, 1525, a new office is disclosed, not carrying additional salary. ' Item to John Heywood player of the virginals, £6 : 13s : 4d.' In 1528 he was

---

[1] *Scriptorum Britanniae . . . Catalogus*, II, 110.
[2] All these entries are reproduced in Prof. Reed's *Early Tudor Drama*, pp. 40–1.

discharged on pension during the economy campaign that followed the French wars. After a period in which his interests lay chiefly in the City, he returned to active court duties in the reigns of Edward and Mary, but his adherence to the Catholic faith cost him his place on the accession of Elizabeth, and he was forced to flee to the Continent.

Heywood married a niece of Sir Thomas More, and four of his interludes published in 1533 and 1534 by William Rastell, another relative of More, belong to the period when he was most intimate with the family. But later associations with the City and court led him to produce interludes for child players and pageants, both of which are closer to Cornish's efforts than to the early farcical dialogues. In the expenses of Princess Mary for March 1537-8 payment is made ' to Heywood playing an interlude with his children before my lady grace. xl s '.[1] Who the children were is not explained. That he was associated with some choir-boy company about that time is suggested by various entries in Cromwell's Book of Accounts for 1538-9, which disclose that in the February of that year he prepared a masque to be performed at Cromwell's house and at court.[2] An entry in the household expenses of Princess Elizabeth for 13 February 1551 reveals his association at a later date with the children of St. Paul's.

Paid in rewarde to the Kinges Maiesties dromer and phiphe 20/-. Mr Heywoodde 30/- ; and to Sebastian, towards the charge of the children with the carriage of the plaiers garments £4. 19. 0. In thole as by warraunte appereth £7. 9. 0.[3]

Professor Reed points out that this entry all refers to one performance.[4] Sebastian Westcott was Almoner of St. Paul's, and the children mentioned were most likely those in his care. In the Revels Accounts for 1552 is mentioned ' a play of the state of Ierland and another of the childerne sett owte by Mr Haywood '.[5] This probably records another performance by the St. Paul's boys.

Heywood's efforts with the Paul's children brought him into contact with Sebastian Westcott, as we have seen. There are also a number of signs of his acquaintance with one of Westcott's predecessors, John Redford, another musician who was apparently concerned with dramatic production. About 1535 he was Master of the Children of St. Paul's. He was a skilful organist and an

---

[1] Royal MS. 17 B. XXVIII, fol. 42, quoted Reed, op. cit., p. 58.
[2] Reed, op. cit., pp. 61-2.   [3] *Camden Miscellany*, II, 37.
[4] *Early Tudor Drama*, p. 59.   [5] *Losely MS.*, ed. Feuillerat, p. 145.

instrumental composer of considerable merit.   Some of his works
are extant, and he figures in Morley's list of praiseworthy ' Prac-
ticioners' at the end of the century.[1]   If the humanist interlude,
A Play of Wyt and Science, be by him, as is usually supposed, he
is equally notable as a dramatist.

Sebastian Westcott, the other St. Paul's musician with whom
Heywood collaborated, is a much more important figure in the
history of drama, though not in the history of music.   As almoner
he instructed the boys of the song school in music and letters.
The grammar school on the same foundation had given Latin
plays for some time.   Wescott was the first to produce dramatic
entertainments with the choir-boys.   He stood high in the favour
of the court and had a good patron in the Earl of Leicester.   Like
several other musicians, he was suspected of Papist views and
occasionally in trouble for them ; but his company nevertheless
appears to have been the most popular troupe of boys at court in
the early years of Elizabeth's reign.   Whether he added authorship
to production is uncertain.   It is possible that he wrote an early
version of *The Contention between Liberality and Prodigality* (printed
1602), and that this was the play called *Prodigality* acted in 1567–8.[2]
He may also have been a poet, for his New Year gift to Queen
Mary in 1557 was ' a boke of ditties, written'.[3]

On 5 August 1559 Queen Elizabeth was entertained at Nonesuch
by the Earl of Arundel with ' a play of the chylderyn of Powlles
and their master Se[bastian], master Phelypes, and master Heywood,
and after a grett bankett'.[4]   The Phillips mentioned is probably
the organist of St. Paul's at the time, and he has been identified
with the John Phillips who wrote *Patient Grissel*, but of this there
is no proof.[5]   When Wescott died, in 1582, his successor, Thomas
Giles, carried on dramatic work until 1600, when he relinquished
his post.   He may be identical with the Thomas Giles who was
appointed music master to Prince Henry in 1606 and composed
music for many masques of James I's reign.

Cornish's successors at the Chapel Royal, Crane and Bower,
are not known to have been dramatists, but the early experiments
at court and the interludes of Heywood were combined to form

[1] Brit. Mus. Add. MSS. 30513, 29996, 17802–5, 15233 contain some of his
compositions.
[2] H. N. Hillebrand, *The Child Actors* (Univ. of Illinois Studies in Lang. and
Lit.), pp. 128 ff.
[3] Nichols, *Progresses of Queen Elizabeth*, I, xxxv.
[4] Machyn's Diary (Camden Society ed.), p. 206.
[5] Chambers, *Elizabethan Stage*, II, 13.

the first court drama by Richard Edwards (1523(?)–1566). A native of Somerset, he graduated at Corpus Christi College, Oxford, in 1544, and was elected a fellow. In 1547 he was nominated a student at Christ Church and became an M.A. He later entered Lincoln's Inn, though he never practised law. The Inns of Court were well-known resorts of young men from the universities, who did not always intend to be called to the bar. They produced entertainments every year that won some reputation, and no doubt they were excellent places for exercising a talent for poetry, music, acting, or stage-management.

Edwards had studied music at Oxford under George Etheridge, an amateur of wide culture. His interests were very similar to those of Campion, to whom we shall refer in the next chapter. They represent a kind of amatuer musicianship that was quite common during the period. Their equal devotion to classical studies and to music was a great factor in maintaining close contacts between literary and musical ideas. Etheridge entered Corpus Christi College, Oxford, in 1534, as a scholar, and graduated there in 1538. In 1545 he became Bachelor of Medicine. Two years later, however, he was elected Professor of Greek, and held that chair until October 1550. In 1556 he was recommended by Lord Williams of Thame for a fellowship at the newly-founded Trinity College, but declined the honour, preferring to practise medicine, which he did in Oxford with great success. His works are a summary of his varied interests. He translated Justin Martyr and presented a Greek poem to Elizabeth when she visited Oxford in 1566 ; he published a treatise on medicine ; made a metrical version of the psalms, and is supposed to have written a great deal of vocal and instrumental music that has not survived. His versatility is a good illustration of the kind of musical amateur in which the period is particularly rich.

Edwards's musical interests may have begun in a similarly amateurish way, but he was to become a professional musician. In 1552 he was admitted a Gentleman of the Chapel Royal, and in 1561 was created Master of the Children of the Chapel. This had now become a semi-dramatic appointment, largely through Cornish's success. Edwards's entertainments were an advance on those of his predecessors. His writing showed the influence of classical tragedy and comedy. In 1564 a tragedy by him was performed by the children before the Queen at Whitehall, probably *Damon and Pithias*, of which the quarto is dated 1571. He accompanied the Queen to Oxford in 1566, and another play by him,

Palamon and Arcite, was produced in Christ Church Hall.   Although it is not extant, its title shows it must have been a tragedy drawn from Chaucer.   Anthony à Wood says that the cry of the hounds in the hunt of Theseus was so realistic that several young men in the hall jumped up to follow them.   The Queen was highly delighted, and complimented the author.   Later generations have not been so kind to him.   But Edwards's work was a great advance on his predecessors' :   it was drama, not a mere organization of existing entertainments, and it united the romantic tradition with classical drama, on which the productions of the universities and schools were modelled.   He apparently wrote comedy too, for Puttenham commends ' Master Edwardes of her Maiesties Chappell for Comedy and Enterlude ',[1] and Meres lists him among the Englishmen who have excelled at comedy.[2]   As a lyric poet his reputation was considerable.   *The Paradise of daynty devises*, issued commercially after his death, contains a number of his poems, with others by his contemporaries, and the mention of his name was evidently thought to assist the sale of the miscellany. His music is a link between the school of Cornish and that of Byrd.   Many of his songs were perhaps sung in his plays.

Edwards's successor at the Chapel Royal, William Hunnis, continued dramatic production on the lines suggested by his predecessor.   *Narcissus*, presented by him on Twelfth Night, 1572, was clearly inspired by Ovid, and was notable for a cry ' off stage ' at one point like a hunt, a realistic effect reminiscent of the hunting scene in *Palamon and Arcite*.   None of Hunnis's original plays has survived, but he is known to have been a dramatist, for Thomas Newton praises his ' Enterludes ' in a poem prefixed to *A Hyve full of Hunnye* (1578).   A fair amount of his poetry and music is extant.   He was a firm Protestant, and was implicated in an attempt to murder Queen Mary in 1555 and in an attempt to rob the royal treasury in 1556.   His religious views led him to spend much time turning passages of the Bible into English metre and setting it to simple music.   In 1549 was printed his *Psalmes chosen out of the Psalter of David and drawen into English meter* ; the following year his *Abridgement, or Briefe Meditation on certaine of the Psalmes in English Meter* ; in 1578 *A Hyve full of Hunnye Containing the first Book of Moses, called Genesis turned into English Meter*.   His most successful book of this kind was *Seven Sobs of a Sorrowfull soule for Sinne*, first published in 1583 and reprinted in 1587 and 1615.   As Master of the Children he assisted in the Kenilworth

---

[1] Gregory Smith, op. cit., II, 65.   [2] ib., II, 320.

festivities of 1575, when Leicester paid lavish homage to his sovereign.

From 1564 Hunnis's dramatic efforts were supplemented by those of Richard Farrant, who resigned from the Chapel Royal in that year to become organist and master of the choristers at St. George's, Windsor, his emoluments being £81 6s. 8d. a year and a ' dwelling house within the castle, called the Old Commons '. As a composer Farrant has a considerable reputation, though there is some uncertainty as to which of the works ascribed to him are his by right. Tudway assigns to him a full morning and evening service found in manuscript at Ely and Peterhouse. Boyce prints two of his supposed anthems; ' Call to remembrance ' and ' Hide not Thou thy face '. There are odd parts of services by him in the Royal College of Music and Additional Manuscript 29289 of the British Museum. More interesting for our present study are some airs with string quartet accompaniment in the library of Christ Church, Oxford.[1] These are thought to have occurred in his plays, for, besides being a very competent composer, he was an active dramatist and producer of plays. In the royal accounts for 1570 is the following entry :

To William Honnyes, Richard ffarante, and Sebastian Westcote mrs of the children of the Q : maiests Chapple Royall, windsore, and powles upon the counsailles warrant dated ultimo Februarii 1570, for presenting of thre plaies before her maiestie at this Shrofted last past, namelye Sondaie, Mondaie and Tuesdaie by waie of her highnes rewarde xxli.[2]

Among the ' emptions and provizions ' for Christmas, 1572-3, we find ' A desk for ffarantes playe—iij s '.[3] An entry in the accounts of 1574-5 supplies a clue to the nature of another of Farrant's plays : ' xj January / for A periwigg of Heare for king xerxes syster / in ffarantes playe / iiij s viij d '.[4] This suggests that he kept to the tradition of Edwards in the choice of subject and perhaps in treatment. In 1576-7 the court enjoyed ' The history of Mutius Scevola showen at Hampton Court on Twelf daie at night, enacted by the Children of windsore and the Chapell '.[5] This time he had charge of the joint forces of the two royal chapels. He had resumed his position as a Gentleman of the Chapel on 5 November 1570, and in 1576 he procured a lease on some of

---

[1] Described by G. P. E. Arkwright, *Musical Antiquary*, Vol. I, p. 30ff.
[2] Pipe Office, Roll 541, fol. 127v, quoted Hillebrand, op. cit., p. 87, n.44.
[3] Feuillerat, *Revels*, p. 175, l. 10.
[4] ib., p. 244, l. 18.   [5] ib., p. 256, ll. 20-1.

the old Priory buildings at Blackfriars and began to give public performances with the Chapel Royal children. After his death, on 30 November 1580, Hunnis ran the theatre with John Newman for a time, but in 1583 their interest was transferred to Henry Evans. When the theatre was forced to close, in 1584, the Chapel boys almost dropped dramatic activity. Their place at court was taken by the Paul's company and by one under the Earl of Oxford's patronage, the plays being written not by a Court musician but by a young protégé of the earl, John Lyly.

The Blackfriars venture marks a change in dramatic conditions. Up to this time musicians had concentrated on plays acted by the children under their care at court. At Blackfriars they sought to attract a wider public. The adult professional companies had revealed a wide demand for plays and were setting a new standard of performance. Burbage's theatre opened the very year Farrant took over his lease of Blackfriars. To compete with them the children's companies needed new material and methods. Their plays were no longer written by the professional musicians but by men of letters specially engaged. Lyly was a young university man of humble origin who made a living by his wits and won the patronage of the Earl of Oxford. He was soon followed by other university men, who turned to the public theatres rather than to the private companies. He sheltered under the influence of the great ; they won the applause of the populace. For those who could not become shareholders the theatre offered a precarious livelihood ; but it did provide some sort of opening for a professional writer, and Shakespeare was to make enough from it to set up as a country gentleman. The press, too, was beginning to afford men of literary ability a source of income and a means of establishing a reputation. The widening of the reading public and the organization of the theatres created a genuine literary profession with remarkable rapidity during the eighties ; and even plays for child actors passed from the hands of musicians and schoolmasters. A new specialization destroyed the union of literary and musical professions that had its roots in medieval minstrelsy.

Yet, though the writing of plays passed to men of letters, the association of musicians with the theatre, and particularly with children's companies, did not entirely cease after the invasion of the university wits. A few composers had interests in dramatic ventures in the first decades of the seventeenth century, when children's companies revived and began once more to filch the bread from the adult actors' mouths. The madrigal composers and church organists did not any longer compete in this business. The lutanists, however, retained the minstrel's adaptability to a greater extent. They were very literary musicians, since part of their duties was to set verses by their noble patrons (see p. 118). John Daniel, composer of a fine set of songs (1606), and in 1625 one of the royal musicians, came to be manager of a theatrical company through the influence of his brother, Samuel Daniel, the poet. The Queen requested the King to grant Samuel the right to form a company of youths and perform comedies and tragedies at Bristol, under the name of the Children of Her Majesty's Royal Chamber of Bristol. To this Sir George Buck, the Master of the Revels, agreed on 10 July 1615,[1] and by a license of 17 July John took his brother Samuel's place as manager. Somewhere about 1617 the company amalgamated with the Queen's Company under Martin Slater, and Daniel's patent was replaced by fresh letters of assistance.[2] In 1618 John Daniel succeeded his brother as censor of the plays performed by the Children of the Queen's Revels. This company, too, was under the management of a famous lutanist, Philip Rosseter, one of the royal musicians in 1604. He had been drawn into the theatrical business by Robert Keysar in 1609, when the Queen's Revels Company occupied Whitefriars, vacated by the bankrupt King's Revels Company. In March 1613 the company amalgamated with Henslow's Lady Elisabeth's men, but in 1615 Rosseter revived it at Puddlewharf, Blackfriars. The premises, Porter's Hall, are said in the patent [3] to be in the possession of Robert Jones, who became one of Rosseter's partners. Jones was another lutanist, who published five books of airs and two volumes of madrigals. Protests by the inhabitants of the neighbourhood eventually led to the demolition of the playhouse in 1616, and Jones dropped out of the company. Rosseter organized another company of the Queen's Revels, in partnership with Robert Lee, William Perry, and Nicholas Long. On 9 April 1623, the company's patent was confirmed, but this time Rosseter's name was omitted. His health was failing, and a month later he died.

Rosseter's theatrical commitments were of unusual magnitude for a seventeenth-century musician. By 1600 the theatre and the literary profession had become distinct from the musical profession. But the existence of such men as Rosseter, and the shortness of the

---

[1] *Calendar of State Papers, Domestic, 1611–18*, p. 294.
[2] ib, p. 549.　　　　　　　　[3] Chambers, *Elizabethan Stage*, II, 472.

time since a great deal of play-writing and production had been in the hands of musicians, served to keep men of letters and musicians in close touch with each other and to remind them that the separation of their callings was comparatively recent. In the streets they might still hear the ballad-singer retailing at once the poetry and the music of the illiterate, and they would be conscious that they themselves had the minstrel tradition not so very far behind them. Moreover, the constant needs of theatrical production would bring the composer into the theatre still. In a society with such traditions and with professional men so close to each other in their little world (if we compare it with ours), musicians and men of letters must have been peculiarly responsive to each other's ideas and knowledgeable about each other's problems.

CHAPTER IV

THE NEW POETRY AND MUSIC

IT is remarkable how responsive poets and composers of the Renaissance were to each other's ideas. Any movement of opinion was very quickly reflected in both arts. The explanation must be sought in the social life of the time. Humanist coteries had from their beginning included musicians and amateurs very interested in music, and a good deal of time was spent by the Italian academies in discussing the place of music in a gentleman's education. Songs and dances, too, were a great feature of these assemblies, even when they were primarily meeting to discuss literature and manners. Italian palace society, from which these coteries and academies sprang, was full of music. In Boccaccio's *Decameron* each day's story-telling is concluded with a song, accompanied on the lute or viol, or a dance, often a *carole*, in which the entire company sings to keep the rhythm of the dance. The work that established the vogue of Platonic love, Bembo's *Gli Asolani*, opens with three songs for the wedding of one of the Queen of Cyprus's maids of honour, and the rest of the discussions are largely suggested by the sentiments of the songs, while other songs are performed during the course of the book. The book is undoubtedly based on life at Asolo, where Catherine Cornaro held court. Of Urbino, the most elegant and cultured court during part of the early sixteenth century, a picture is preserved in Castiglione's *Courtyer*. The company taking part in the discussions there is very representative, and includes Bembo, one of the leaders of the New Poetry, whose connexion with Asolo has just been mentioned. Several of Castiglione's characters were skilful musicians, and a considerable time was spent on the question of how far music should be allowed to occupy a nobleman's attention. There was general agreement that no courtier could afford to be ignorant of it. The whole court at Urbino, in fact, was devoted to music. Castiglione avers that 'thither ran continually Poets, Musitions, and all kinds of men of skill, and the excellentest in every faculty that were in Italy', and the brilliant company gathered round the Duchess would often, after supper, enjoy 'among other recreations, musicke and dauncing, which they used continually'.[1]

---

[1] Everyman ed., pp. 21-2.

The social conditions of Italian courts were reproduced in the more formal academies, which bore a strong resemblance to gatherings like those at Urbino and Asolo, and which came to exercise so great an influence in formulating humanist doctrine. From Italy the academy spread to France. The Accademia della Nuova Poesia, with its concern to adapt humanist principles to Tuscan poetry, became a model for the Pléiade group. Here again musicians were in the centre of the discussions. The Académie de Musique et de Poésie, of which mention must be made in a later chapter, was an attempt of poets and musicians to collaborate in the reform of French versification. Ronsard and the other poets of La Pléiade were very sympathetic to it.

No formal academies were founded in England, but the Italian and French examples were not without influence. The New Poetry in England was particularly affected by the Pléiade. Ronsard was a friend of the Earl of Leicester, and was living in the Louvre in 1572 when Sidney, Leicester's nephew, visited Paris. Sidney must have met the French poet and have known of the Académie de Musique et de Poésie. He himself was a member of an informal and somewhat mysterious group with aims similar to those of the Pléiade and the Accademia della Nuova Poesia. The Areopagus, mentioned by Spenser in a letter to Gabriel Harvey, was probably only a name to cover those sharing Sidney's main ideas, but discussions about the New Poetry were certainly going on in England during the seventies, and Sidney, Spenser, and Harvey had some part in them. Like the French poets, they tried to trim between extreme classicism, which despised the vernacular tradition, and patriotic medievalism, which had lost touch with contemporary interests. The Spenser–Harvey letters of 1579–80 mention quantitative metres as an important field of investigation. How far they tried to justify quantitative metres by setting them to music, as the French Académie did, is a matter for conjecture. Sidney himself was not a musician, but seems to have been keenly interested in music. He regrets that he had not better training for it, writing to his brother that ' you will not believe what a want I finde of it in my melancholie times '.[1] The family to which he belonged was famous for its patronage of music. In the Penshurst papers are many references to the purchase of instruments, and Sidney himself encouraged musicians. He spent a good deal of his time at Salisbury, which, in the next generation, became a well-known music centre, and may have

---

[1] *Sidney Papers,* I, 285.

been one already in Elizabethan times. There he gave private concerts, as is proved by a letter from Sir Arthur Basset to Sir Edward Stradling, dated 6 February 1584. Sir Arthur speaks of one Thomas Richards, a musician, and continues :

I have giuen some commendacions of the man and his Instrument knowledge, but cheefly for the rareness of his instrument with wyars, unto sondry of my good friends, namely to my cosen sr Phillippe Sydney, whoe doth expecte to haue yor man at Salsbury before the VIIth of Marche next, where there will be an honorable assemblye and receyte of many gentlemen of good calling.[1]

Several of Sidney's poems have been found set to music. One of the composers was Charles Tessier, a French lutanist resident in England for a time, who published a volume of airs in London in 1597, dedicating it to Lady Penelope Rich, the Stella of Sidney's sonnets. This would seem to imply a connexion of some sort between Tessier and Sidney's circle. Sidney's appreciation of music is also shown by the fact that he wrote some of his poems to French and Italian tunes and one to the English country-dance *Greensleeves*.[2] In the *Arcadia* all the lyrics are described as being sung by various characters, and the accompanying instruments are carefully chosen to underline the moods of the different songs. Turning over a few pages at random one comes upon numerous passages like these :

. . . she might perceive the same voice, deliver itself unto musicall tunes, and with a base Lyra gave foorth this songe. . . .

But as if the Shepheard that lay before her, had bene organes, which were onely to be blowen by her breath, she had no sooner ended with the joyning her sweete lips together, but that he recorded to her musick, this rurall poesie. . . .

. . . she haply saw a Lute, upon the belly of which Gynecia had written this song. . . .

. . . which she taking a Citterne to her, did laye to Auroras chardge with these wel songe verses. . . .

Zelmane, first saluting the muses with a base voyal hong hard by her. . . .

Sidney, in fact, is always knowledgeable about music, though apparently ignorant of its technique. One cannot help wondering to what extent music entered into the discussions of quantitative metre and the measures of the New Poetry. It is significant that in the *Defense of Poesie*, comparing modern accentual poetry with

---

[1] *Sidneiana* (Roxburgh Club), p. 81.   [2] See pp. 174-5, 179-80.

quantitative verse, he finds 'the Auncient (no doubt) more fit for Musick, bothe words and tune obseruing quantity'.[1] There seems to be another relic of the French Académie in a rejected portion of the *Arcadia*.

Dicus said that since verses had their chief ornament if not one in musicke, those that weare iuste appropriated to musicke did agree with musick, since music standing principally upon the sound and the quality, to answer the sound [the poets] brought words, to answer the qualitie they brought measure, so that every semibreif or mynom had its sytlables matched accordingly with a long foote and a short foote . . .   So that eyther by the time a poet should know how every word should be measured unto yt, or by the verse as sone find out the full quantitie of the music.[2]

This notion of testing quantitative verse by setting its scansion down exactly in musical notes and then singing it, was precisely what led the French Académie to play with quantitative settings ; and Sidney's interest in it probably reflects discussions in the Areopagus group, which owed much to France.

Of the other leading parties to the discussion Harvey was the most likely to be pedantic and to work out quantitati ve scansion by theory rather than by ear.   It is curious, however, that in the quarrel between Nashe and him, Nashe should have laboured the comparison of him to a ballad-singer.   This *motif* runs right through *Have with you to Saffron Walden*.   The alternative title is 'Gabriel Harveys Hunt is up', a reminiscence of the popular tune 'The hunt is up', which gave its name to any prelude played by an itinerant fiddler.[3]   In launching his attack Nashe commends himself to 'Qui Cytheram nervis, & nervis temperat arcum, the melodious God of Gam ut re, that is life and sinnewes of everie thing'.[4]   His ridicule of Harvey's attempts at poetry certainly suggests that Harvey tried to set his verses to music.

Our poeticall Gabriell would transforme and metamorphize it [his own name] from Doctour to Doctor Ty (of which stile there was a famous Musition some yeres since.)[5]

Association with Dr. Tye is not uncomplimentary ; but the sub-title of the book promises harsher vituperation, which is quickly

---

[1] Gregory Smith, op. cit., I, 204.

[2] R. W. Zandvoort quotes this from the Queen's College MS. in his study of the *Arcadia*, p. 11.

[3] Anthony Now-now, an itinerant fiddler mentioned by Deloney (*Gentle Craft*) and Chettle (*Kind-hartes Dreame*), always begins with a 'hunts up'.

[4] Works of Nashe, ed. McKerrow, III, 23.   [5] ib., III, 37.

forthcoming. Harvey's real affinity, it is explained, is not with
Tye but with the tribe of Elderton, the red-nosed ballad-maker.

> Scarce nine yeeres of age he attained too, by engrossing al ballets
> that came to anie Market or Faire there-abouts, he aspired to bee as
> desperate a ballet-maker as the best of them.[1]

The equation of Harvey's verse with low balladry is never allowed
to drop throughout the book. Nashe is full of contempt for his

> Poetrie . . . having writ verses in all kindes . . . yet I can see no
> Authors he hath, more than his owne Naturall Genius or Minerva, except
> it bee Have with ye to Florida, The Storie of Axerxes and the worthy
> Iphijs, As I went to Walsingham, and In Crete when Dedalus, a song
> that is to him food from heaven.[2]

All these ' authors ' that served as Harvey's models are, of course,
popular ballads of the day. Harvey's hexameters are compared to
stage jigs, crude verses fitted to dance tunes and mimed after plays.
Finally, Nashe offers a parody of his own,

> The trick or habit of which I got by looking on a red nose Ballet-
> maker that resorted to our Printing-house. They are to the tune of
> Labore Dolore, or the Parlament tune of a pot of ale and nutmegs and
> ginger, or Eldertons ancient note of meeting the divell in coniure house
> lane. If you hit it right, it will go marvellous sweetly.[3]

Undoubtedly the suggestion that the scholarly Harvey was a mere
ballad writer was meant to wound. It may only have been
another way of saying that Harvey's verse was doggerel, but the
labouring of the point is interesting. It would be more damaging
if there were a germ of truth behind the allegation. Is it not
possible that Harvey, with the rest of his humanist friends, had
been studying the experiments of Baïf and the French Académie
and saw the relevance of musical time to discussions of quantitative
metre ?

Spenser was the most cautious of those discussing such metrical
experiments. His *English Poet*, as far as can be judged from E. K.'s
glosses, probably covered much the same ground and adopted much
the same critical position as Sidney's *Defense*, and he may therefore have held the views of the Pléiade about the importance of
music in studying the time problems of verse. His poetry gives
the impression of one not indifferent to music. Sometimes he
is intentionally vague in his references to it, as in the description
of the Bower of Bliss, and the vagueness is part of the poetry's

[1] ib., III, 63.   [2] ib., III, 67.   [3] ib., III, 133.

enchantment. He can be more definite. Like Sidney, he knows
the proper instruments to choose for his effects. Calliope and the
Muses sing to 'Luyts and Tamburins', the accompanying instruments for singing and dancing. King Arthur finds

> . . . in her delicious boure,
> The faire Paeana playing on a Rote,
> Complayning of her cruell Paramoure,
> And singing all her sorrow to the note,
> As she had learned readily by rote.[1]

Spenser's rustics play the bagpipe, the traditional English pastoral
instrument. At his own wedding the music well befits the shepherd Colin Clout.

> Harke how the Minstrels gin to shrill aloud
> Their merry Musicke that resounds from far,
> The pipe, the tabor, and the trembling Croud,
> That well agree withouten breach or iar.
> But most of all the Damsels doe delite,
> When they their tymbrels smyte.[2]

Queen Radigund, the Amazon, is

> Guarded with many damsels, that did waite
> Uppon her person for her sure defence,
> Playing on shaumes and trumpets. . . .[3]

—the appropriate military band of Elizabethan times. Sometimes he is conventional. When he compares the birds to a
choir—

> The merry Larke hir mattins sings aloft,
> The thrush replyes, the Mauis descant playes,
> The Ouzell shrills, the Ruddock warbles soft,
> So goodly all agree with sweet consent,
> To this dayes merriment [4]—

he is merely echoing Chaucer. Perhaps he was thinking of the
emotional effect of the suspension in contrapuntal music when he
remarked that

> . . . Discord oft in Musick makes the sweeter lay.[5]

His instruments and sounds always have a pleasant definiteness
that contrasts with the vague unearthly kind of music in (say)
Romantic and nineteenth-century poets ; but that is not unusual

---

[1] *Faerie Queene*, IV, ix, 6.   [2] *Epithalamion*, ll. 129–34.
[3] *Faerie Queene*, V, v, 4.   [4] *Epithalamion*, ll. 78–84.
[5] *Faerie Queene*, III, ii, 15.

for his period. One of the songs in the *Shepheardes Calender* is written to a popular tune (see pp. 173–4) ; but it remains doubtful to what extent Spenser was interested in music, and to what extent he shared the ideas of Sidney and, above all, of his model Ronsard.

In *Foure Letters* (1592) Harvey alludes to others sympathetic to the Areopagus movement. These ' deere Lovers of the Muses and professed Sonnes of the same ' were ' Edmond Spenser, Richard Stanihurst, Abraham Fraunce, Thomas Watson, Samuell Daniell, Thomas Nash, and the rest '.[1] Stanihurst was a crank who played with quantitative verse and spelling reform : he need not detain us. Abraham Fraunce owed much to the Sidney family. His education at Cambridge had been under Sir Philip's patronage, and his gratitude to the family found expression in the dedication of various works to the Countess of Pembroke. Spenser refers to him in *Colin Clout's Come Home Again*, and in the *Faerie Queene* there is a reference to his translation into English hexameters of Watson's Latin version of Tasso's *Aminta*.[2] Watson had a considerable reputation as a classicist, which alone would explain his gravitation towards the Areopagus discussions. But he had personal relations with the Sidneys too. In words reminiscent of Spenser, he salutes Sidney as Astrophel ; and he had evidently seen *Astrophel and Stella* in manuscript before the printed version appeared.[3] In another poem Sidney's death is mourned along with that of his father-in-law, Sir Francis Walsingham,[4] to whom Watson also devoted a collection of poems in Latin and English, *Meliboeus*. He shared the desire of Sidney and Harvey to adapt classical imitation to the genius of the English language, and, like them, his eyes were turned towards Italy and France for guidance in revitalizing vernacular literature. He was something of a pioneer in naturalizing the Petrarchan style and forms. His *Hecatompathia, or Passionate Centurie of Love* (1582) is the first of the sonnet cycles of the Elizabethan period, and a very important milestone in the progress of the New Poetry. Even more interesting in the present context is his next work. *The First Sett of Italian Madrigalls Englished* is a selection of Italian compositions with their texts translated into English ' more after the affection of the note than the dittie ' (i.e. so that the words will sound well when sung, without bothering very much about how they sound when read). Two years previously Nicholas Yonge had published a similar anthology. But Watson was more up-to-date than

[1] *Works*, ed. Grosart, I, 218. [2] III, vi, 45.
[3] *Italian Madrigalls Englished* (1590), No. 1. [4] ib., Nos. 23, 27.

Yonge in his study of the Italians.   Twenty-three of his twenty-
eight compositions are by Luca Marenzio, the most advanced and
most brilliant of the Italian school, and they are from quite recent
works, thirteen of them being printed in Venice only three years
previously.   Watson's musical taste deserves credit, though he
was probably assisted by William Byrd, for, as the title-page
informs us, 'there are also here inserted two excellent Madrigalls
of Master William Byrds, composed after the Italian vaine, at the
request of the said Thomas Watson'.

    This statement gives the impression that Watson was the
leading spirit in *Italian Madrigalls Englished*; but both he and Byrd
were closely associated with the introduction of Italian music as a
whole.   Byrd had probably had something to do with Yonge's
venture two years before, for Yonge included 'the first and second
part of La Virginella, made by Maister *Byrd*, vpon two Stanz's of
Ariosto, and brought to speake English with the rest'.   Indeed,
the very fact that both these volumes were printed at all points to
Byrd's collaboration, for he virtually inaugurated English music
publishing.   He secured a monoply for printing music and ruled
paper in 1575, in partnership with Thomas Tallis, and imported
a fount of music type from John Petreius, the famous Nuremberg
type-cutter and printer.   With this Thomas Vautrollier prepared
a set of Latin *Cantiones*, composed by the two monopolists themselves, and published it in 1575.   The type, however, lay idle, until
Thomas East was put in charge of it and in 1588 began issuing
volumes of music by Byrd himself.   *Psalmes, Sonets, and Songs*
appeared in 1588 ; *Songes of sundrie natures* and *Liber primus Sacrarum
Cantionum* in 1589.   Yonge's and Watson's volumes were thus the
first works not by the monopolists themselves to be printed, and
it is difficult to imagine their being so except with Byrd's co-
operation.

    Byrd was a very influential personality in the musical life of
his time.   The pupil of Tallis, the leading figure in the Reformation school of church music, he was the master of Thomas Morley,
the first English composer to feel completely at home in the Italian
style of the madrigal.   Byrd had already composed some remarkable songs in the English tradition, but he was keenly interested
in Italian achievements, and, when he published his first set of
songs in 1588, he arranged them so that they should approximate
to the Italian madrigal, although they had originally been written
for solo voice and string quartet, after the English manner (see pp.
85-8).   He must have learned a great deal about Italian madrigals

from Alfonso Ferrabosco, a native of Bologna who had settled at the English court some time before 1567. That the two were well acquainted is certain, for Morley records a

vertuous contention in loue betwixt themselues made vpon the plaine song *Miserere*; but a contention, as I saide, in loue : which caused them to strive euery one to surmount another without malice, enuie, or back-biting; but by great labour, studie, and paines, each making other Censor of that which they had done; Which contention of theirs (specially without enuie) caused them both to become excellent in that kinde, and winne such a name, and gaine such credit, as will neuer perish so long as Musick endureth.[1]

The results of their labours were printed by East in 1603 under the title *Medulla Musicke*.[2] They also both set two French *chansons* that served as texts for Orlando di Lasso, ' The Nightingale ' and ' Susanna fair '. Fourteen of Ferrabosco's madrigals were included in *Musica Transalpina* of 1588, six in the second edition of 1597, and five in Morley's *Italian Madrigals* of 1598. In addition to his friendship with Watson, Byrd may have had direct contact with the Sidneys. Not only does he set a poem by Sidney in his 1588 volume, but two of the other songs are headed ' The funerall Songs of that honorable Gent./*Syr Phillip Sidney*, Knight'.

The collaboration of Watson and Byrd supports the belief that music must have entered the discussions about the New Poetry in England as in France. Others of the Areopagus circle were not ignorant of music. Samuel Daniel's obligations to the Sidney family are acknowledged in the dedication of his *Defense of Ryme* (1607) to Philip Herbert, Sidney's nephew, and his *Delia* (1592), *Cleopatra* (1594), and *Civil Wars* (1609) to the Countess of Pembroke, Sidney's sister. It is not surprising Harvey should name him as a sympathiser with the Areopagus group, and, if music had a place in the deliberations, he was probably able to judge its relevance. He was brother of John Daniel, the great song-writer, and supplied some of the verse for his brother's *Songs* (1606). His own knowledge of music may have been one of the reasons he was well fitted to reply in his *Defense of Ryme* to Campion's plea for a wholesale adoption of quantitative metres into English, for Campion based his arguments partly on musical experience.

What Nashe had to do with the Areopagus it is difficult to see. Harvey's approval of him did not last long, and we have

[1] *Plaine and Easie Introduction*, p. 115.
[2] Stationers' Register (Arber's reprint), III, 246.

already quoted some of Nashe's compliments to his former friend. But Nashe apparently moved in circles that discussed the humanist ideals of Castiglione's *Courtyer*, and his reference to a meeting of such people includes the customary question how far music should be encouraged in a gentleman's training.

> Not long since lighting in company with manie extraordinarie Gentlemen, of most excellent parts, it was my chance (amongst other talke which was generally traversed amongst us) to moove divers Questions, as touching the severall qualities required in Casalions Courtier : one came in with that of Ovid, *Semper amabilis esto*, another stood more strictly on the necessitie of the affabilitie, which our Latinists entitle *facetus*, and we more familiarlie describe by the name of discoursing : the third came in with his carpet devises and tolde what it was to tickle a Citterne, or have a sweet stroke on the Lute, to daunce more delicatelie, and revell it bravelie.[1]

Musical analogies spring readily to Nashe's mind. He talks about harping on the ' two strings of praise and reproofe . . . as it were a Dirige in pricksong I have harpt upon ' ; [2] refers to ' my old Sarum plainesong I have harpt upon ' ; [3] declares ' I have sung George Gascoignes Counter-tenor ' ; [4] and avers that Harvey ' looks like a case of tooth-pikes, or a Lute pin put in a sute of apparel '.[5] More significant is an allusion to Marenzio's madrigals and the current terms in which they were praised. Sarcastically recommending Harvey to tune his rimes like a fiddler, he exclaims : ' O they would have trowlt it off bravely to the tune O man in Desperation, and, like Marenzos Madrigals, the mournefull note naturally have affected the miserable Dittie.' [6] There are other evidences that Marenzio was especially admired for the suitability of his music to the text, and this allusion of Nashe probably reflects the opinions of the musical-literary circles for which Watson intended his editions.

Nashe had musical friends among the younger writers of the day. Thomas Campion most completely realized the aspirations of Ronsard, for he set his own verses to music : with him Nashe seems to have been well acquainted. Perhaps they first met at Cambridge, where they were contemporaries, Nashe at St. John's and Campion at Peterhouse. Later Campion addresses a complimentary epigram to him in the *Poemata* of 1595. They both taunt poor Barnabe Barnes, who was either a common friend that

---

[1] *Works*, ed. McKerrow, III, 177.   [2] ib., II, 285.
[3] ib., III, 184.   [4] ib., II, 310.
[5] ib., III, 38.   [6] ib., II, 265.

had annoyed them or a common enemy whom they united to discredit.

Campion was typical of a kind of amateur who combined music and poetry. He was not an aristocratic dilettante in the tradition of the *trouvères*. He came from the same social class as most of the dramatists and pamphleteers, who, as we saw, constituted the first real literary profession. He had been educated with them at the university and at Gray's Inn, and he too had to find a profession when his small patrimony was exhausted ; but he did not choose either the literary or the musical profession. The son of a cursitor in the Court of Chancery, he graduated at Peterhouse, Cambridge, and then spent some time at Gray's Inn, where he assisted in the *Gesta Grayorum* of 1593. He later studied medicine abroad, and returned to practise it very successfully in London. But his fame depends on his amateur interest in music and poetry. If he is exceptional in his mastery of both arts, his viewpoint is similar to those of many contemporaries : he is a very representative figure. Such amateurs as he—and many had his twofold interest without his eminence as a creator in both arts— helped considerably to keep music and poetry in touch with each other. In music, he was the first to state clearly the harmonic ideas that were coming to replace the contrapuntal theory of the middle ages : his book on counterpoint contains nothing new, but it implies progression in chords, not the harmonization of rhythmically independent melodies, which the orthodox theorists still pretended was the only kind of composition. As a literary critic, Campion shared the views of the neo-classicists, being himself a very good Latin poet. In his English poems he often uses the classics—Catullus, for example—in a seventeenth-century manner rather than an Elizabethan ; but his quantitative experiments are related to the discussions of the earlier Areopagus group. He acknowledges his debt to them by addressing epigrams to both Sidney and Spenser.

Campion's circle, as we should expect, included many interesting literary and musical personalities. There were, for instance, the three Mychelburnes and Charles Fitzgeffery, author of two sets of Latin poems, *Cenotaphia* and *Affaniae*, and of a eulogistic English poem on Sir Francis Drake. In 1597 Fitzgeffery contributed complimentary verses to *The Cittharn Schoole* of Anthony Holborne, a professional musician, who would seem to have been a friend of several of Campion's associates, and who perhaps owed obligations to the Sidneys, the centre of the earlier group that did so much for Italianate poetry and music.   One of Holborne's lute pieces is called 'The Countess of Pembruth funeralle'.[1]   Like many lutanist composers, and as one would expect in a friend of Campion and Fitzgeffery, he was a very literary musician.   He contributed Latin verses to Farnaby's *Canzonets* (1598) and English verses to Morley's *Introduction*.   In Robert Dowland's *Musicall Banquet* (1610) there is a setting by him of a poem by the Earl of Cumberland, another friend of Campion and perhaps the Maecenas of the whole group of poets and musicians.   *Two Bookes of Ayres* Campion dedicated to this earl, declaring his house the palace of the Muses.

> What patron could I chuse, great Lord, but you ?
>   Graue words your years may challenge as their owne,
> And eu'ry note of Musicke is your due,
>   Whose house the Muses pallace I haue knowne.

When the earl provided an entertainment for James I at Brougham Castle in 1617, Campion wrote the words.   It is possible from the last line of the dedication just quoted that many of Campion's airs were written to be sung at the earl's house.   Rosseter says that they were intended to be privately imparted to his friends (see p. 36).

In the preface to his *Fourth Booke of Ayres* Campion says that some of the poems in the volume 'haue beene cloathed in Musick by others, and I am content that they then serued their turne : yet giue mee now leaue to make vse of mine owne'.   This remark makes it likely that, when a good text of a poem by Campion is found in a book of airs by somebody else, especially if it appeared before Campion's own setting, the author gave permission for its use.   One such is in a volume by Dowland, and nothing is more probable than that Dowland had many acquaintances in Campion's circle and knew the poet himself.   It has already been mentioned that Anthony Holborne's setting of some words by the Earl of Cumberland is included in *A Musicall Banquet*, edited by Dowland's son, and this suggests the Dowlands, like Campion and Holborne, may have had works performed at the earl's house.   Campion addressed a very laudatory epigram to Dowland in his *Poemata*.   Dowland was more than a skilful virtuoso and a sensitive song-writer ; the choice of poems in his volumes is exceptionally discriminating.   He may have written a number of the texts himself ; it seems certain that he

---

[1] Egerton MS. 2046.

had some literary taste. To Farnaby's *Canzonets* he contributed a witty poem, twitting Farnaby on his love of strange progressions.

> Thou only shalt have Phyllis,
> Only thou fit (without all further gloses)
> Crouned to be with everlasting Roses,
> With Roses and with Lillies,
> And with Daffadoundillies,
> But thy songs sweeter are (save in their closes)
> Then are Lillies and Roses :
> Like his that taught the woods sound Amaryllis.
> Goldings : you that have too too dainty Noses,
> Avaunt, go feed you them els where on Roses.

Other verses by him are to be found in Richard Alison's Psalms. Alison was an acquaintance also of Campion, who wrote verses prefixed to his *Howres Recreation*. Dowland had relations with the Sidney family, the fountain-head of the whole movement of the New Poetry in England. One of the poems in his *Pilgrimes Solace* (No. 1) is by William, Earl of Pembroke, Sidney's brother-in-law. His son, Robert Dowland, dedicated *A Musicall Banquet* (1610) to Sir Robert Sidney, Viscount Lisle, in acknowledgement of

that dutie I owe vnto your Lordship for two great respects ; in regard (your Lordship vndertaking for mee) I was made a member of the Church of Christ, and withall receiued from you my name : the other the loue that you beare to all excellency and good learning, (which seemeth hereditarie aboue others to the Noble Familie of the Sidneys).

Viscount Lisle's standing godfather to Robert Dowland argues a regard for Robert's father. John Dowland would also seem to have been acquainted with Anthony Holborne, who has already been mentioned as a member of Campion's circle. The fine song 'I saw my lady weep', in *The Second Booke of Ayres*, is dedicated to 'the most famous Anthony Holborne'. Moreover, the Dowlands owed something to another friend of Campion, Sir Thomas Monson. To him Robert dedicated *Varietie of Lute Lessons* (1610) in token of 'the gratefull remembrance of your bountie to me, in part of my Education, whilst my Father was absent from England'. Monson was somewhat compromised by the Overbury murder, and Campion was questioned, because of the friendship between the two. Dedicating *The Third Booke of Ayres* to 'my honourable friend sr Thomas Monson, Knight and

Baronet', Campion congratulates him on being at length free from suspicion and asks him to accept

> These youth-borne Ayres then, prison'd in this Booke,
> Which in your Bowres much of their beeing tooke.

Another lutanist who set some of Campion's verses was Robert Jones. In the preface of one of his books of airs, as has been pointed out in an earlier chapter, Jones says that he attired the poems for some gentlemen of his acquaintance, and Campion was evidently one of them. Nothing is more natural than that they should know each other. Jones was partner in a theatrical venture with Philip Rosseter, Campion's closest friend, to whom in his will he left all that he had 'and wished it had bin far more' (see p. 59). Rosseter's patent for the Queen's Revels Company was obtained through the influence of Sir Thomas Monson, whose friendship with Campion has just been mentioned.

Campion was interested not only in the adaptation of quantitative measures to English verse, a question that had occupied so much attention among the early disciples of the New Poetry, but also in the later Italian experiments in equating poetic and musical rhythm. Only two English composers of that time affected the declamatory style that emerged from these experiments. One was John Coprario, an Italianate Englishman, for whose *Songs of Mourning* Campion supplied the texts, and the other Alfonso Ferrabosco, son of Byrd's friend, whose *Ayres* (1609) contained a complimentary poem by Campion and another by Ben Jonson. Most of the airs in the latter were composed for Jonson's masques. Whether Jonson also knew Campion it is impossible to tell, but it is likely that he did. Certainly Jonson moved among musicians, both amateur and professional. One amateur with whom he was acquainted was Richard Martin, a lawyer and M.P. with a reputation as a poet and composer. He was one of the 'chief doers and undertakers' in a masque before the King in February 1612–13, when John and Robert Dowland played lutes. Further evidence of his association with the Dowlands is a musical setting by him of a poem by the Earl of Essex, which was published in Robert Dowland's *Musicall Banquet*.

There is plenty of evidence in Jonson's plays that he rubbed shoulders with musicians and those who fancied themselves musicians. In *The Poetaster* a musician, Hermogenes, is among the men of letters satirized. His vanity is pricked by the poet-master's attempts at music, but he displays all the assumed modesty of the minor singer. When asked to sing he replies churlishly, 'Cannot sing', wanting to be pressed. But when Crispinus sings instead, Hermogenes adds the second stanza of the song, and he can hardly be quieted, so anxious is he to add more displays of his talent. Jonson is undoubtedly hitting at types he knew only too well, and a particular musician may be intended.[1]

Many other instances might be added of the contacts between musicians and men of letters, but enough has been said to suggest that the ties were very close. The society in which both lived and the traditional union of the two arts drew them together. The amateur who practised both arts was an important link. The New Poetry was discussed in an atmosphere that was musical as much as literary; the madrigal was one of the early fruits of Petrarchan poetry; and the younger poets at the turn of the century were just as much in contact with the lutanist song-writers as their elders had been with the contrapuntal composers. This very inadequate sketch of the involved relations of a few leading figures will perhaps help to explain how literary pre-occupations so frequently determined musical developments during this period, and how musical ideas constantly modified the theories about poetry and the structure of actual verse.

[1] The fact that this particular behaviour of a musician is suggested by Horace (*Satires*, I, 3) does not make it any the less likely that Jonson has a contemporary in mind.

CHAPTER V

MUSICAL AND POETICAL FORMS

THE organization of sound into rhythm is fundamental to both poetry and music. Rhythmical sound has always helped to relieve the tedium of physical activity, whether work or marching, and to guide the expressive bodily movements of dancing. Music has therefore been associated not only with poetry but with the dance; and, while poetry was commonly sung, the interactions of the three arts were bound to be particularly significant. Dance routines suggested musical forms, on which in turn verse forms were modelled; speech rhythms were reproduced in music, while tunes provided moulds in which poetic ideas could be cast.

In speech a word acquires its full meaning only as a member of a sentence group, but a single note of music is even less intelligible than an isolated word. The unit of musical expression is the phrase, and it is in the nature of music that the phrase invites response, until a tune has been created from two or more phrases somehow related in rhythm, melodic curve, and cadences. It is a fair presumption that in the tune, the primary and fundamental musical form, strophic verse found its origin.[1] The stanza represents no poetic necessity : the line furnishes a sufficient metrical underpart on which to counterpoint the rhythm of the sentence. The earliest extant English poetry is not strophic; but if it, or any later English narrative verse, were ever sung to music similar to that which accompanied the French *chansons de geste*, a single phrase being repeated for each line of the verse, the music was acting merely as a vehicle for the oral transmission of the poetry and refraining from development along the lines dictated by its own nature. Song requires the stanza. Folk-song illustrates this. Although the popular ballads are narrative, like Old English heroic poetry and medieval romance, they are sung to tunes, and therefore their form is strophic.

Verse fitted to a tune has its own form, but its general outline is parallel to that of the musical form. Similarly a simple tune set to a stanza of verse takes a form satisfying in itself as music. The line corresponds to the musical phrase, and rime commonly marks the

[1] 'Das Dichten eines Volkes beginnt nicht mit der Zeile, sondern mit des Strophes, nicht mit der Metrik, sondern mit Musik.' W. Meyer, *Gesammelte Ablandlungen zur mittellateinischen Rhythmik* (Berlin, 1905), I, 51.

cadence ; but identity between the forms of verse and tune cannot be complete, for meaning in poetry and melody in music impose their separate structural principles. Rime, for instance, does not fulfil the same function as cadence : if a tune comprises two repeated phrases of equal length in the order ABAB, the first couplet ending in a half-close and the second in a perfect cadence, then the lines might just as well rime abab or abba. The forms of music and poetry are parallel, however, and modify each other.

The music of every age and society falls into rhythmical and melodic habits. Association with music would create in medieval and Renaissance verse certain standard formal patterns, based on contemporary musical habits, and to these poetry would tend to conform, even when it was not written with some particular music in mind. The tendency is visible in folk-song. Of English folk-songs Cecil Sharp writes :

> The usual stanza of poetry contains four measured lines, not necessarily of equal length, though forming a just balance ; and the music to which such a stanza is set consists, normally, of four phrases, the points of division being marked off by means of cadence. Of these the middle cadence is the most important.[1]

Not only is there a normal number of phrases, however, but the phrases themselves have a normal length equivalent in modern terms to two bars of compound time (C or 6/8). Of course, there are many tunes not of this strict pattern, but it is sufficiently common to be regarded as a standard one, and one can easily see how, with such a pattern at the back of their minds, composers could develop more varied forms by combination and repetition of phrases, addition of a refrain, insertion of measures in irregular time, &c. As each note generally has a syllable set to it, we should expect the standard pattern to produce in verse a normal stanza of four lines, each with four stresses, or else one of alternate four-stress and three-stress lines, since the middle and final cadences are usually marked by held notes and the former often followed by a rest. This is, in fact, just what is found. By far the commonest stanza is the one significantly termed ballad metre—i.e. a quatrain of alternate four-stress and three-stress lines—and the next most common is the quatrain of four-stress lines. The pattern is not peculiar to folk-song. The prevalence of the four-stress line in medieval English and Latin and in sixteenth-century verse suggests that it is related to a pattern of medieval music. The fourteener, so common in the

[1] *English Folk-Song : Some Conclusions,* p. 73.

earlier sixteenth-century poetical miscellanies, obviously derives from it ; in fact, it is nothing else than ballad metre written as couplets.

Melodic variation and repetition would produce more elaborate patterns in art music than in folk-song ; but, while the lyric continued to be sung, we should expect a tendency to construct verse on metrical patterns related to the structure of contemporary music. It is to this that Dante refers when he says : ' It will become plain how the art of the Canzone depends on the division of the Musical Setting.'[1] He does not mean that the poem is to be written to existing music ; rather is he thinking of the usual forms that tunes take, and insisting that the stanza must be made ready to fit one possible form of tune. ' We say, then, that every stanza is set for the reception of a certain Ode ' (i.e. melody).[2] Every detail of the stanza may not perfectly correspond with every detail in the form of the music it is expected to receive. It is important, however, that the general structure of both should be the same.

It appears to us that what we call the Arrangement [of the parts of the stanza] is the most important section of what belongs to the art of the Canzone : for this depends on the division of the Musical Setting, the putting together of the lines, and the relation of the rhymes.[3]

The purport of this somewhat obscure statement becomes plainer as Dante proceeds to divide the possible kinds of musical form into two main kinds.

Some proceed to one continuous ode—that is, without the repetition of any musical phrase, and without any Dieresis : and we understand by Dieresis, a transition from one ode to another : this, when speaking to the common people, we call Volta. And this kind of stanza was used by Arnaut Daniel in almost all his Canzoni, and we have followed him in ours beginning—

Al poco giorno ed al gran cerchio d'ombra.[4]

By continuous ode he apparently means a simple tune composed of a number of distinct phrases moving to a final cadence. More elaborate patterns result from the repetition of certain parts of the tune to new words.

There are some stanzas which admit of a Dieresis, and there can be no Dieresis (in our sense of the word) unless a repetition of one ode be made either before the Dieresis, or after or both. If the repetition takes

---

[1] *De Vulgari Eloquentia*, trans. Howell, p. 73.
[2] ib., p. 72. [3] ib., p. 74. [4] ib., pp. 72–3.

place before the Dieresis, we say that the stanza has Feet : and it ought to have two, though sometimes (but very rarely) we find three. If the repetition takes place after the Dieresis, then we say that the stanza has Verses. If there is no repetition before the Dieresis, we say that the stanza has a Fronte ; if there is none after, we say that it has a Syrma or Coda.[1]

The easiest way of making clear Dante's meaning is to quote a thirteenth-century lyric constructed according to his rules.

Musical Sections

Lenten is come with love to toune,	Foot	A
With blosmen and with briddes roune		
That al this blisse bryngeth.		
Dayes-eyes in this dales	Foot	A
Notes suete of nyhtegales ;		
Uch foul song singeth.		
The threstelcoc him threteth oo ;	Verse	B
Away is huere wynter woo,		
When woderove springeth.		
This foules singeth ferly fele	Verse	B
Ant wylteth on huere wynter wele,		
That al the wode ryngeth.[2]		

Behind this stanza is a musical form consisting of two repeated sections, each of which contains three phrases. There is no reason why the two sections should be alike in the number and relationships of the musical phrases. The same principle of structure recurs in a lyric set by John Dowland in the sixteenth century, but the second half of this poem requires in his music a different number and arrangement of phrases from the first half.

Music

Awake, sweet loue, thou art returnd.	Foot	A
My hart, which long in absence mournd,		
Liues now in perfect ioy.		
Let loue, which neuer absent dies,	Foot	A
Now liue for euer in her eyes,		
Whence came my first anoy.		
Only herselfe hath seemed fair,	Verse	B
She only I could loue ;		
She only drave me to dispair,		
When she vnkind did proue.		
Dispayer did make me wish to die,	Verse	B
That I my ioyes might end.		
She only, which did make me flie,		
My state may now amend.[3]		

---

[1] ib., pp. 72–3.
[2] Chambers and Sidgwick, *Early English Lyrics*, p. 8.
[3] *First Book of Ayres*, No. 19.

As the man of letters acquired a function more and more separate from that of the composer, stanzas originally derived from musical patterns would come to be regarded purely as metrical structures ; but the artificiality of some medieval literary *genres* is due to their imperfect detachment from their musical antecedents. The roundel may be cited as an example. A simple French type of roundel occurs with music in Royal MS. 12 C. 6 in the British Museum. The music consists of two themes only, repeated in the order ABAAABAB. To sing only two lines of verse to these two phrases would be extremely monotonous, and therefore five lines are employed, in the following arrangement :

Faus semblant ciel estes vous	A
Mis m'aves ou rent destous	B
Vous enpartez bien les vos	A
Faus semblant ciel estes vous	A
Mieux a dieux fais i'aime vous	A
Je vous en averez destous	B
Faus semblant ciel estes vous	A
Mis m'aves ou rent destous.[1]	B

This simple type was elaborated, either or both of the musical themes being given to a couplet instead of a single line, the repetitions occurring in the same order. Chaucer wrote a roundel with a couplet for the first theme and a single line for the second :

Your yen two wol slee me sodenly,	A
I may the beaute of hem not sustene,	
So woundeth hit through-out my herte kene.	B
And but your words wol'helen hastily	A
My hertes wounde, whyl that hit is grene,	
Your yen two wol slee me sodenly,	A
I may the beaute of hem not sustene.	
Upon my trouthe I sey yow feithfully,	A
That ye ben of my lyf and deeth the quene ;	
For with my deeth the trouthe shal be sene.	B
Your yen two wol slee me sodenly,	A
I may the beaute of hem not sustene,	
So woundeth hit through-out my herte kene.	B

To Chaucer the roundel was a poetic exercise, but no literary effect is achieved by the repetition of the words, which is merely a relic of the original musical form of the roundel.

The progress from musical pattern to verse structure can be seen from a glance at forms ultimately derived from the dance. The

[1] Reproduced with music in J. Wolf, *Geschichte der Mensural-Notation*, III, 27.

earliest dances seem to have been round dances, the formal principle of which was an alternation of verses sung by the leader and an unvarying refrain sung by the chorus as a whole. The ring of dancers moved right or left while singing the refrain, and made some sort of marking-time gesture while the soloist sang his part. At first the leader sang a couplet and the chorus a single line of refrain, and this primitive form has survived in a quotation by Robert of Brunne in his *Handlyng Sinne* :

> By þe leued wode rode Beuolyne,
> wyþ hym he ledde feyre Merswyne ;
> why stonde we ? why go we noght ? [1]

The very words of the refrain suggest the movement that was to accompany them. Quite early, however, three-line stanzas for the soloist and couplets for the refrain became common, and the necessity for giving a cue to the chorus led to the addition of a further line to the stanza, riming with the refrain. This form— aaar RR (the large letters standing for the refrain)—becomes the ordinary pattern of the English carol. There is no need to follow its history, for that has been done with great scholarship by Dr. R. L. Greene. [2] He points out that by the fifteenth century the dance had ceased to be necessary to the carol, which had been stylized into a musical form. The scoring of the voice parts no longer followed the division between soloist and chorus. Any number of voices was assigned to either section of the poem indifferently, though the refrain was kept distinct from the stanza. The dance rhythm had given place to a free contrapuntal style. The distinction between stanza and refrain, however, assists musical coherence, for repetition is a normal element of musical form, and a recurring refrain can be set more freely than words the audience must hear distinctly. It is likely that poets like Henry VIII, Wyatt, and Skelton were encour- aged to write carols because it was a recognized contemporary musical form. Once the musical texture had become free from dance associations, however, poets elaborated the metrical structure of the early carol. Stanza and refrain might be of any length and in any metre the poet chose, and the composer was left free to deal with the verse as best suited him.

The history of the carol is very typical of the general develop- ment of dance patterns into poetic forms. First a musical form is detached from its dance associations, and then a poetic form is

---

[1] Ed. Furnivall (Early English Text Society), ll. 9049-51.
[2] *Early English Carols* (1935).

derived from the musical form. In Italy the ring dance developed into the *ballata*. This was still danced as well as sung in Dante's time, for he distinguishes the *canzone* from the *ballata* by declaring that

> *Canzoni* produce by their own power the whole effect they ought to produce, which *Ballate* do not, for they require the assistance of the performers for whom they are written ; it therefore follows that *Canzoni* are to be deemed nobler than *Ballate*.[1]

The early *ballata* was similar in form to the early English carol, but it gradually became more complicated as it detached itself from the dance. The French *ballade* became an even more completely literary form, losing the distinction between stanza and refrain. De Machaut's *ballades* are set to elaborate contrapuntal music and usually have the rime scheme ababbcc, only the last line serving as a refrain. This metrical pattern is imitated by Chaucer, to whom it was a purely literary form.

It is apparent that, while lyrics continued to be meant primarily for singing, up to the seventeenth century, musical pattern was behind the form of the poetic stanza in a general way ; but stanza forms became standardized and written for literary effect, composers being left to fit music to them after their completion. The kind of musical structure implied by this general influence on poetic metres was song-form, the kind we know in folk-song and in the simpler *lieder* of modern composers, in which the musical phrase corresponds to the line of verse and the tune to the stanza. The relationship between the two arts would have been quite different if a variety of musical forms had been developed. But song-form was virtually the only musical form consciously realized before the seventeenth century. Poems were set line by line, the whole tune corresponding with the stanza. This does not mean that the text had a particularly direct influence on the music, except for the formal framework. In a sense medieval music is often instrumental in conception, although it is not certain what part instruments took in its performance. Attention was largely concentrated on the sensuous effect of combining different voices rather than on the sentiments of the text or indeed on emotional expression at all. But, however independent the harmonized voices were felt to be, one of the parts had to be composed first and the others adapted to it, and this basic song melody provided the framework on which the whole composition was built. Church

---

[1] *De Vulgari Eloquentia* (ed. cit.), p. 53.

music took a liturgical melody phrase by phrase, often treating it very freely, and weaving counterpoint around it. Except for the end of the liturgical *canto fermo*, there was no reason why the flow of polyphonic sound should ever stop : listeners must sometimes have feared it never would. In the fifteenth century rhythmical tunes, like ' Westron Winde ' and ' L'homme armé ' were frequently used instead of plainsong, in an effort to give more point to the succession of contrapuntal episodes built on the phrases of the song melody. Secular music kept closer to the rhythmical melodies round which it was composed, although it, too, often aimed at an impressive flow of sound, and the words were lost in melismatic ornament and contrapuntal ingenuity. Still it was only the basic song melody that gave the music any shape. The periods of the music were determined by the metrical form of the text, if it were verse, or by the phrases into which its meaning caused it to fall, if it were prose.

If song-form was virtually the only musical form up to the seventeenth century, the only real principle of development was the fugal one. This was brought to perfection by the Netherlands school of the late fifteenth century, and nearly all sixteenth-century music merely worked out the implications of their technique. Their ingenuity sometimes outran artistic effect, and they were excessively fond of displaying their mastery of canon ; but there was much more purposeful progression and greater harmonic propriety in their music than in any that had gone before. They did not merely build their *chansons* round a song melody but developed the material in the melody itself : there was therefore greater coherence and concentration of interest in their works than in most medieval music. Each phrase of the song melody in turn was introduced with a point of imitation, the phrases being dovetailed so that a clear cadence was reached only at the end of the composition. The relations of the episodes were provided chiefly by those of the phrases in the song melody, which might be adapted to suit the counterpoint, but the musical interest was sustained by the succession of fugal entries and was so far dominant as to make the declamation of the text comparatively unimportant.

It is rather difficult to gain an adequate idea of early sixteenth-century English music because of the lateness of music printing in this country. As far as one can judge from manuscripts, English secular composition at the beginning of the century followed its own fifteenth-century tradition. Netherlands influence was bound ultimately to be felt. Names like ' Guillaum Deventt ', ' Peter

Vanwilder' and 'Hans Aseneste' among Henry VIII's musicians indicate the presence at court of Flemish professionals.   Church music shows signs of Netherlands influence fairly early in Henry's reign.   Until the middle of the century, however, English secular music seems to have kept a character of its own.   There appears to have been a good deal of plain note-against-note counterpoint, the tune in the tenor, each note of it bearing a syllable of the text, and two other parts in the same rhythm being harmonized with it. This type of composition could develop only into the part-song. It was inevitable that sooner or later the tune should be set in the highest part and the accompanying voices be conceived harmonically instead of contrapuntally.   Netherlands influence would affect this development only by increasing the customary number of parts and perhaps suggesting little points of imitation, which would nevertheless merely decorate the harmony.   Some of Thomas Whythorne's *Songes of three, fower, and fiue voyces* (1571) are already part-songs of this kind, anticipating the airs of the end of the century.   The three-part songs surviving from Henry VIII's reign are by court composers, such as the king himself, Cornish, and Cooper, but they are very suitable for amateurs and related to the popular ' three men's song '.   The growth of a demand from amateur singers, who would be more interested in the tune than in counterpoint, was all that was needed to stimulate development towards the modern part-song.

Of the more elaborate music for trained singers the florid counterpoint in which the song melody was ornamented with melismatic runs in some or all the voices was a medieval barbarism the sixteenth century rejected fairly early.   Church music had much more to repent than secular music.   The drowning of words in long runs was a feature of late medieval church music all the reformers ridiculed :   they were determined the liturgy should be heard distinctly.   Cranmer, in a letter to the king, in 1544, declared that ' The song that shall be made for the English service would not be full of notes, but, as near as may be, for every syllable a note, so that it may be sung distinctly and devoutly.'   The Injunctions issued at York and Lincoln in 1547 similarly directed that ' no anthems were to be allowed but those of Our Lord, and they in English, set to a plain and distinct note, for every syllable one '. Queen Elizabeth's Injunction of 1559 repeated the direction, adding the reason ' that the same might be as plainly understanded as if it were read without singing '.[1]   This change in church music was in

[1] *Tudor Church Music*, Vol. I, pp. xxvi–xxvii.

part due to the reformers' veneration for Holy Writ. But it was also due to a generally increased attention to the words of singers. As the prestige of secular music caught up with that of church music the interest in rhythmical melody, too, would discourage long rambling vocalizations.

One type of song intended for skilled performers is more interesting. It is represented mainly in the Fairfax Book (Additional MS. 5465), the principal composers being Fairfax himself, Newark, Sheringham, and Turges. Each line of the text is set in duple measure, a note to a syllable as a rule, and at the end of the line each voice breaks into long, quick runs in six-time. It is probable, though not certain, that these runs were performed by instruments, which doubled the voice parts while the words were being sung. Sometimes the voices enter with a slight point of imitation and sometimes in plain chords. The usual number of voices is two or three. The idea was apparently to fill in the pauses between the phrases of the song melody and maintain a continuous interplay of parts. The whirling runs in six-time were a clumsy way of doing that. By the middle of the century the English had learned, probably from the Netherlanders, how to connect the phrases of the song melody by weaving round them a more relevant contrapuntal texture. From the middle of the century there survive a number of rather stately songs, many of them apparently sung in the early court plays, for solo voice accompanied by string quartet.[1] Each line of verse is set quite plainly to a musical phrase. To make the singer's entry more effective and to give him his pitch the viols anticipate his opening notes, generally with a slight point of imitation, and between the singer's phrases they maintain the flow of contrapuntal sound with material from his part. The texts of the songs are strophic, but it is doubtful whether more than one stanza was ever sung, for the delayed entries make a rather long composition from one stanza.

This English school of secular music culminates in the first two printed volumes of William Byrd, in 1588 and 1589. Dr. Fellowes has included them in his *English Madrigal School*, and it is convenient to have them there; but, as Prof. Dent has pointed out, they are not really madrigals. As printed, they differ from the string quartet airs just mentioned in having words for all parts;

[1] Peter Warlock has edited a number in his *Elizabethan Songs, that were originally composed for one voice to sing and four stringed instruments to accompany* (Oxford University Press, 1926). They are discussed, with examples, by G. P. E. Arkwright in *The Musical Antiquary*, I, 30, and IV, 112.

but Byrd explains in his preface to the 1588 volume that they were written as solo airs, and that the words have later been fitted to the accompanying string parts. ' Heere are diuers songs, which being originally made for Instruments to expresse the harmonie, and voyce to pronounce the dittie, are now framed in all parts for voyces to sing the same.' The reason for the change is not hard to find. The Italian madrigal was just coming into fashion in England, and Byrd himself was very interested in it. Since it was an unaccompanied part-song of contrapuntal texture, he sought to present his airs in the same guise to meet the change of taste. The original form is easy to detect, however. The former solo voice is usually marked ' the first singing part'. It is not necessarily the top part ; more often it is the second soprano. This does not generally repeat the words more than once ; it just sings them through, a syllable to a note, except in a few places where an ordinary solo song might repeat a phrase to underline the sentiment, or else at the end of a stanza, where perhaps there has been an instrumental coda to which words have later been set. The three-part psalms, from paucity of voices, are forced to treat all the parts more equally, and in some others repetition is necessary to fill up gaps in which the leading voice would have a disproportionate amount of silence. Sometimes two voices divide the leading melody between them (Nos. 27–8 and 38–9 in the second set). The two carols in the 1589 set (Nos. 24 and 35, 25 and 40) conclude with elaborate choruses in which all voices freely assist the florid counterpoint and there is no one part with the underlying song-melody. This is like a refrain at the end of a song, intended to give the composer freedom from the text for an outburst of pure music.

Compared with his immediate successors of the madrigal school Byrd is a very unliterary musician. His inspiration is entirely musical, as was that of the Netherland masters and the early church school in which he learned his art. If there were no words at all to his songs, the effect would be just as great : one cannot imagine the same of Marenzio's madrigals. Yet Byrd was not indifferent to the text. He tried, he tells us, to frame his music ' to the life of the words ',[1] and he had found by experience that meditation on the text caused the right music to come spontaneously into his mind.

Porro, illis ipsis sentenijs (ut experiendo didici) adeo abstrusa atq ; recondita vis inest ; vt diuina cognitanti, diligenterq ; ac serio peruolu-

---

[1] *Psalmes, Songs, and Sonnets* (1611).

tanti ; nescio quonam modo, aptissimi quiq ; numeri, quasi sponte accurrant sua ; animoq ; minime ignauo, atq ; inerti, liberaliter ipsi sese offerant.[1]

He was anxious to learn all the Italians had to teach about enlivening his music with suggestions from the text, and his 1611 volume shows how completely he later mastered this technique.

In his 1588 and 1589 volumes he was hampered not only by the rather stiff declamation he inherited from his predecessors but by the regular periods and inflexible rhythms of his texts. No fewer than ten in the first set and nine in the second are metrical psalms in the familiar jog-trot alternation of eight- and six-syllable lines. The fondness of the early Elizabethans for this sort of doggerel is hard to explain. Twelve in the first set and five in the second are in the common stanza rimed ababcc, with six, eight, or ten syllables to the line, and Thomas Churchyard contributed one with the medieval rime-scheme ababbcc. Two sonnets appear in the first set and five in the second. With so much uninspired accentual iambic verse it is not possible to expect very flexible declamation. Byrd has a fairly varied number of means for representing the iambic foot, and takes full advantage of the rhythmic freedom accorded the separate voices in contrapuntal music.

Little more is attempted in most of the songs. Compared with the earlier English composers, he is very successful at representing the verbal rhythm ; compared with his successors, who had learned Italian methods, he is rather heavy. But when his texts are less pedestrian he takes advantage of his opportunities. In ' Though Amaryllis dance in green ' the idea of dancing leads him to employ with great effect the mixture of 3/2 and 6/4 rhythms that are typical of the galliard ; and the short second and third lines are a real help in getting away from the square periods of the more regular poems.

Byrd 1588 Set no. 12.

Though Amaryllis dance in green, Like Fai-ry Queen, And sing full clear

Co-rin-na can with smi-ling cheer

The New Poetry, in fact, just peeps into Byrd's first two volumes. Beside the early court poetry of Dyer and Lord Oxford, there is

[1] *Gradualia*, I.

a letter from Penelope to Ulysses in quantitative hexameters, probably the work of Byrd's friend Watson, and two lyrics by Sidney, in addition to three texts from Italian madrigals—' La virginella ', ' The nightingale ', and ' Susanna fair ' (the last from a French text but set by Ferrabosco and Di Lasso).

The tradition of Byrd was not lost. In 1594 John Munday published a volume of *Songs and Psalms*, whose very title proclaims its kinship. Orlando Gibbons, too, is in a sense a disciple of Byrd. Fine as his one set of madrigals is, its gravity of tone reminds us that he was chiefly a church composer. Though he treats his texts very scrupulously, one feels that the counterpoint comes first : like Byrd's, his imagination was essentially musical, and he had not Wilbye's delicacy in handling poetry. The English tradition modified what it borrowed from Italy. But in itself that tradition carried no possibility of further development. It needed to gain flexibility and emotional colour from poetic imagination ; and a new and richer poetry was entering England to teach it how to distil from the text not only a basic form as expressed in the song melody, but a passion and dramatic force medieval music had never known.

CHAPTER VI

THE MADRIGAL

SIDNEY and Spenser realized that the medieval tradition had degenerated into a 'rakehellye route of our ragged rhymers'; that conditions had changed so much a new poetry was needed, if the English language were ever to be worth the attention of intelligent people. They turned their eyes to the New Poetry of Italy and France, trying to learn from the examples of those countries how to rejuvenate English poetry. Musicians were in no better plight. They too realized that their inherited medium no longer sufficed for what they wanted to express. They had at their disposal an art created for the service of the church and, like it, detached, restrained, impersonal. The time in which they lived needed a more vivid, dramatic, and personal art. Moreover, there was nothing further to be done within the old limits; the system of harmony and melody had been explored as far as was profitable. Only a more imaginative poetry could inspire the old material with contemporary meaning. This the Italians and the Netherlanders had already discovered; and it was to them that English composers directed their attention, just as the poets went to school under Bembo and Ronsard.

The madrigal, which appeared first in England at the end of the century, was near enough to the English style of Byrd to be readily accepted and naturalized here. It owed a great deal to the Netherland School, whose influence had already modified the English musical tradition. But it was equally Italian in nature, and the circumstances of its origin had linked it closely with the New Poetry. Though its fame spread throughout Europe, it never lost the distinctive marks of its native country, and it never became absolutely acclimatized to any country but England, where, as in Italy, it always remained in alliance with the kind of poetry that had helped to determine its nature.

Italian secular music had never developed very far in a contrapuntal direction. The *trecento* school had been one of the first to use canon freely, but the entries were so far apart that there was little artistic purpose in it; and, after initiative passed to the north of Europe, the Italians contributed little to the great medieval polyphony. In the fifteenth century most of their secular music was slight and homophonic. The verse associated with it probably helped this, for it was semi-popular in style. The vernacular languages were not yet benefiting from the Renaissance ; they were neglected in the enthusiasm for the classics ; and in Italy no medieval tradition survived that any longer seemed relevant to the contemporary situation. The leading *genres* in the musical collections were the *frottola* and the *strambotto*. These were written by courtly poets, such as Galeotto del Caretto and Niccolo da Correggio, and set to music by court musicians like Cara and Tromboncino. Though obviously intended for educated people, they were frivolous in tone and semi-popular in form. The music was homophonic and strophic. The highest voice had the tune and set the words fairly syllabically. If there were any imitations in the accompanying parts, they were very slight and merely decorative, the real structure being harmonic. The melodic phrases were few and uniform. The *frottola* was descended from the *ballata* and had the four-line *reprise* of that form, while the *strambotto* usually repeated some of the musical phrases to make up its stanza of eight lines. The periods tended to be regular, since the *frottola* consisted of eight-syllable trochaic lines, and the *strambotto*, in which the lines were often of eleven or twelve syllables, usually had a caesura in the middle of the lines. The minor forms all had equally fixed rime-schemes. The sonnet had lines of equal length, allowing repetitions of musical phrases. The *capitolo* had a three-line stanza and the ode a four-line. All these forms, which appeared in miscellanies under the general name of *frottole*, thus employed exceedingly simple musical material, and their fixed metrical schemes allowed very small scope for rhythmic variety.

The *frottola* maintained its popularity during the first three decades of the sixteenth century. Ottaviano de'Petrucci, the first Venetian music printer, published nine separate volumes of *frottole* between 1501 and 1508, and several of them ran into second editions. But alongside the *frottole* the *chansons* of the Netherland masters had a following in Italy. This school had long held a commanding position in church music, and the Papal chapel had frequently sent special emissaries to the Low Countries to recruit singers. As early as the first half of the fifteenth century, Guillaume Dufay, one of the leaders of the First Netherlands School, had spent seven years in Savoy. Jacob Obrecht had left his position as *kapellmeister* of Utrecht Cathedral in 1474-5 to become a singer at the court of Hercules d'Este at Ferrara. The great Josquin des Près himself had made his reputation to a large extent in Italy. He had served Lorenzo il Magnifico, joined the Papal Choir at the invitation of

Sixtus IV, and then gone to Ferrara, leaving Italy in 1490 to take up a position in the chapel of the King of France. The Sforza Duke of Milan had patronized Agricola and Caspar van Weerbeke; and Johannes Tinctoris, the great theorist of the Netherlands School, had spent some years as choirmaster and singer to Ferdinand of Aragon at Naples. Most decisive for the future of Italian music was the settlement at Venice of Adrian Willaert. He began his career as a pupil of Jean Mouton at Paris, and later became a singer at the court of Ludwig, King of Bohemia. In 1527 the Doge of Venice, Andrea Gritti, prevailed upon the authorities of the city to waive the rule against employing foreigners and to appoint Willaert *maestro di cappella* at San Marco. It was at Venice, under Willaert's influence, that the character of sixteenth-century music was to be decided, for some of the leading composers of the next generation were his pupils—Zarlino, Andrea Gabrieli, Cyprian de Rore, and Constanza Porta among them. In 1539 another important Flemish musician, Jacob Arcadelt, settled in Rome as choirmaster of the Julian Chapel.

The elaborate art of the Netherlanders did not suit semi-popular forms like the *frottola*. Their *chansons* were well received in Italy, but kept quite distinct from the Italian tradition. They did not even trouble to set Italian texts to any great extent. The vogue they had among discriminating patrons of music may be seen from the early printed volumes. Petrucci's first venture was a gigantic collection of *chansons*, published in three parts—the *Harmonice Musices Odhecaton A* and the *Canti B* in 1501, and the *Canti C* in 1503. In 1535 Ottaviano Scotto, another Venetian printer, issued *Il Primo Libro de le Canzoni Francese*, and in 1536 Antonio Blabate (?) published *La Courone et Fleurs des Chansons a troys*, while Antonio Gardane, a Frenchman settled in Venice, produced *Venticinque Canzoni Francesi* in 1538.

Between 1500 and 1530 a new critical outlook was slowly being created that was to help the Netherland art make closer contact with the Italian. The vernacular was rising in the estim-ation of men of taste. The fifteenth century had practically exhausted the possibilities of Latin writing. New combinations of the elements found in classical authors were becoming increas-ingly difficult, and the unreality of composition in a dead language was evident. It was realized that the vernacular was not as un-promising as it had seemed in the first enthusiasm for the recovery of antiquity. Its traditions were not entirely crude and barbarous, and it could be refined by application of lessons learned from the classics. This new interest in the vernaculars as mediums of artistic expression was strengthened by the growing nationalism of the time, which even Italy did not escape. Among the leaders of the New Poetry, which was to combine the native tradition with the classical, was Bembo, whose ecclesiastical and philological eminence gave him special authority. He edited the poems of Petrarch, who had been one of the pioneers of humanism and yet a successful poet in the vernacular. The spirituality of Petrarch's love poetry appealed to a generation familiar with the Platonism of Ficino and Pico della Mirandola, and the polish of his technique differentiated him from the extravagant semi-popular styles that had more recently gained control of vernacular poetry.

Petrarch had excelled as a writer of short poems, and it was therefore on the kind of poems found in the musical volumes that the new movement had most immediate effect. Bembo taught that 'lo scrittore non debba al populo accostarsi', that the poet must be a man of learning and his technique sophisticated. Attention was therefore turned from the semi-popular forms of the fifteenth century to the more elaborate and polished forms of the fourteenth century, especially the madrigal and the sonnet. To suit the sophistication of the poetry a less obvious type of music was required than that of the *frottola*. Moreover, the Netherland art, which had the artifice appropriate to the new poetry, had always been too elaborate for strophic verse, and the new forms were largely non-strophic. The fifteenth century forms all had fixed metrical schemes, but the new ones were mainly free, the sonnet being the only important one that was fixed. The madrigal consisted chiefly of lines of seven and eleven syllables numbering from seven to eleven, the rimes being at the discretion of the poet. Thus greater variety and flexibility were at the composer's service.

The development of more complex musical structure followed the Petrarchan movement very closely. Bembo's edition of Petrarch in 1501 was followed by 30 years of increasing interest in the fourteenth century poet, culminating in Vellutello's *Life* in 1525 and Bembo's own *Rime* in 1530. The first musical volume to bear the title Madrigals appeared in 1533 – *Madrigali noui de diversi excellentissimi Musici Libro primo de la Serena*. But the new style had begun to filter through to the press before that. Manuscript copies of madrigals had been circulated, and a few madrigals had found their way into volumes of *frottole*. As has been said, the name *frottole* on a title-page never meant that all the contents were actually *frottole*. Minor forms were also included, and the name *frottole* was given to the whole by a sort of majority vote. Madrigals insinuated themselves into the *frottole* volumes increasingly during the first three decades of the century. They took precedence on the title-pages when they began to constitute the majority in most collections. Canzonets, belated *frottole* and *villanelle* often rubbed shoulders with their more exalted relatives. But the *frottola* had ceased to concern educated people. Its popular appeal passed to the *villanella*, while literary circles deserted it for the madrigal. Cesari has demonstrated the close interest which courtly circles took in the changes of musical style.[1] The courtly adherents of the New Poetry demanded music fit for poetry modelled on Dante and Petrarch, and the musicians quickly adapted their art to their patrons' requirements. In doing this the Netherland composers had an advantage from the start because of their more sophisticated technique.

Though there was greater artistry lavished on the madrigal from the beginning, there was no sudden break between it and the *frottola*. The first madrigal texts were treated in much the same way as the *frottole*. The structure was still largely homophonic and the declamation syllabic. The greater variety came from the freer rime-schemes and more varied lengths of line. Niccolo da Correggio, on being asked by Isabella d'Este to set some verses of Petrarch, replies that he has chosen ' Si e debile il filo a cui s'atiene' because the lines ' vanno crescendo e sminuendo,'[2] He means that the lines are of different lengths, which allowed greater variety in the periods of his music. The leaders of the new style were nearly all Netherlanders, but the structure of the *frottola* was preserved and elaborated rather than laid aside for that of the *chanson*. The most famous of all madrigals, Arcadelt's ' Il bianco e dolce cigno ', is a good example of the early type. It is almost all in plain chords ; only at the end is there imitation among the parts. The early ones of Willaert are more florid but not essentially different. Gradually the basic structure was filled out with points of imitation. But the madrigal never entirely forgot its origins. The degree of polyphonic development was restrained by the basic song melodies, which were generally longer than those used for the Netherland *chansons*. Sections of homophony were introduced into most polyphonic madrigals for

[1] G. Cesari, *Le origini del madrigale cinquecentesco* (*Rivista musicale italiana*, XIX [1912]).

[2] L. Renier, *Niccolo da Correggio* (*Giornale storica della letteratua italiana*, XXI, 247).

contrast.   Some of the simpler madrigals, like those of Farmer, Gibbons's ' Silver swan ', and Morley's ' On a fair moring ', are little more than part-songs.   There was also a minor form, the canzonet, which had the same general texture as the madrigal but less contrapuntal development.

Terminology is never very exact in the sixteenth century, and the form of the canzonet has been obscured by carelessness in naming the English volumes.   Farnaby's canzonets are so elaborate that it is difficult to see why he did not call them madrigals.   But Morely had a clear idea of the distinction between the two.   He published a set of Italian madrigals for five voices and a set of Italian canzonets for four voices.   Some madrigals have strayed into the canzonet volume and some canzonets into the madrigal volume, through the accident of their having the number of parts appropriate to the wrong volume.   But, on the whole, his two sets reveal the difference fairly well, and an examination of the Italians themselves leaves little doubt as to what constituted the differentiating qualities.   Etymologically ' canzonet ' means little song, and the canzonets of Morley are little madrigals.   He defines madrigals as the best kind of light music, and then continues :

> The second degree of grauetie in this light musicke is giuen to Canzonets, that is little shorte songs (wherein little arte can be shewed being made in straines, the beginning of which is some point lightlie touched, and euerie straine repeated except the middle) which is in composition of the musick a counterfet of the *Madrigal*.[1]

In accordance with his own definition, Morley always attached the sub-title ' Little Short Airs ' or ' Little Short Songs ' to his volumes of canzonets.   The madrigal set each line of poetry to a musical phrase introduced with ' some point lightly touched '. The canzonet counterfeited this procedure.   Each line of poetry was set to a musical phrase introduced with ' some point lightly touched ', but the lines were not treated equally.   The first and last musical phrases had two entries for each voice, while those in the middle sang the words once only.   In the simplest form of canzonet a three-line poem would be set thus :

> Line 1 :   Each voice sings the words twice.
> Line 2 :   Each voice sings the words once.
> Line 3 :   Each voice sings the words twice.

Examples of three-line canzonets are ' Lo, here another love ' and ' I should for grief and anguish ' in Morley's two-part set.

[1] *Introduction*, p. 180.

In addition the whole of the music set to the first line is repeated to balance the conventional repetition of the last two.

In the five- and six-part canzonets Morley usually repeats the music for the last line of the text, but uses the repetition of the first musical phrase to cover the first two lines of text. If he has a four-line text the musical phrases are thus distributed :

Our Bonny-Boots could toot it, yea and foot it.	A
Say, lusty lads, who now shall bonny-boot it ?	A
Who but the jolly sheoherd, bonny Dorus ?	B
He now must lead the morris dance before us.	C (*bis*)

The second line is a simple repetition of the first. The third is sung only once by each voice, except for a slight reiteration of a few words to allow the delayed entry of the various voices. The last line is repeated. When the stanza is longer the first line is generally more or less in plain chords ; the second introduces a point of imitation ; then the music for the first and second lines is repeated for the third and fourth lines (Nos. 1, 2, 7, 15, and 16 of *Canzonets . . . to fiue and sixe Voices*). The principle is evidently that the canzonet is too slight for every phrase of the song melody to receive contrapuntal development. Those at the beginning and those at the end are therefore more fully treated than those in the middle.

The madrigal and its related forms kept closely to the outlines of a rhythmical song melody, which was filled out with various degrees of polyphonic elaboration. Yet a contrapuntal texture is characteristic of the madrigal in its later development. It was its capacity for a continuous nonstrophic texture with imitation among the voices that commended the madrigal to musicians as a form that exhibited the best musical technique of the time. Morley declared that ' it is next vnto the Motet, the most artificiall and to men of vnderstanding the most delightfull '.[1] Its basis is song-form, and the declamation is generally quite syllabic. Each line of poetry is taken in turn and set to a musical phrase, and with this, or a variant of it, each voice enters. The fugal possibilities of the theme are just lightly suggested, and then the next line is taken in the same way. While some of the voices are finishing the phrase another voice enters with the next line, so that there is no clear cadence until the end of the composition. Each voice repeats the words of the line once or twice, so that the entries can be completed. The voices have rhythmical and melodic

[1] ib., p. 180.

independence ; indeed rhythmical contrasts among the voices are among the chief points of interest.   Though there is no exhaustive use of canon, as in the Netherland *chanson*, all the devices of contrapuntal technique can find a place.   ' You may maintaine points and reuert them, vse triplaes and shew the verie vttermost of your varietie, and the more varietie you shew the better shal you please.' [1]

The madrigal was thus a compromise between the art of the Netherlands and Italian tradition, and it revealed throughout its history the circumstances of its birth.   The poetry to which it was set was a distinguishing mark wherever it was composed. The only formal requirement was that it must be non-strophic. It might be of any suitable length, and the lines might have any rhythm and be rimed in any way.   The sonnet found its way into the madrigal volumes because of its association with Petrarch. It was really too long to be quite satisfactory, and it was usually divided into two madrigals, one taking the octave and the other the sestet.   Even borrowings from strophic poetry could be pressed into service : single stanzas of Ariosto and Spenser were frequently used.   There was no absolute rule about the musical texture : it might be simple or elaborately contrapuntal.   But the text had to be Petrarchan.   That was the only real criterion of what constituted a madrigal.   Morley could think of only that definition, apart from the desirability of variety.   ' Vse sheweth that it is a kinde of musicke made vpon songs and sonnets, such as *Petrarcha* and many Poets of our time haue excelled in.' [2]

The first English volume to bear the word madrigal on its title-page is Thomas Morley's *Madrigalls to Foure Voyces* (1594) ; the first that can definitely be said to belong to the *genre* is Morley's *Canzonets or Little Short Songs to Three Voyces* (1593).   Why the English should have been so late in producing madrigals is not clear.   A manuscript collection of Italian compositions has been found dating from the sixties.[3]   Striggio had visited England in 1567, and the elder Ferrabosco had been in England twenty years before English composers began to imitate the style of his country. It must be remembered, however, that music printing started very late in England.   Nicholas Yonge complains about the difficulty of getting hold of copies of good vocal music, and perhaps other musicians and amateur singers felt the same desire for it before the

[1] *Introduction*, p. 180.   [2] ib., p. 180.
[3] In the Fellows' Library, Winchester College, dated 1564, and containing madrigals by Arcadelt, Willaert, and Orlando di Lasso.

printers had thought of satisfying the demand. Another reason for the lateness of English madrigals may have been the lack of suitable texts. We have already seen how closely the beginning of the madrigal was linked with the Petrarchan movement, and how close were the relations between the English disciples of the New Poetry and the musicians who actually introduced the madrigal to England. Sidney and Spenser had to show that English could adapt itself to the New Poetry before composers could think of following the lead Italy had given. The two go together. The sonnet sequences of the nineties are contemporary with the first wave of English madrigals. The lateness of the English was an advantage in one respect. They learned the most advanced technique of Marenzio at the same time as the simpler technique of the early madrigal composers. It is impossible in their works to detect much progress ; they took over the madrigal as a fully developed form, and in some ways Morley's first efforts were never surpassed, though his outlook was rather conservative and not particularly literary. He excelled at the lighter madrigal ; he cannot compare with Wilbye or Weelkes for boldness of style or emotional force. But this lightness was just what English music most lacked. His declamation is much livelier than Byrd's. Dainty, tripping quaver figures are common, and one constantly comes across typically Italian rhythmic figures like

Morley's declamation is Italian ; in fact, the madrigal itself always remained Italian. A large proportion of the texts in the English volumes are translations ; the others are largely imitated from the Italians. Lines of seven and eleven syllables and with feminine endings are often good evidence when the debt cannot be certainly proved. The music is no less conclusive. The English composers are original as individuals, but there is scarcely any feature of their style that is without Italian antecedents. Their patrons admired Italian music, and Italian music was what the English composers tried to provide. There is some reason to believe that Morley's music was set to Italian words, which were then translated. The Ballets of 1595 were published under the title : ' Of Thomas Morley the First Booke of Balletts to fiue vqyces.' But at the same time there was issued an Italian edition with the title : ' Di Tomaso Morlei Il Primo Libro delle Ballette a cinque voci.' Both editions are extant. Of the two-part canzonets, published in the same year, only the English edition has been found, but there can be no doubt that an Italian one was printed. The title-page itself gives the clue. The usual word-order on a title-page is something like this : ' Canzonets. Or Little Short Songs to Three Voyces : Newly published by Thomas Morley.' But the volume of Ballets, it will be noticed, had a different order of words ; it had the usual Italian order, and the English edition translated the Italian title-page quite literally, without altering the order of the words. One's suspicions are therefore aroused by the word-order of the two-part canzonets' title-page : ' Of Thomas Morley the first booke of Canzonets to Two Voices.' All doubts are resolved by an entry of the printer, Thomas East, in the Stationers' Register, among a list of copy-rights transferred to him on 6 December 1596: ' 8. Of THOMAS MORLEY, The first booke of Canzonettes to 2 voices with the same sett also in Italian.' [1] On East's death, when his copyrights were made over to his successors, the list again included : ' Morleyes 2 partes Englishe and Italian.' [2] A number of the ballets were to texts already set by Gastoldi, and some of the two-part canzonets to words set by Anerio in his four-part madrigals. Morley's music goes just as well to the Italian words as to the English. The translations are by no means exact ; they have tried to keep the verbal rhythm rather than the meaning. Even more remarkable is the similarity between the music of the Italians and that of Morley. The words have almost the same stresses and quantities ; even the rise and fall of the melodies are almost identical. Had the volumes of Anerio and Gastoldi and the English works of Morley all been lost, the Italian editions of Morley would have been accepted as the music of an Italian composer.

The madrigal was a very satisfactory compromise between the claims of music and poetry, as we should expect from a form that had grown up under literary patronage. It respected the shape of the poetry, being built on song-form and setting the verse line by line. It made great efforts to follow the verbal rhythm in the individual voices. That is what still makes madrigals so singable. The declamation may be Italian in origin, but it is English in effect. Despite the exigencies of counterpoint, the individual musical phrase always seems to do justice to the words. A com-poser like Wilbye manages not only to give the syllables the right quantity and stress, but at the same time to suggest by the shape and tempo of the melody the emotional significance of the poetry.

[1] Arber's *Transcript*, III, 76.   [2] ib., III, 465.

Both Zarlino and Morley attach much importance to the correct setting of words. They strongly disapprove of long runs that take no account of the verbal rhythm : in this respect medieval music seemed as barbarous to them as did medieval poetry to the humanist literary critics. Morley criticizes Dunstable severely for putting a rest in the middle of a word.

We must also haue a care so to applie the notes to the wordes, as in singing there be no barbarisme committed : that is, that we cause no sillable which is by nature short be expressed by manie notes or one long note, nor no long sillable bee expressed with a shorte note, but in this fault do the practitioners erre more grosselie, then in any other, for you shall find few songes wherein the penult sillables of these words, *Dominus, Angelus, filius, miraculum, gloria,* and such like are not expressed with a long note, yea many times with a whole dossen of notes, and though one should speake of fortie he should not say much amisse, which is a grosse barbarisme, & yet might be easilie amended. We must also take heed of seperating any part of a word from another by a rest, as som dunces haue not slackt to do, yea one whose name is *Ioannes Dunstaple* (an ancient English author) hath not onlie deuided the sentence, but in the verie middle of a word hath made two long rests thus, in a song of foure parts vpon these words, *Nesciens virgo mater virum.* . . . For these be his owne notes and wordes, which is one of the greatest absurdities which I haue seene committed in the dittying of musicke.[1]

The madrigal is careful of the words without being fussy ; it does not sacrifice musical interest to them—a merit that was to bring it adverse criticism in its later career. It was as complex a composition as the time knew how to create ; the fugal principle, the only method of development then perfected, was given adequate play. The discussion of the theme by the various voices still affords singers a pleasure few other kinds of vocal music can equal. The text may mean little, but it nearly always sounds natural and attractive when sung. Take the text away, and musical interest will remain. This was often done ; many volumes of madrigals are described as ' apt for voice or viols '. That they are satisfactory enough as string fantasias is perhaps a sign that the music is more important than the poetry : one could not do that with the best madrigals, Marenzio's for example, any more than with a song of Wolf's, without losing something. The suspicion that the majority of ordinary madrigals really did put the music before the poetry led ultimately to a reaction against counterpoint in the very literary circles that had encouraged the madrigal.

[1] *Introduction,* p. 178.

But, even if music were the dominant partner, it dealt fairly with the words. It was a great improvement on anything that had gone before from a literary point of view, as well as being the most attractive contrapuntal music the age could conceive.

A good deal of its attractiveness it really owed to its poetry. The literary amateurs admired the madrigal not only for its fidelity to the form and rhythm of the verse but also for its success in depicting the sentiments of the text. This is the great innovation of sixteenth-century music, and it was very largely due to the nature of the texts themselves. The century did not add much to the resources of the great Second Netherlands School; it refined away some of its crudities, but it did not extend its technical resources very much, except that it made a tentative beginning at true instrumental style. But the impression sixteenth-century music makes on the listener is very different from that made by fifteenth-century music. A greater picturesqueness is one of the most noticeable features of Renaissance secular music. The madrigal did mark a great advance in the employment of the inherited technical resources for emotional effect. It did so much to exploit the pictorial and emotional possibilities of its resources that in its later stages it was driven to seek new technical devices, the old ones having gone stale from constant repetition. And its alliance with the Petrarchan convention helped it considerably. The uniformity in the style of the poetry inspired freshness in the music. The stock Petrarchan situation describes the pangs of a lover, the beauty of his mistress, his fire and her coldness, his devotion and her aloofness, always in much the same terms. Whatever sincerity there may have been in Petrarch's handling of the theme, it rapidly became one of the shallowest and most tiresome clichés in sixteenth-century literature. But that mattered little to composers. All a musician needs from his librettist is an atmosphere, a mood sustained for some time; and contrasted moods are even better, provided the transition from one to another is not too sudden, for music takes a little time to establish its atmosphere—a single chord in isolation has nothing like the suggestiveness of a single word. Good music can be made from indifferent poetry, and the Petrarchan convention had all a composer wanted. Its emotions were broad and simple, its contrasts as clear as that between black and white. The more intellectual a poet's imagery the more difficult is it for a composer to give the impression of meaning the same thing, for the intellectual pleasure of music is not the equivalent of anything in another medium; on the emotional level only do the two meet. Each art needs a certain liberty. One is appropriate to the other if the general atmosphere of both appears broadly the same. The contrast between the lover's ecstasies and the lover's miseries was just what a musician could depict. The madrigal was the first music to apply itself consistently and whole-heartedly to the illustration of the text. Medieval music had always been rather mathematical; it concentrated on the sensuous effects of harmony and counterpoint. The madrigal forged from the traditional resources of music a language of emotional expression. The whole disposition of the music was governed by the suggestions of the text. In some of the works of Marenzio or Weelkes almost every phrase in the text is represented in the music, which changes from point to point as new emotional suggestions occur in the words. This was only possible within the framework of the Petrarchan convention, in which the emotions were not complex but followed well-worn paths. The constant variability of the music at the instance of the poetry is the distinctive feature of the madrigal. To compose one, says Morley,

you must possesse your selfe with an amorus humor (for in no composition shal you proue admirable except you put on and possesse yourselfe wholy with that vaine wherein you compose) so that you must in your musicke be wauering like the wind, sometime wanton, sometime drooping, sometime graue and staide, or herwhile effeminat.[1]

'Word-painting', the wish to give emotional 'meaning' to music, was a manifestation of that quickened interest in the psychology of the individual which is at the very centre of the Renaissance. The drama is its characteristic expression. Opera is the seventeenth-century culmination of a dramatic tendency that runs through sixteenth-century music. Horatio Vecchi actually tried to turn madrigals into drama. He had so far experimented with the technique of pictorial and emotional expression that the natural sequel was to make scenes and passions objective in the interaction of characters, to create a drama to be heard instead of seen.

That the Renaissance temper rather than the fashion of a short period was behind the dramatic conception of music is shown by the early appearance of programme music in Italy. When the northern nations were building Gothic cathedrals and constructing the great polyphonic masses, Italy had already felt the first stirrings of the new spirit. The *trecento* composers were very fond of

[1] *Introduction*, p. 180.

pictorial music. In the *caccie* there are descriptions of hunting and fires, crowds in the street and other lively scenes. The sixteenth-century witnessed a great increase in programme music all over Europe. The French composer Clement Jannequin was especially noted for it. The contents of his *Verger de Musique* (1559), a re-issue of some of his most popular pieces, gives an idea of the sort of subject he liked to depict.

Le chant des oyseaux	Le siège de Metz
Le chant du Rossignol	La bataille a 5
Le chant de l'Alouette	Le caquet des femmes
La prinse de Boulongne	La ialouzie
La reduction de Boulongne	La chasse
	La guerre de Renty.

Bird-songs have always been popular. A crowd of gossiping women is portrayed in a famous *chanson* by Orlando di Lasso. There were several renderings of the Battle of Pavia, and in England Byrd's Battle was often played on the virginals or the lute. Tobias Hume tried a more difficult feat in representing a battle with a solo voice and a bass viol,[1] marking different passages 'The great Ordenance', 'Kettle Drumme', 'Trumpets'. In another piece his poor bass viol had to play the role of an organ.[2] Giovanni Croce wrote some comic pictures of a carnival —*Mascarate Piacevoli et Ridicolose per il Carnevale* (1590). Striggio's *Il Cicalamento delle Donne al Bucato* (1567) is a set of five-part madrigals describing various contemporary scenes. Banchieri (1598–1630) wrote a number of onomatopoeic madrigals.

The madrigal was generally too sophisticated to be content with such obvious programme music as this, but it did not disdain realism. To Morley it appeared axiomatic that straightforward physical details in the text should be sketched in the music. Height and depth, for instance, were constantly recurring in madrigal poetry, and Morley reminds his pupils that

you must haue a care that when your matter signifieth ascending, high heauen, and such like, you make your musicke ascend : and by the contrarie where your dittie speaketh of descending, lowenes, depth, hell, and such others, you must make your musicke descend, for as it will be thought a great absurditie to talke of heauen and point downwarde to the earth : so it will be counted great incongruitie if a musician vpon the wordes hee ascended into heauen shoulde cause his musicke descend, or by the contrarie vpon the descension should cause his musicke to ascend.[3]

---

[1] *The First Part of Ayres*, fol. C.   [2] ib., fol. Q2.   [3] op. cit., p. 178.

Composers followed Morley's counsel to the letter. When Weelkes wants to tell us that Hecla's flames ascend higher than the flames of Etna, he employs not only an ascending musical phrase but a rising sequence, divided between two sopranos.[1] The mention of heaven necessitates an aspiring phrase, although the actual sentence in which the word occurs might well have suggested a descending phrase—'What, have the gods their comfort sent *from* heaven?'[2] When Wilbye's text says, 'At thy feet I fall', he must run down the scale,[3] and Ward rushes down in quavers to declare, 'I would lay down my life at her proud feet.'[4] Morley cries out, 'Help, I fall!' with leaps of a fourth and a fifth.[5] Weelkes even descends a fifth to invite us to 'sit down'.[6] Tomkins imparts a contented serenity to 'heaven' by using a sustained note in the soprano over descending thirds in the tenor and bass.[7] Descending quavers suggest pouring through a strainer in one of Farnaby's canzonets.[8] Wilbye illustrates 'steps' with a figure built from notes rising step by step in the scale.[9]

Various kinds of movement were another easy outlet for realism. Haste was always expressed by means of quick runs: Morley was particularly fond of running figures. For 'stand' East employs a long note passing into a pedal point,[10] and on the word 'cease' Ward places in the two upper voices crotchets preceded by rests, while the bass moves in minims.[11] The mention of numbers in the text was also easy to illustrate. If anyone were said to be alone, then a single voice would sing that line,[12] while 'pair' required two voices. In the famous madrigal, 'As Vesta was from Latmos hill descending', Weelkes gives the phrase, 'first two by two', to two voices, while a third enters at 'then three by three'.[13] In another of Weelkes's madrigals the four voices act roles in the story. 'Three virgin nymphs', represented by three sopranos, are walking sedately along, when 'rude Silvanus', a bass, meets them. His approach is depicted in a sequential passage, and a vigorous rush in the bass signalizes his snatching at one of them. Meanwhile the three sopranos apprehensively cry 'Ay me'.[14] This is more entirely programme music than the madrigals usually become. But they contain all

[1] *Madrigals of 6 parts*, No. 7.   [2] ib., No. 3.
[3] *Second Set*, No. 6.   [4] No. 9.   [5] *Madrigalls to Foure Voyces*, No. 5.
[6] *Madrigals* (1597), No. 1.
[7] *Songs* (1622), No. 12.   [8] No. 18.   [9] *Second Set*, No. 2.
[10] *First Set*, No. 24.   [11] No. 13.   [12] Farmer, No. 15.
[13] *Oriana*, No. 17.   [14] *Madrigals* (1597), No. 10.

kinds of pictorial effect, from the dotted quaver and semi-quaver runs with which Ward describes thunder,[1] to the more subtle suggestiveness of Weelkes, who, at the lover's self-surrendering ' Take here my heart, I give it thee for ever ', lets us hear a peal of wedding bells.[2]

Programme music, then, is a regular feature of the madrigal ; but it is far from being the most important link between the sentiments of the text and the music. The composers tried to re-create the poems they were setting in their own medium. In doing this they had a recognized set of conventions corresponding to the conventions of Petrarchan poetry. Every situation or emotion to be expected in verse of the prevailing style had a corresponding kind of progression in music. Individuality was possible inside the convention, but the means of illustration followed certain well-defined paths. The English merely imitated the Italians, and, as they learned the later Italian madrigals almost as soon as the early ones, it is impossible to see in their work the gradual extension of technical resources the Italians achieved in their desire to impart extra vividness to the text. The English copied the musical effects of the Italians ; the Italians had their eyes fixed on the poetry. The chromaticism of Gesualdo is unintelligible without the text. He was not straining primarily after musical novelty but after more vivid realization of the possibilities in the text, since he felt the older methods of illustration were going stale. The English, however, admired the Italians' novel music as much as their fidelity to the suggestions of the poetry. Weelkes, one of the most enterprising in the portrayal of the text, disclaimed any literary interests at all.

I confess my conscience is vntouched with any other arts, and, I hope, my confession is vnsuspected, many of our Musitians thinke it as much praise to be somewhat more then musictians, as it is for golde to bee some what more than golde.[3]

Yet the mere form of Weelkes's disclaimer bears testimony to the presence among other English composers of literary preoccupations, even though the literary history of the English madrigal is comparatively unimportant. Since they adopted a style of composition already fully developed in Italy, there is little progress between the first madrigal volumes and the last ; all have the same conventions, which stand out in greater relief and can be more easily studied on that account. Morley was quite prepared to teach his

[1] No. 17. [2] *Madrigals of 5 parts*, No. 3.
[3] Dedication to *Madrigals* (1600).

pupils ' how to dispose your musicke according to the nature of the words which you are therein to expresse, as whatsoeuer matter it be which you haue in hand, such a kind of musicke must you frame to it '.[1]   Once he had learned these rules, the individual could use his own judgement in the handling of them, just as he let his taste direct the application of the rules of counterpoint.   But we are not concerned here with individual genius ; only with the conventions it presumed.

Broad differences between lightness and seriousness of tone, between gaiety and sadness, were mainly expressed by differences in movement.

If the subiect be light, you must cause your musicke go in motions, which carrie with them a celeritie or quicknesse of time, as minimes, crotchets and quauers : if it be lamentable, the note must goe in slow and heauie motions, as semibreues, breues, and such like, and of all this you shall finde examples euerywhere in the workes of the good musicians.[2]

Thus Wilbye must slow down the movement of a madrigal when he comes to the words, ' So heavy is my heart ',[3] as must Morley on the words ' Grief tormenteth '.[4]   On the other hand, Weelkes impresses on us that Mars was in a fury by a vigorous roll of quauers.[5] The function of tempo is best seen by contrast.   A famous madrigal by Weelkes, ' Our country swains ',[6] begins with a picture of the morris dance, a subject also of one of Morley's best madrigals ; but when, in the last couplet, the poem goes on to contrast the poet's feelings with the heartiness of the dancers, there is an immediate change from the complicated and abandoned rhythms of the morris to slow progressions in minims, often with suspended discords.   Weelkes is so careful to follow the tiniest detail of the text that in the space of one line a change of feeling will often cause him to alter the movement of his music.   ' All our merry jigs are quite forgot ', exclaims the poet in one place.   On the words ' All our merry jigs ' Weelkes prances gaily along in a triple rhythm ; but at ' quite forgot ' he immediately lapses into slow movement, with suspended discords to aggravate the melancholy.[7]   Dancing was generally represented by triple rhythm, the parts moving more or less homophonically.   To Weelkes any kind of pleasure seemed to suggest dancing, and he uses triple time for words like ' joy ' and ' pleasure ' when there is no mention of actual dancing in the text.

[1] op. cit., p. 177.   [2] ib., p. 178.   [3] Second Set, No. 4.
[4] Madrigalls to Foure Voyces, No. 3.   [5] Madrigals of 6 parts, No. 8.
[6] 1597 Set, No. 11.   [7] ib., No. 2.

The use of rests was an important adjunct to the management of movement to depict the text. They were chiefly employed to express sighing—an important office, since the lover's sighs were a constant feature of a very constant convention.

> When you would expresse sighes, you may vse the crotchet or minime rest at the most, but a longer than a minime rest you may not vse, because it will rather seeme a breth taking then a sigh, an example whereof you may see in a very good song of *Stephano venturi* to fiue voices vpon this dittie *quell'aura a che spirando a Paura mia?* for comming to the worde *sospiri* (that is sighes) he giueth it such a natural grace by breaking a minime into a crotchet rest and a crotchet, that the excellency of his judgment in expressing and gracing his dittie doth therein manifestlie appeare.[1]

The standardized sigh ' Ay me ' has a figure involving a suspension. A few other words were occasionally treated like ' sigh '. Wilbye thus sets ' pity ' and Ward ' rests ', while Morley illustrates ' break ' with detached notes followed by rests.[2]

Rhythm was another of the composer's tools. It is true that the madrigal, like all polyphonic music, encouraged considerable rhythmic independence among the voices. Of the variety so obtainable there was no greater master than Morley. He was not particularly subtle in portraying the sentiments of the verse, and he modelled himself on the more orthodox Italians rather than on the bold innovators who were stretching the traditional system to find more picturesque ways of illustrating the text. His conservatism as well as his great learning made him alive to all the possibilities of rhythmic contrast among the voices. His morris dance madrigals are masterpieces of rhythmic ingenuity. Yet even here the text is the warrant for energetic cross-rhythms. Wilbye and Weelkes use cross-rhythms cleverly and consistently to express a variety of ideas in the text. The fact is that, despite the independence of the voices, there is a sort of basic regularity behind madrigals. The Elizabethans clearly realized the difference between metre and rhythm. In poetry there is a regular pattern that continues in the mind throughout the reading—the metre ; but this implicit pattern is not always evident in the actual sound of the verse, which gains its interest from innumerable tiny variations from the fixed metre. The metre is subconscious most of the time, once the poet has set the mind ticking the right pattern ; the rhythm is the tune counterpointed on that subconscious pattern by the natural stresses and

---

[1] Morley, op. cit., p. 178.
[2] Wilbye, II, 14 ; Ward, No. 19 ; Morley, *Madrigalls to Foure Voyces*, No. 6.

quantities of the words. The madrigal, too, has metre behind its rhythmic fluidity. To bar madrigals regularly would be a good way of representing it if one could rid the mind of inevitable overt stress at the beginning of each bar. Excessive fluidity of rhythm, leaving the mind in real doubt as to the metre behind the variations, or emphatic cross-rhythms in all the parts together, have usually some textual significance. Farnaby is very fond of both. He uses them to illustrate phrases like 'In fury down he flang her', or 'He pulled her and he hauled her', to suggest the search for someone lost, or to add force to 'cursed' and 'sware'.[1]

As melody is always one of the composer's chief means of illustrating the text, it is not necessary or possible to describe in any detail the aptness of the themes to the lines of verse. To outline the melodic conventions alone would require a large volume, without taking into account individual genius. It is only possible to mention that the contour of the single voice-part is moulded not only by the exigencies of counterpoint but also by pictorial intentions. When Wilbye rises a sixth in the soprano and alto and falls a sixth in the two lower parts, he is trying, by the unusually large leap (which appears more striking among the restricted leaps of sixteenth-century melody), to add force to the words 'Change me'.[2] The subtler relations between melody and text are innumerable ; but we are dealing here with the conventions common to the whole school. One point only need be mentioned because it is purely conventional. This is the setting of more than one note to a syllable. The whole tendency of the century is towards a syllabic declamation. In the madrigals, however, ornaments and runs do occur. They are exceptions that prove the rule, since they are always used for special effect. Dr. Fellowes observes that 'the madrigal writers frequently set musical phrases or groups of notes of considerable length to single words or syllables that sometimes are of small importance'.[3] This may give a wrong impression unless it is realized that Dr. Fellowes means a number of notes may be set to a syllable which is rhythmically unimportant. Some picturesque intention is generally behind the run. Dr. Fellowes himself quotes an example from Morley, in which the text is : 'In nets of golden wires . . . my heart entangled.' The runs occur on 'wires' and 'entangled', and surely the pictorial purpose is very clear. Wilbye has a similar passage on the phrase 'silken twining'.[4] Nearly always when there is a run the phrase contains some word of pictor-

[1] Nos. 4, 6, 8, 14.   [2] *Second Set*, No. 11.
[3] *English Madrigal School*, I, iii.   [4] *Second Set*, No. 14.

ial or emotional import. The effect depends a great deal on performance. Sung smoothly it may imply pleasure or beauty ; sung boldly, more turbulent emotions. A short list, chosen at random from a few leading madrigal volumes, will indicate the variety of associations this means of expression might have : it is never used without regard for the text.

Adieu—Weelkes, *Balletts*, 21.
Adorning—Morley, *2-part Canzonets*, 2.
Beautify—Oriana, 9.
Bite—Farnaby, 9.
Blindness—Morley, *3-part Canzonets*, 9.
Burning—Farmer, 5
Cheerful—Ward, 12.
Cunning—Oriana, 14.
Darling—Morley, *2-part Canzonets*, 1 and 4.
Delightful—ib., 8.
Eternal—ib., 1.
Entangled—ib., 10.
Fancy—Morley, *Introduction*.
Feature—Weelkes, 1597 *Madrigals*, 16.
Feeling—Ward, 6 ; Tomkins, 5.
Fire—Weelkes, *6-part Madrigals*, 7 and 8.
Fly—Ward, 6 ; Tomkins, 9 ; Wilbye, II, 19 ; Farmer, 11.
Fortune—Tomkins, 2.
Frolic—Ward, 20.
Flame—Tomkins, 3, 12 ; Wilbye, II, 19 ; Farmer, 5 ; Morley, *Italian Canzonets*, 8.
Fury—Weelkes, *6-part Madrigals*, 6.
Gentle—Ward, 18.
Gladness—Tomkins, 11.
Inspiring—Morley, *Italian Canzonets*, 9.
Jewel—Wilbye, II, 8.
Jocund—Ward, 25.
Kisses—Tomkins, 5.
Laughs—Tomkins, 10 ; Morley, *3-part Canzonets*, 9.
Light—Wilbye, II, 32.
Live—Morley, *Madrigals*, 12.
Love—Ward, 15.
Melodies—ib., 13.
Merriment—Morley, *Balletts*, 11.
Mirth—Ward, 13.
Morning—Morley, *2-part Canzonets*, 2.
Murmur—Ward, 18.
Pleasure—ib.
Quailed—Farnaby, 10.

Rainbow—ib., 4.
Rays—Morley, *2-part Canzonets*, 1.
Regard—Farmer, 16.
Relenting—Morley, *3-part Canzonets*, 15.
Runs—Ward, 7.
Satyrs—Ward, 14.
Showers—ib., 24.
Smile—Ward, 20 ; Wilbye, I, 13, and II, 18 ; Morley, IV, 8.
Sweet—Ward, 16 ; Morley, II, 14 ; III, 5.
Swell(ing)—Wilbye, II, 6.
Thunder—Ward, 17.
Twining—Wilbye, II, 14.
Venus—Ward, 22.
Weep—Morley, *Madrigals*, 3 ; East, 1604 volume, 17.
Whistle—Wilbye, II, 8.
Wires—Morley, *2-part Canzonets*, 10.
Wounding—ib., 5.
Wavering—Farmer, 16.
Waxeth—ib., 3.

The rise of chromaticism is an interesting chapter in the use of melody to express the text. The English composers were much later to attempt it than the Italians. As early as the forties Cyprian di Rore, the pupil of Willaert and his successor at San Marco, was composing chromatic madrigals. The later Italians, particularly Marenzio, handled chromaticism with great delicacy, and Gesualdo produced effects with it that must have startled his hearers. The English, however, did not approach chromaticism as a new way of making the text more vivid ; they were attracted to the musical effects the Italians had created. This is shown by references to chromaticism in the texts of English madrigals. A poet in Byrd's 1611 volume invokes chromatic music to provide a fit setting for his mourning.

> Come, woeful Orpheus, with thy charming lyre,
> And tune thy voice unto thy skilful wire ;
> Some strange chromatic notes do you devise,
> That best with mournful accents sympathise ;
> Of sourest sharps and flats uncouth make choice,
> And I'll thereto compassionate my voice.[1]

And a poet in Daniel's *Songs* asks :

> Can doleful notes to measured accents set
> Express unmeasured griefs that time forget ?
> No, let chromatic tunes, harsh without ground,
> Be sullen music for a tuneless heart ;

---

[1] No. 19. *English Madrigal Verse*, p. 65.

> Chromatic tunes most like my passions sound,
>> As if combined to bear their falling part.
> Uncertain certain turns, of thoughts forecast
> Bring back the same, then die, and dying last.[1]

These lines incidentally explain what the Italian composers were seeking in their chromatic experiments. Orthodox counterpoint had exhausted its possibilities for expressing sombre passion. Doleful notes and measured accents had become clichés. To give the music sufficient intensity novel progressions had to be invoked. The English merely copied the Italians, but their chromaticism was always correlated with the sentiments of the text; it was used to add poignancy to suggestions of melancholy and pain. It occurs on words like 'cruel', 'pain', 'dolorous', 'languish', 'weary', and 'crying'.[2] A remarkable sustained chromatic passage comes at the beginning of Weelkes' 'O Care, thou wilt dispatch me'.[3]

Chromatic harmony too was an early feature of the madrigal. Arcadelt's 'Il bianco e dolce cigno' opens in F major tonality; then at the word 'piagendo' the chord of E♭ is unexpectedly taken. The effect is impressive because of the simplicity of the chords. The same transition occurs in Weelkes' 'Thule, the period of cosmography' on the words 'These things are wondrous.'[4] The madrigal composers had a very good appreciation of harmonic effect, although they thought contrapuntally. The false relation, quite frequent in the English school, comes from thinking of the voices' horizontal movement, though again it is used to illustrate the text. Weelkes, for instance, has false relations on the words 'pain and anguish' and 'deadly sting',[5] and Ward on 'bitter'.[6] But Morley has something to say about chords. He recommends flat (minor) thirds and sixths, as being more grateful to the ear, when the composer would represent 'a lamentable passion', but major thirds and sixths to 'signifie hardnes, cruelty or other such affects'.[7] This is a rather arbitrary notion of little consequence. The English composers often use major third and minor sixth together to 'signifie hardnes, cruelty or other such affects'. Weelkes does so on the words 'wanteth concord' and 'Why weep ye?'[8] Within the framework of the traditional counterpoint the only dissonance allowable was the suspension. This was normally used with slow movement to give an effect of melancholy. Ward

[1] No. 19. *English Madrigal Verse*, p. 405.
[2] Ward, Nos. 17, 23, 28; Wilbye, II, 16, 20.
[3] *5-part Madrigals*, 4–5.   [4] *6-part Madrigals*, 7–8.
[5] 1597 Set, 15; *5-part Madrigals*, 4.   [6] No. 21.
[7] op. cit., p. 177.   [8] *Balletts*, 3 and 8.

has rather a distinctive way of using double suspensions. The
upward resolution of the discord was not permitted, but Wilbye
has an effective line of concords resolving upwards. The text
reads : 'For tears, being stopped, will swell.' The upward
resolutions convey the sense of obstruction and at the same time
carry the listener forward as on a wave to the bursting out of the
long roll of quavers on ' swell '.[1]

It was mainly by extension of the rules about resolving suspensions
that bolder discords were introduced. The seventh, and even the
ninth, occur fairly often, and there are instances of bolder discords.
Dr. Fellowes has given a very scholarly account of dissonances
found in the English school.[2] It is only necessary to say that they
always occur where the text requires a poignant effect. Even
without dissonance, however, the composers knew how to handle
harmony for pictorial ends. The emphatic chords, with their
tonic, dominant, and sub-dominant suggestions, in the first part of
Weelkes' ' Like two proud armies ', help to give the air of martial
confidence which the words need.[3]

Chromaticism and the exploitation of harmony as an end in
itself were disruptive elements in the contrapuntal scheme the
madrigal had inherited. The urge for emotional expression had
stretched and twisted the conventions, and, without a system of
tonality, the later madrigals—those of Gesualdo, for instance—
tended to become a succession of splashes of colour destitute of
form. Literary pressure had transformed music from sensuous
sound into a romantic medium for the transmission of emotion.

[1] II, 6.   [2] *English Madrigal Composers, passim.*   [3] *6-part Madrigals,* 1.

The service of poetry had taught it how to absorb into itself some of the emotional appeal of poetry. When it learned that lesson it no longer needed words to prompt it. It could turn to the new problems of form its experiments had rendered acute. For these problems the seventeenth century was to furnish solutions that lasted until our own day.

CHAPTER VII

THE AIR

THE songs of Byrd reveal a long tradition of accompanied song in England. There is nothing primitive about them, and they must have required very capable performers. Solo songs will be composed in all ages, because everybody can appreciate a good tune, and while there are professional singers there will always be elaborate music for solo voice. Sixteenth-century elaboration was bound to be contrapuntal ; no other kind of accompaniment was known. Byrd's songs therefore did not differ very much in construction from the part-music of contemporary schools, and, as the madrigal came into vogue, they could easily be dressed up to look like the fashionable new Italian music. Professional singers, however, would continue to want solo songs that would display their talents, and amateurs would still like a good tune, however fond they were of part-singing. From the musical idiom of the time the demand of both kinds of singers created at the end of the century a distinctive type of song known as the air.

The term ' air ' can be restricted to a school of composition represented by a series of publications appearing between 1597 and 1622. The leader of the school was John Dowland. In 1597 he published a work entitled : ' The First Booke of Songes or Ayres of fowre parts with Tableture for the Lute : So made that all the partes together, or either of them seuerally may be song to the Lute, Orpherian or Viol de gambo.' Actually two little songs with lute accompaniment had been published the year before in William Barley's *Newe booke of tabliture*, and a number in manuscript are considerably older than Dowland's. But it is convenient to reckon the 1597 volume as the beginning of the school. Its end can be as conveniently marked by the publication in 1622 of John Attey's *First Booke of Ayres*. Later songs, although still often called airs, well into the seventeenth century, are composed in a different idiom. Those published between 1597 and 1622 have so many common characteristics of style and technique as to constitute a distinctive type.

The essence of the air is the tune. Its distinction lies in its being the first English song in which the accompaniment is carefully composed yet purely subsidiary to the solo voice. Strumming on an instrument to support the voice is as old as instruments themselves ; but there is nothing improvised about the airs. Their best composers were as technically accomplished as the contemporary madrigal composers ; they just did not choose to employ their technique as Byrd had employed his when he tried his hand at solo song. His song melodies had been adapted to the requirements of the contrapuntal texture into which they were woven. The song melody, on the other hand, *is* the air. The accompaniment is generally harmonic, but, even if it becomes contrapuntal, it is subordinate to the solo part.

Because of the range of demand they satisfied, from the amateur's to the professional singer's, the airs had not only a variety of style but two methods of performance. The rather obscure wording of Dowland's title-page, quoted above, means that they could be performed either as solos with instrumental accompaniment or by four unaccompanied singers. They were printed with the instrumental tablature underneath the soprano part and the lower three parts facing the three other points of the compass, so that one person could sing the tune to his own accompaniment or four people could sit round a table and sing together from one book. The latter arrangement was a concession to the contemporary fondness for part-singing. Several of the volumes of airs are for soloist and lute only, but Campion explains why it was generally considered advisable to add alternative voice parts, even when the composer had thought of his airs in the first place as accompanied solos. In the preface to *Two Bookes of Ayres* (1613) he says :

These Ayres were for the most part framed at first for one voyce with the Lute, or Violl, but vpon occasion, they haue since beene filled with more parts, which who so please may vse, who like not may leaue. Yet we doe daily obserue, that when any shall sing a Treble to an Instrument, the standers by wil be offring at an inward part out of their owne nature ; and true or false, out it must, though to the peruerting of the whole harmonie.

The composer began with a tune. This he treated as the treble of his air, not as the tenor, which had been the traditional practice, even in plain note-against-note counterpoint. '. . . if wee consider well, the Treble tunes, which are with vs commonly called Ayres, are but Tenors mounted eight Notes higher.' [1] To the treble was added first a bass and then two inner parts. The air was then ready for four voices, or the three lower ones could be arranged for the lute. The tune could actually be sung by either a man or a

---

[1] To the Reader, *Two Bookes of Ayres*.

woman, but it was treated as though it were the highest part and supported by chords. A few qualifications could be made to this summary of the general way of meeting the air's dual purpose (Dowland's later airs, for example, have genuine instrumental accompaniments) ; but it is sufficiently correct for present requirements.

The identity of the accompanying instrument was immaterial. Tobias Hume thought the bass viol the most suitable. It was often added to the lute as an extra bass part, and sometimes, as in Robert Jones's *Second Booke of Ayres* (1601), it might be tuned ' lyra-way ' and replace the lute. But by Hume's own admission the lute was ' the most received instrument that is '.[1] Dowland, indeed, replied rather sharply to Hume's aspersions on it.[2] It was most frequently used partly because most of the composers of airs were lutanists, and partly because it was the most popular domestic instrument of the time. It was the sixteenth-century pianoforte. It was found everywhere. It hung even in the seaman's cabin,[3] and its poor relation, the cither, beguiled the time of waiting in barbers' shops.[4] Just as modern works are often arranged for the piano, that amateurs may become acquainted with their structure, so elaborate contrapuntal works were often arranged for the lute. Willaert published lute versions of some of Verdelot's madrigals, and church music can be found in some English manuscripts arranged as lute solos or as pieces for single voice and lute.

In a sense, therefore, the choice of the lute as the usual accompanying instrument meant simply that airs were regarded as popular songs that amateurs could amuse themselves by singing. It does not follow that they were originally composed for a very large public. Dowland would first of all sing his songs to his patrons and friends, and most of the other composers would have no idea of printing their songs when they first produced them. Rosseter can be credited when he says that Campion's airs were privately imparted to his friends. But there was a wider public available when the composers thought of gaining its ear. Some do seem to have wanted to print their airs. Jones announced his *Third Booke of Ayres* as his last and called it *Ultimum Vale* (1608). Yet the very next year he published another volume, and to cover up his inconsistency he pretended to have dreamed

---

[1] *The First Part of Ayres* (1605), fol. B2v.
[2] *A Pilgrimes Solace* (1612).
[3] *Sanderson's Travels* (Hakluyt Society), pp. xxxii, 5, 233.
[4] Jonson, *Epicoene*, III, ii.

all the airs in it, entitling the work *A Musicall Dreame*. He did not bother to invent any excuse for his fifth set, *The Muses Gardin for Delights* (1610). It must be admitted that he may not have had much to do with the issue of these two volumes. There are so many misprints in them that it is not likely he supervised the printing. But that merely means that the printer, if not he, saw a possible market for his songs. There was, indeed, a public demand for airs. Dowland's first set ran into four editions, in 1597, 1600, 1606, and 1613. The second set is known to have been printed in an edition of 1,000 copies.[1] If the first set had the same number of copies in each edition, it must have been widely bought and have brought a fair profit to the printer, if not to the composer. There is plenty of evidence that airs were on everybody's lips. Madrigals are very seldom referred to in plays or pamphlets, but airs frequently are. Sir Toby and his friends in *Twelfth Night* bawl out a song by Jones in their cups, and the citizen and his wife in *The Knight of the Burning Pestle* ask the playhouse consort to strike up Dowland's *Lachrimae*. These characters are not represented as very refined, so their choice probably reflects a popularity of the airs among the bourgeoisie. From one point of view, the air is simply a popular song closely related to the anonymous tunes everybody sang and whistled in the street. Campion realized that the air owed much to English traditional music, and censured those who pretended to like only foreign airs. 'But some there are who admit onely French or Italian Ayres, as if euery Country had not his proper Ayre, which the people thereof naturally vsurpe in their Musicke.'[2] Campion is not referring to the madrigal but to the lighter tunes of the Italians. Morley groups together the canzonet, the neapolitan, the *villanella*, and the *ballata*, saying that 'these and all other kinds of light musicke sauing the *Madrigal* are by a generall name called ayres'.[3] There are always snobs who prefer foreign music simply because it is foreign. Campion reminded them that Italian airs were founded on Italian traditional melody, and so English airs must be founded on native melody. It is difficult sometimes to draw a rigid line between the air and other popular songs. A few of the printed airs were circulated as broadsides, and the two kinds of verse rub shoulders in commonplace books of the period. One of Dowland's airs became very popular as a tune to which ballads

[1] M. Dowling, *The Printing of John Dowland's Second Booke of Ayres* (*The Library*, 4th Series, XII, No. 4).
[2] *Two Bookes of Ayres.*   [3] *Introduction*, p. 180.

were written (see p. 172). The two forms are distinct enough in a general way, but the air was just popular enough for there to be a doubtful region around the frontier between them.

Yet the air is not only a popular song. The verse in the song-books is of the same type as that of the madrigals and much better in quality. This is partly because the airs are strophic and allow more scope than madrigals, but that is not the only reason. Literary attention was directed more to the air than to the madrigal. Campion, one of the leading composers of airs, was the finest lyric poet of his age. Dowland's volumes, too, contain some of the best lyrics of the period. Nor was the music popular in the sense of lacking deliberate art. John Dowland and John Daniel, the masters of the form, were as perfectly skilled in their craft as any madrigal composer. Dowland could style himself 'Batcheler of Musicke in both the Universities' and later Doctor of Music. He was well read in the theory of the day, and translated the rather old-fashioned *Micrologus* of Andreas Ornithoparcus. Few would question Fuller's judgement of his abilities : ' He was the rarest musician that his age did behold ; having travelled beyond the seas, and compounded English with foreign skill in that faculty, it is questionable whether he excelled in vocal or instrumental music.' [1] If some of the airs approach popular song in their simple tunefulness, those of Dowland and Daniel approach the madrigal in the elaboration of their part-writing. The norm between the two tendencies is a simple but artistic song set to poetry of the same kind as the sonnet sequences, though very free in form. Both poetry and music were intended for cultured people, who could appreciate technique and taste.

The majority of the composers of airs were professional lutanists. Dowland held an appointment at the Danish court from 1598 to 1606, and was later lutanist to Lord Howard de Walden and to King James I. John Daniel and Philip Rosseter were also in the king's service, while Alfonso Ferrabosco and Thomas Ford belonged to the household of Henry, Prince of Wales. The other class of composer particularly attracted to the air was the literary amateur, of whom Campion is the most interesting example. It was not only the customary lute accompaniment that drew lutanists to the air. Their instrument had obvious defects as a solo instrument, and it was recognized that its virtues shone most clearly when it was supporting the human voice. Its lack of sustaining power prevented more than a slight sketch of con-

[1] *History of the Worthies of England* (1662).

trapuntal ideas and led to a constant twinkle of quick runs and arpeggios. It is true that a number of virtuosi made considerable reputations by their fantasias and variations on popular tunes, and such famous lutanists as Anthony Holborne and Francis Cutting do not seem to have written many songs. Still, the musicianship of the lute solos that have survived is inferior to that of the compositions for the virginals. Dowland had a very great reputation as a solo performer, but he would be quite aware of the restricted art possible in writing for such an instrument. The position of lutanist, therefore, usually entailed singing as well as playing. At court the lutanists had charge of six boy singers. Composition was part of their duties as well as performance ; it was not so easy then as it is now to procure a supply of music by other composers. The madrigal composers had to produce vocal music for their patrons : Wilbye wrote his works for the family at Hengreave Hall. Lutanists had to keep up a fresh supply of songs for their patrons, and particularly to set the poems of their patrons and friends. Jones speaks of the gentlemen who asked him to set their songs (see p. 35).

This function of lutanists at court and in the large houses was similar to that of the Italian *improvisatori*, descendants of the medieval minstrels who survived into the eighteenth century. The *improvisatori* had a stock of simple traditional tunes, to which they improvised verses, and to which they were ready to fit other people's verses, accompanying themselves on an instrument. Lyrics were meant to be sung, not read, and the poet either sang them himself or had them sung by somebody with a better voice : it was thus he published them to his friends. Humanist circles had always included men who could sing their own verses and those of others. Typical of such presenters of vernacular poetry to courtly circles was the fifteenth-century poet Serafino del'Aquila (1466–1500). He acquired his education at the court of Naples, where his music teacher was the famous Guglielmo Fiamengo. Later a few years in Rome, part of the time in the service of Cardinal Ascanio de Sforza, brought Serafino to the notice of influential people. At twenty-four he knew all the arts of the courtier ; he sang, played the lute, and was fond of dancing. He travelled with the Cardinal, and enjoyed the entrée of the literary academies. His own settings of *frottole* and *strambotti* were sung in the Roman Academy, meeting-place of poets and wits. They were taken up by other singers, and his fame spread throughout Italy.[1] Returning to Naples in the

[1] Life of Serafino by Calmeta, prefixed to Serafino's poems (1505).

service of Ferdinand II, he attended another academy, of which Sannazaro, Caritheo, and Cara were members. He was in demand not only for singing his own songs but for setting the poems of men of letters he met in these circles.[1] Though his poetry seems extravagant and superficial, he won a considerable reputation in his own day, and on his death Paolo Cortese compared him with Petrarch, whom he imagined to have been the first to sing songs of the same type to the lute.

Quod quidem genus primus apud nostros Franciscus Petrarcha instituisse dicitur, qui edita carmina caneret ad lembum. Nuper autem Seraphinus Aquilanus princeps ejus generis renovandi fuit, a quo ita est verborum et cantuum conjunctio modulata nexa, quo nihil fieri posset modorum ratione dulcius. Itaque ex eo tante imitantium auledorum multitudo manavit, ut quicquid in hoc genere Italia tota cani videatur, ex ejus appareat carminum et modorum praescriptione natum.[2]

The collocation of the two names is important, for the sixteenth century recognized Petrarch as the first to write the sort of poetry it was interested in, and his fame as a humanist satisfied neo-classicists of the propriety of imitating even features of his work that did not come from the ancients. The singing of lyrics was medieval ; Petrarch inherited it from the troubadours ; but the Renaissance saw in it a revival of the Greek lyric, which was sung to the lyre. The lute became the poet's particular companion. Airs to the lute continued to be popular in Italy right through the Renaissance period, and they remained in literary favour even while the Netherland composers were bending their contrapuntal dexterity to the service of the Petrarchan revival in developing the madrigal. Among the works printed by Ottaviano de'Petrucci, the first Italian music printer, in the first decade of the sixteenth century, were volumes for the lute by Francesco Sprinaccino (1507 and 1508), Juan Ambrosia d'Alza (1508), and Francesco Bossinensis (1509). The circles in which the New Poetry was born continued to patronize the successors of Serafino. In Castiglione's *Courtyer* the Count praises

the manner of singing that Bidon useth, which is so artificiall, cunning, vehement, stirred, and such sundrie melodies, that the spirites of the hearers move all and are inflamed, and so listing, a man would weene they were lift up into heaven.

---

[1] ib.

[2] *De Cardinal*, quoted Tiraboschi, *Storia della Letteratura Italiana*, Bk. VI, pt. III, p. 1244.

And no lesse doth our Marchetto Cara move in his singing, but with a more soft harmony, that by a delectable way and full of mourning sweetenes maketh tender and perceth the mind, and sweetly imprinteth in it a passion full of great delite.[1]

Cara was a composer of *frottole*, and associated with one of the academies in which Serafino performed. Calmeta, who wrote Serafino's life for the edition of his poems in 1505, was present during part of the discussion recorded in *The Courtyer*, and Serafino himself spent some months at the court of Urbino, where he was well received by the Duchess. Sir Thomas Wyatt, himself a lover of the lute, would hear poetry sung to the lute in circles such as Castiglione's during his visit to Italy, and would return to England convinced that to sing poetry thus was to follow Petrarch and to restore the classical lyre to poetry. Ronsard, too, was acquainted with Italian fondness for lute songs, and he set himself to imitate what he thought was the Italian restoration of the Greek manner of singing lyrics. ' Et ferai encore revenir (si je puis) l'usage de la lire aujourdhui resuscitée en Italie, laquelle lire seule doit et peut animer les vers et leur donner le juste poix de leur gravité.'[2] With satisfaction he afterwards boasts of being the first to introduce what had become a fashion in France.

> Premiere j'ay dit la façon
> D'accorder le luth aux Odes.[3]

Thus, even while the madrigal was establishing itself as the appropriate musical counterpart of Petrarchan poetry, there lingered in Italy a predilection for the solo air with lute accompaniment. The literary circles who patronized the air had quite clear reasons for preferring it. They felt that contrapuntal music, however much it tried to underline the text, distracted attention from the poetry. It was difficult even to hear the poetry properly with so much else to occupy the ear. Sir Frederick, in *The Courtyer*, thought contrapuntal music

a faire musicke, so it be done upon the booke surely and after a good sorte. But to sing to the lute is much better, because all the sweetnes consisteth in one alone, and a man is much more heedfull and under-standeth better the feat manner, and the aire or veyne of it, when the eares are not busied in hearing any moe than one voice : and beside

---

[1] Trans. Hoby, Everyman ed., p. 61.
[2] *Œuvres*, ed. Vagaray, III, 368. [3] ib., III, 69.

every little errour is soone perceived, which happeneth not in singing
with company, for one beareth another out.

But singing to the lute with the dittie (me thinke) is more pleasant
than the rest, for it addeth to the wordes such a grace and strength,
that it is a great wonder.[1]

An amateur's difficulty in following the independent movement of
each part is here joined with a belief that the words are more
fairly treated in solo music. The Italian makes this more apparent
than Hoby's clumsy translation. 'Singing to the lute with the
dittie' is a poor rendering of 'singing to the viol by way of
recitative'.[2] The speaker clearly had in mind such singing as
would give the words the same emphasis as recitation. It could
not be pretended that contrapuntal music was as respectful as this
to the text. Even if the declamation of the individual voices
were particularly careful, the listener could not hear the words
easily. The musical interest of the madrigal was sure to dwarf the
literary. The music could exist apart from the words, could be
'apt for viols or voices'. It was possible to write a very impressive madrigal to nonsensical words. Robert Jones proved it
by setting as a madrigal a few of the tags used in printing a volume.

> Here is an end of all the songs
> That are in number but four parts ;
> And he loves music well, we say,
> That sings all five before he starts.[3]

The most impressive words were often treated cavalierly. Excla-
mations were added and adjectives inserted to fill out the individual
parts. The madrigal composers made great pretence of following
the text, but one had not to look too closely at the details of their
handling of the verse.

In this undercurrent of criticism against counterpoint the
moderate literary amateurs put first the necessity for a simpler
texture, which would not distort the accentuation of the words
and would leave opportunity for hearing and appreciating the
words as poetry. This did not in itself imply much special preference for the solo air ; the homophonic part-song would almost
have fulfilled their desires. The more radical neo-classicists, however, saw a peculiar virtue in the accompanying instrument,
equating the lute with the Greek lyre. It was the simplification
of texture that received most attention from the practical musicians.
The French school, which had great influence in England, was

---

[1] op. cit., p. 101. [2] 'Il cantare alla viola per recitare.'
[3] *First Set of Madrigals*, No. 12.

producing a fairly homophonic type of part-song even before the madrigal had reached England. When Ronsard asked the leading composers of his day to provide settings for the *Amours* of 1552 the style of the music was very plain compared with that of contemporary madrigals. Goudimel's settings are the most elaborate, but they are nearer the early madrigals of Arcadelt than the later ones of Marenzio and Vecchi. There are points of imitation, but the contrapuntal development is very slight. Each voice sings the words only once and gives the same accentuation and quantity to each syllable, as far as the musical continuity allows. The other composers approximate more closely to the harmonic part-song. The influence of the Pléiade is to be suspected in the choice of style ; but it cannot be pressed too far, since there were always fairly homophonic *chansons*. All it would be fair to suggest is that a tradition already in existence was perhaps strengthened by the Pléiade's preference for a plain setting of poetry.

The left wing of the Pléiade interpreted Ronsard's view on the close relationship between music and poetry as a justification for using music to solve the problems of quantitative metre. In 1571 Jean-Antoine de Baif joined with Thibaut de Courville, a lutanist, to found the Académie de Musique et de Poésie. Baif himself was a very capable musician as well as a poet. In 1562 he published twelve hymns set to his own music, and in 1578 a number of songs in four parts, the words and music again both being his own. He reasoned that if the classical longs and shorts were set to music exactly, it would then be possible to see whether the sound of Greek metres were tolerable enough to justify a change-over to quantity as the basis of French versification. Baif's Académie did not last very long, but its ideas did, and a later Académie du Palais, in which Claude Lejeune and Jacques Maudit were the chief musical figures, continued to amuse the court circle with quantitative poems set to music. Of course, the music had to be strictly homophonic, since the quantities had to be the same in all parts and repetition of words would have been very unliterary. Sometimes the settings were for four voices and sometimes for solo voice and lute. They seem to have enjoyed remarkable success, and many are still to be found in Bataille's lute books in the early seventeenth century.[1] The decoration of the simple quantities displays a good deal of ingenuity, and the rhythmical effects are often strangely fascinating. M. Prunieres

---

[1] H. Expert has reprinted some of Lejeune's and Maudit's works in his *Maîtres musiciens de la Renaissance* series.

has suggested that they attracted Monteverdi during his visit to France.[1]

Experimenters like Baif preferred homophonic settings not only because the poetry could be heard more distinctly but because the rhythm of the verse could be more exactly reproduced. The French neo-classicists did not pay much attention to the sentiments of the poetry. There were, however, Italian neo-classicists who wanted to restore not just the metres of Greek poetry but its aesthetic power ; and they too looked to music for assistance, knowing that the Greek lyric had been sung. By concentrating on the force of music to sway the passions they delivered a harder blow at counterpoint than the French theorists, for the madrigal's chief claim as an interpreter of poetry was that it illustrated vividly the sentiments of the text. From their deliberations the seventeenth-century opera was to emerge. The Camarata of Count Bardi in Florence was a typical Renaissance academy, of which Florence had always been a stronghold. The fashion had started there with the Platonic Academy, founded by Cosimo, the Father of his Country, and supported by Lorenzo de' Medici, Ficino, Poliziano, and Machiavelli, among others. It came to an end in 1522. In 1540 an academy began to meet in the house of Giovanni Mazzuoli. It first took the name of Accademia degli Umidi, then became known as the Florentine Academy. Its chief aim was the perfection of Tuscan language and literature, and it gave special attention to the poetry of Petrarch. Another important academy in Florence was founded in 1568 in the house of Giambatista Strozzi il Cieco and called the Accademia degli Alterati. The Accademia della Crusca was founded in 1582 by members of the Florentine Academy, and again directed its attention to the Tuscan language, publishing a Vocabulary in 1612. Now Giovanni Bardi, Count of Vernio, had been a member of both the Accademia degli Alterati and the Accademia della Crusca, and his interests were what we should expect in a member of those bodies—literary and philosophic. He was the author of eleven works no longer extant, and his one surviving work reveals him as a man of urbane temper and considerable learning. From about 1570 he gathered round him a number of men attached in different capacities to the Medici court, and they continued to meet at his house until he received a call to Rome, when his place was taken by his friend Jacopo Corsi. The previous experience of its founder in other academies indicates the sort of group the

[1] *Monteverdi* (English ed.), p. 17.

Camarata was. It was an academy of the kind that has been mentioned several times in this book, a meeting-place of scholars and men of letters. The madrigal had been in favour with such circles half a century earlier. Now the discussion still centred round the application of the classics to the enrichment of the vernacular literatures, but the musical opinions of people who moved in this society had solidified into definite prejudices. The Florentine Camarata concentrated on the relations between music and poetry. It did not produce any new ideas about them, but it formulated clearly what neo-classical amateurs tended to think. It was representative.

The members were practical musicians, scholars, and men of letters. Girolamo Mei, the author of works on Aristotle and Aeschylus and of a huge commentary, *De modis veteris musiae libri quattuor*, was the scholar and philosopher of the party. The chief literary figure was Ottavio Rinuccini (1565–1621), a lyric poet whose fame had travelled to France and won him invitations to visit Marie de' Medici and Henry IV. He was later to produce libretti for the first operas. Vincenzo Galelei, born about 1533 of a noble Florentine family, was the most scientific of the group. He knew a great deal about the construction and technique of Greek and modern instruments. His *Dialogo . . . della musica antica e della moderna* (1581) attacked counterpoint so bitterly that a cabal, led by Zarlino, is said to have tried to suppress it ; but he returned to the attack in his *Fronimo* (1583). Emilio del Cavalieri, a Roman born about 1550, was inferior to those just mentioned in his knowledge of antiquity, according to Doni, but he brought to the Camarata great experience of stage management and vocal music. He directed entertainments at the court of the Grand Duke Ferdinand. It was he who first actualized the dramatic purpose of the group with his *Rappresentazione di Anima et di Corpo* (1600). Jacopo Peri, director of music at the Medici court and from 1601 master of the chapel of the Duke of Ferrara, and Giulio Caccini, a famous singer, were the practical executants of the Camarata. They both composed solo songs on the group's principles, and collaborated in the two early operas *Dafne* and *Euridice* (1594–7 and 1600).

When an academy of this kind set out to discuss the relations of music and poetry there could be no doubt about the course the discussion would take. It was sure to begin with Greek practice. That was the routine procedure for improving any modern art. The Camarata was not antiquarian in its interest ; it wanted to apply Greek practice to modern conditions. Pietro Bardi, the Count's son, explains :

Uno de' principali scopi di questa Accademia era, col ritrovare l'antica Musica, quanto però fosse possibile in materia si oscura, di migliorare la Musica moderna e leverla in qualche parte dal misero stato, nel quale l'avevano messa principalmente i Goti dopo la perdita d' essa e delle altre Scienza e Arti piu nobili.[1]

The attitude reminds one of Ascham's stigmatism of rime as the invention of barbarous Goths. It arose from the same process of reasoning. As all the members of the Camarata expressed the same views, and as we are interested primarily in the aims and assumptions common to the whole period, we may conveniently summarize the Camarata's position.[2]

It did not know much about Greek music, but it believed all the accounts of the ancient writers about the power of music.[3] Dryden's Timotheus was a novice compared with a Greek musician as the Camarata imagined him. Why was it, then, that modern music could not tame wild beasts and alter the characters of men ? Either human nature had changed or else modern music had lost something Greek music had. Only the latter seemed conceivable. The Camarata therefore felt bound to inquire what was the secret the Greeks knew and the moderns did not. It lay, they decided, in the realization that music was a blending of words, rhythm, and harmony. Vocal music was supreme among the Greeks, and the words governed it. Rhythm was latent in the words ; it was produced by a succession of justly measured syllables. Harmony too was implicit in the text, in the grave and acute accents of the words as spoken. The musician, then, had to start from the words as they were generally pronounced ; his music

[1] Letter to J. B. Doni (Bandini, op. cit., p. 118).
[2] The chief expositions of the Camarata's views are : G. Bardi, *Discorso mandata a Guilio Caccini sopra la musica antica e'l cantar bene* ; G. Caccini, Prefaces to *Euridice* and *Nuove Musiche* (1601) ; V. Galelei, *Dialogo* (1581), *Fronimo* (1583) ; G. Mei, *Discorso sopra la musica antica e moderna* (1602). There is a useful summary by H. Martin in *La Revue de Musicologie*, May 1932–August 1933.
[3] During the Renaissance knowledge of Greek music was as scanty as the enthusiasm for it was great. Much of it came from sources already known to the middle ages. Boethius' *De Musica* was printed at Venice in 1491–2 and 1497–9, and Capella's Ninth Book as late as 1599 by Hugo Grotius at Leyden. Latin versions of Euclid and Plutarch were published in 1498 and 1532. Zarlino persuaded Gogavinus to publish a Latin version of Ptolemy, Aristoxenes, and part of Aristotle at Venice in 1562, and Daniello, also at Zarlino's suggestion, translated Vitruvius. The actual music of the Greeks remained unintelligible.

for them simply noted definite quantities and definite pitches for the different syllables, according to their positions in the verse. Counterpoint was unknown. Choirs sang in unison, and the accompanying instrument of a soloist merely doubled the voice part. Often the composers were poets as well, and improvised simple settings. Everything depended on a single tune, which reproduced faithfully the sound qualities of the words. Harmony meant only the right singing of the text.

No wonder, thought the Camarata, modern music is so inferior in power to Greek music. Anything more unlike the Greek conception than the madrigal could scarcely exist. Words, they complain, are the last concern of modern composers. Some manipulate unsuitable texts to make them fit music already composed. Ordinarily one cannot distinguish verse from prose, for the endings of the lines are obliterated : while one part is finishing a line another is beginning the next line. The technique is instrumental, not vocal.

So the whirligig of time had brought its revenges. The madrigal's attempts to illustrate the text by contrapuntal elaboration was condemned as effacing the poetry. For it won no praise from the Camarata as a means of expression. 'Word-painting' might please the vulgar ; it had no interest for a man of taste. It appealed to the senses, whereas true music should appeal to the soul. Modern music had lost the

parte piu nobile importante e principale della musica, che sono i concetti dell'animo espressi col mezzo delle parole, e non gli accordi delle parti come dicono e credono i moderni prattici ; i quale hanno la ragione fatto schiava degli appetiti loro.[1]

The purpose of music was to ennoble the hearers. The Camarata invoked the Platonism of earlier academies to testify to this truth. Both Plato and Aristotle had said that music was an education of the soul, and the conceits of the soul were expressed in words. Let the text be heard clearly and its emotions would communicate themselves to the listener. The characters of the persons speaking the words must be studied, and the nature of the verse must be a guide. For instance, Petrarch's 'Italia mia, ben ch'il parla sia in darno' should be given to a tenor ; it should be set in the Dorian mode, *tempo moderato*, so as to be dignified and imposing. Then the intervals of the speaking voice under the stress of emotion must help to determine the rise and fall of the melody. This is

[1] Galileo, *Dialogo della musica antica e della moderna*, p. 83.

impossible in contrapuntal music, in which extraordinary leaps, far beyond the compass of the speaking voice, occur at every turn, and in which one voice rises while another descends. Contrary motion sacrifices the natural appeal of the words. The listener remains unmoved by it, like a pillar tugged two ways at once. The *tempo* of the music should be according to the speed at which the words would be spoken, this being dependent on the emotion. On phrases like ' Cor mio ' or ' Deh, non languire ' there should be *crescendo* and *diminuendo*. In fact, the general principle is to hold fast

à quella maniera cotanto lodata da Platone e altri Filosofi che affermarono la musica altro non essere, che la fauella, e'l rithmo, e il suono per vltimo, e non per lo contrario, à volere, che ella possa penetrare nell'altrui intelletto, e fare quei mirabili effetti, che ammirano gli Scrittori, e che non poteuano farsi per il contrappunto nelle moderne musiche.[1]

The words are to be the determining influence in all music. Only one voice is to be admitted because it allows the words to be more distinctly heard, and its rhythms and melody are to reproduce the natural stresses and quantities of emotional speech. The Camarata had advanced beyond the French theorists. It no longer bothered with classical metres ; it saw that speech rhythms were more complicated than the classical alternation of longs and shorts could suggest. The music should rather be framed to the life of the words, as Byrd finely expressed it. Caccini refers to his recitative as talking in music (' quasi in musica favellare ').

It is clear, then, that there were two lines of literary criticism both tending to discard the madrigal for solo song. One was concerned with the form of the poetry and the other with its feeling. Both agreed that counterpoint obscured the verse. The French school was anxious that the rhythm of the music should be correct, the Italian that the emotions should be natural. Both were extremists, of course. The insistence of the Camarata that modern music did not affect the listener sufficiently is an amateurish point of view : madrigals were intended not only for listeners but for singers. But there can be no doubt that criticisms of this kind had influence, and it is easier to detect the general movement of ideas by taking these extreme examples, especially when one realizes that they came from circles that had had much to do with the success of the New Poetry and of the madrigal in a previous generation. England did not produce any theorists as extreme as the ones we have just discussed, but the same ideas were vaguely

[1] Caccini, *Nuove Musiche.*

stirring here. The French neo-classicists had the more influence
during the sixteenth century; it was not until the seventeenth
century that Italian recitative invaded both England and France.
Literary amateurs, however, without going to the lengths of either
French or Italian neo-classicism, were inclined to prefer the air
to the madrigal for reasons not very different.

Campion's viewpoint owed something to Baif. His airs were
not the primary source of his reputation. 'His selfe neglects
these light fruits as superfluous blossomes of his deeper studies.' [1]
They are merely 'eare-pleasing rimes without Arte'; Latin verse
was his chief interest. One cannot take this too seriously; it was
the correct attitude. He was the only English composer who had
something like a complete theory of the air. Nevertheless, as a
Latin poet it was natural he should be inclined to the discussions
of quantitative metre that had wasted so much of the time of the
earlier Areopagus group. He must have been aware of Baif's
experiments and have been attracted by their invocation of music
to settle the difficulties of naturalizing classical prosody. It is not
surprising that he should have published a treatise on quantitative
metres in English.

Observations in the Arte of English Poesie (1602) came just too
late to be taken seriously. Sidney and Spenser had made the
whole question academic by their defence of English tradition,
backed by the success of their own poetry. An additional mis-
fortune of Campion was to provoke a reply from the ablest of
Sidney's younger protégés, Samuel Daniel. The *Defense of Ryme*
is full of good sense, and it settled the matter for three centuries.
Ben Jonson told Drummond that he intended to reply to both
Campion and Daniel, and the world is poorer for his failure to
carry out his intention : there was more to be said. Campion's
prejudices discounted, there are many interesting points in his
treatise, and he has received rather less than justice. He was not
laying down arbitrary laws but trying to start a discussion.

These rules concerning the quantity of our English sillables I haue
disposed as they came next into my memory ; others more methodicall,
time and practise may produce. In the meane season, as the Grammarians
leaue many sillables to the authority of Poets, so do I likewise leaue many
to their iudgments ; and withall thus conclude, that there is no Art
begun and perfected at one enterprise. [2]

Unfortunately the discussion was not joined.

[1] Rosseter's preface to *A Book of Ayres* (1601).
[2] *Works* of Campion, ed. Vivian, p. 56.

The idea behind the attempt to classify quantities is not just that the Greeks used longs and shorts and so we must. Campion is conscious all the time of practical problems in setting poetry to music. His aim in his airs was the perfect union of poetry and music. 'In these English ayres I haue chiefely aimed to couple Words and Notes louingly together, which will be much for him to doe that hath not power ouer both.'[1] This entailed scanning verse quantitatively as well as accentually. 'There is nothing more offensiue to the eare than to place a long sillable with a short note, or a short sillable with a long note, though in the last the vowell often beares it out.'[2] It is a problem all song composers must resolve. They are justly allowed some licence, but Campion is right in advising them to take as little as they can.

Rhythm in music depends on both stress and time. Poetry is also an organization of sound, and it is logical to assume its rhythm must be similar to that of music. Verse has duration as well as stress, and Campion's musical training helped him to time the periods of verse. He did not deny that stress marked the rhythm, but contended that stress alone was inadequate to explain it; that the regular succession of time periods, in poetry as in music, was the foundation of rhythm, though stress was an inevitable feature of the periods. Daniel rather missed the point when he found Campion's iambic pentameter was only the normal English blank verse : of course it was, but Campion was giving a new explanation of its structure. Indeed, he tried to account for its being the natural measure of English unrimed verse and gave a reason for its being the English equivalent of the classical hexameter.

I haue obserued, and so may any one that is practis'd in singing, or hath a naturall eare able to time a song, that the Latine verses of sixe feete, as the Heroick and Iambick, or of fiue feete, as the Trochaik, are in nature all the same length of sound with our English verses of fiue feete ; for either of them being tim'd with the hand, quinque perficiunt tempora, they fill up the quantity (as it were) of fiue sem'briefs. . . . The cause why these verses of differing feete yield the same length of sound, is by reason of some rests which either the necessity of the numbers or the heauiness of the sillables do beget. For we find in musick that often-times the straines of a song cannot be reduced to true number without some rests prefixt, in the beginning and middle as also at the end if need requires. Besides, our English monosillables enforce many breathings which no doubt greatly lengthen a verse, so that it is no wonder if for

---

[1] *Two Bookes of Ayres* (1613). [2] *Works*, ed. Vivian, p. 35.

these reasons our English verses of fiue feete hold pace with the Latines of sixe.[1]

Campion was not alone in thinking English ' clogged with consonants' and ' our monosyllables inapt to slide' : Dryden makes the same complaint in the preface to his translation of Virgil, and a similar feeling is behind the general belief that English is inferior to Italian as a language for singing.

Campion's recognition that pauses as well as syllables must be counted to fill the time periods of a metrical pattern is a real contribution to prosody. It is a corollary of his preliminary assumption that the metre of poetry, like that of music, is based on a succession of time periods felt to be equal. The rhythm heard against this regular metrical pattern is that of the words as pronounced in ordinary speech : that is why Campion is interested in the ' natural' length of syllables, although he fails to appreciate the extent to which words owe their stresses and quantities to their functions in the sentence. The metrical measure, like the bar of music, can be divided among any number of time values, provided the total duration remains constant. The ' iambic licentiate' may contain feet of three syllables instead of the ordinary two, and the ' English elegiac' may contain feet of several different types : the constant element is not the dispositions of the syllables but the duration of the foot. The result may only be free blank verse, but Campion has tried to include in his system of prosody what most systems have not mentioned, the variety of rhythm which distinguishes interesting from monotonous verse.

It is curious that, having started to time verses and got very near to a perception of the equality of time in feet of different patterns, he should have been deflected into a discussion of feet in terms of the classical longs and shorts. The great variety of consonant groups in English should have warned him that there were many classes of long and half-long syllables. He did not consider that Greek quantity might have been arbitrary, and that such arbitrary division of all syllables into long and short might be permissible in a language like Latin, which has few heavy blocks of consonants, but would not work in a language like English. Modern barring makes it more obvious than sixteenth-century scoring, but it is still strange Campion did not remember the time periods in music can be broken into notes of more than two different values. From that he might have perceived more than two lengths of syllable were possible. But his classical training

[1] *Works*, ed. Vivian, pp. 39–40.

blinded him, and his one published experiment in quantitative metre set to music is marred by following the example of the French neo-classicists and restricting himself to two time values. The metre he chose for his experiment was sapphic.

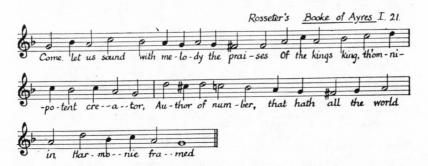

Rosseter's *Booke of Ayres* I. 21.

Come, let us sound with me-lo-dy the prai-ses Of the kings 'king, th'om-ni-
-po-tent cre--a--tor, Au-thor of num-ber, that hath all the world
in Har-mb--nie fra--med

It is a composition not without some rhythmical attraction, but it suffers from the drabness of the melody. The quantities are fairly good but have too narrow a range, and the effort of setting the metre exactly evidently exhausted Campion's very remarkable gift for melodic invention. He must have felt this himself, for he never repeated the experiment.

Although his attempts at strict quantitative metre proved unsatisfactory, Campion still thought of his airs as related to the classical lyric. ' The Lyricke Poets among the Greekes and Latines were first inuenters of Ayres, tying themselues strictly to the number, and value of their sillables.'[1] The relation is expressed in echoes of Catullus, but not in that only. He believed the association of poetry and music to be another ' classical ' feature the modern lyric should imitate. He often achieved empirically what eluded him when he worked from theory. As he composed both words and music, perhaps sometimes both together, it is scarcely accurate to say his verse derives unusual rhythms from the music or that his music succeeds admirably in following the quantities and stresses of the words : both poetry and music often owe delightful rhythmical effects to a just appreciation of the time values of syllables, in attending to which he felt he was in the tradition of the classical lyric. The beauty of the last two lines in this song is greatly enhanced by the initial long syllables, coming after the anapaestic movement of the previous line, and by the two long syllables at the end.

[1] Rosseter's *Booke of Ayres.*

It is the quantity rather than the stress that gives character to the lines, and verse and music correspond perfectly. Both stress and quantity are judged by ordinary speech rhythm, not by any preconceived metrical form. On the other hand, Campion is not pedantic : he knows that a singer can be trusted to make little adjustments to compromise between the requirements of musical pattern and those of syllabic quantity. The following song, were the music not known, would probably be thought to consist of four-stress trochaic lines.

> Shall I come, sweet Loue, to thee,
>> When the eu'ning beames are set ?
> Shall I not excluded be ?
>> Will you finde no fained lett ?
> Lett me not for pitty more,
> Tell the long hours at your dore. [1]

Campion, however, decides that the speech rhythm is more appropriate to three-stress lines. Once he has seen to it that the first two syllables are short, the lines fall naturally into the required rhythm. The other syllables are nearly all comparatively long : at least he apparently considers their differences too unimportant to worry about, and even the obviously short preposition ' to ' in the first line bears a crotchet, for Campion knows that its position between ' love ' and ' thee ' will ensure the singer's making it as unobtrusive as a crotchet can be. The other words to be watched are ' pity ', which must have a strong stress on the first syllable, and ' long ', the key-word of the last line. The stress on ' pity ' is reinforced by pitch-accent, while ' long ' is underlined by repetition. Campion's sense of proportion prevents him from

[1] *Third Booke of Ayres*, No. 17.

being fussy and concentrates his attention on the important stresses and quantities.

In the following couplet, 'shadow' consists of two short syllables, represented in the tune by two quavers.[1]

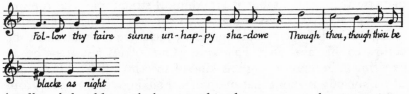

'Follow' should strictly be treated in the same way, but its position in the line allows it to be set to a dotted crotchet and quaver, which is more suitable to the shape of the tune. The second line begins with two long syllables, the second of which can, however, be pronounced quickly when the word is not to be emphasized. Campion gives, as it were, two scansions of the line—one showing the first two syllables as both long, by virtue of their vowel sounds, and the other shortening the second syllable because of its context. As it happens, this same tune was set by Campion to other words, and he succeeded in matching musical with metrical quantity better in his other version than in the one just quoted.

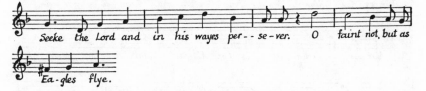

[1] In this and the following example the note values of the original have been *halved* to give modern readers a readier notion of the tempo.

The dotted crotchet at the beginning this time falls on the word 'seeke', which needs a long note because of its emphatic position in the sentence and because of its long vowel, reinforced by the two consonants after it. At the end of the first line there is again an accented short syllable. The second line opens with two syllables containing long vowels, which are given their proper quantities. In the previous example quoted the correspondence between musical and verbal quantities was sufficiently close for ordinary purposes, but here it is remarkably close. Without being pedantic, Campion does study quantity as well as stress and ensures that verse and music have the same time values, although he never allows a rigid interpretation of quantity to interfere with the pattern of either verse or music.

Campion was nearer to the French theorists than to the Italian, although he certainly knew what the Italians were trying to do. He was not interested so much in the musical representation of dramatic and impassioned speech as in copying in music the reading of verse that brought out its rhythmical structure. The tone of his own verse was less emotional than that of the poetry the Italians used for their experiments in recitative : significantly he compared his airs with epigrams. One of his airs may be an experiment in reproducing this kind of speech rhythm. The range of the melody is about that of a normal talking voice : apart from one note, it does not exceed a fifth.

Rosseter's Book of Ayres. I. 1.

My swee-test Les-bia let us live and love, and though the sa--ger sort our deedes re---prove, let us not way them heav'ns great lampes doe dive in--to their west and strait a--gaine re--vive, but soon as once set is our lit-tle light then must we sleepe one e---ver---du-ring night, e---ver---du-ring night.

If this is an attempt to reproduce the natural declamation of the speaking voice, it bears the same relation to the experiments of the Camarata as Tennyson's reading of his own verse bore to Browning's reading of his. The emphasis in the one case is on the rhythmical qualities of the verse and in the other on the emotional and dramatic possibilities of the words. Because of this difference in temper, Campion felt no incentive towards recitative : provided the rhythm of the music did not clash with that of the verse, he could add the interest of melody to be enjoyed for its own sake.

The air seemed to Campion a better ally of poetry than the madrigal because it allowed the values of the syllables to be distinctly heard and reproduced in the music. He admitted that counterpoint had musical interest ; there is none of the exaggeration of the Italians in his theories. But he insisted that the art of the air was as genuine in a humbler way.

As in poesie we give pre-eminence to the Heroical Poem, so in Musick we yield the chiefe place to the graue, and well inuented Motet, but not to euery harsh and dull confused Fantasie, where in multitude of points the Harmonie is quite drowned. Ayres haue both their Art and pleasure, and I will conclude of them as the Poet did in his censure, of *Catullus* the Lyricke, and *Vergil* the Heroicke writer :

> Tantum magna suo debet Verona Catullo :
> Quantum parua suo Mantua Vergilio.[1]

Significantly he made a criticism of the madrigal's word-painting similar to that of the Camarata. His example of its ridiculousness recalls Galileo's remark that an orator who drew attention to every important word would be laughed at. Like Galileo, he concludes that the proper declamation of the words is all that is required to move the hearer.

But there are some, who to appeare the more deepe, and singular in their iudgement, will admit no Musicke but that which is long, intricate, bated with fuge, chaind with sincopation, and where the nature of euerie word is precisely exprest in the Note, like the old exploded action in Comedies, when if they did pronounce *Memini*, they would point to the hinder part of their heads, if *Video*, put their finger in their eye. But such childish obseruing of words is altogether ridiculous, and we ought to maintaine as well in Notes, as in action a manly cariage, gracing no word, but that which is eminent, and emphaticall.[2]

---

[1] Rosseter's *Booke of Ayres*.   [2] ib.

Campion was too interested in the words for their own sake to bother about illustrating them ; all he wanted was that they should be heard, and that their stresses and quantities should be correct. An air was like an epigram, ' short and well seasoned '. The tune was the main thing. ' A naked Ayre without guide, or prop, or colour but his owne, is easily censured of euerie eare, and requires so much the more inuention to make it please.' [1] It is as a writer of pretty tunes that Campion excels ; of tunes that admirably fit the poetry, which was obviously his chief strength.

The air as Campion conceived it remained a very miniature form. The fact that it did try to be tuneful is a reminder that composers of airs were not only anxious to fit the verse with music not too complicated for the words to be heard. Like other movements of thought, the revolt against counterpoint included less exalted motives than those of its leaders. Rosseter, Campion's friend, is very similar to Campion in his outlook, and was a better musician : his airs have a haunting quality few of Campion's attain. But many of the other members of the school cared little for theories ; they wrote simply popular songs. Robert Jones excels as a writer of comic songs. When he is serious and tries to imitate Dowland, he is merely dull, but he can create a tune with a fine swing in it. The slender talents of John Bartlet and William Corkine could never rise above the popular air. Thomas Ford seems to have conceived his airs as homophonic part-songs, and Francis Pilkington's are nearer to the madrigal than any other airs in the period. Michael Cavendish's too have some madrigal characteristics : two of them are given in his volume as both solo airs and madrigals.

There is, then, a good deal of variety in the handling of the form. One must not forget the popular side of the air, nor over-emphasize the importance of the literary amateurs' revolt against counterpoint. Yet it was important, even if it only rationalized changes that were happening anyhow. The theories of the Florentine Camarata were undoubtedly discussed in England. Two of Campion's friends accepted them more thoroughly than he did. One of them, John Cooper, had lived in Italy for a time and changed his name to Coprario ; the other, Alfonso Ferrabosco, was of Italian descent, though of English birth and education. Campion's views were nearer to those of the French neo-classicists than were those of his friends. They were attracted by the

[1] Rosseter's *Booke of Ayres.*

recitative style, with its claim to follow the tones of the emotional speaking voice. They relied almost entirely on the voice and little on the accompaniment for their effects. Not only the rise and fall but also the speed of the declamation was regulated according to the sentiments of the words. Already they had some of the tricks of the Lawes brothers in the next generation of composers. As music these efforts are not very important ; Ferrabosco is better when he is not declamatory, and Cooper is better in instrumental music. The lack of invention in the music is laid bare to anyone who compares Cooper's setting of 'In darkness let me dwell' with the setting of the same words by Dowland.[1] Even in the light of their own principles these early declamatory songs are not very successful, for they manage to imitate only the clichés of the Italian style and not to adapt it to their own language. They are interesting only as straws to point the direction of the wind.

The real justification of the English air is found in the songs of Dowland and Daniel. These are of much greater dimensions. Both composers excel as painters of intense and sombre passion. John Daniel's output is very small—only one volume of songs— yet he must rank among the great English song-composers. With two of the poems in his volume he throws aside the cramping strophic form and sets each stanza to its own music, dictated by the sense of the words. An expressive contrapuntal texture is woven round the voice part, whose intervals and free rhythm reinforce all the emotional suggestions of the text. The harmony is boldly chromatic. In such a passage as this there is much more than faithful declamation of the words, though the treatment of the words is quite impressive : the diminished intervals in the voice part and the harmonic structure add something to the expression of the emotion in the words :

Danyel's Songs. no. 9

Since Joy can weepe as well as thou, Dis-daine to

---

[1] *Funeral Teares*, No. 4 ; *A Musicall Banquet*, No. 11.

sigh for so can slen-der cares, which but from i--dle cau-ses grow,

All the resources of the most daring madrigals are employed, and yet the solo voice enhances the expression in a way impossible in the madrigal. The ending of the song just quoted, for instance, dying away on a monotone, is an effect that only a solo singer could attempt.

Danyel's Songs, no. 11.

Pine, Fret, Con-sume, Swell, Burst and

Dye. Pine, Fret, Con-sume, Swell, Burst and

Dye, Pine, Fret, Con-sume, Swell, Burst and Dye.

A similar expansion of the simple air takes place in the work
of Dowland. He excels at all types of air, but his songs progress
from the tuneful strophic air to works of tremendous power, in
which the emotions of the poetry seem to dictate their own form.
The early books contain some delightful tunes suggestive of the
dance, and some that have clearly been conceived as part-songs.
In the later books the texture becomes more contrapuntal, the
harmony more chromatic ; the strophic form is sometimes abandoned, the text no longer treated line by line.   In three great songs
of *A Pilgrimes Solace* a viol and a viol de gamba reinforce the lute.
The part-writing becomes fuller, the vocal line often more florid.
At the same time he tries to stylize the declamation of the voice,
adjusting the intervals and the speed of utterance to the emotions
of the speaker. A song to an Italian text, ' Lasso vita mia ',[1]
shows how near he was to what the Italians were attempting.
The chromatic rise on ' crudel'amor ', the fourths on ' mio cor
consume ', and the quickening of *tempo* on ' Da mille, mille, mille
ferite ', with the pitch accent on the third ' mille ', are all dramatic
rather than melodic.

In places, indeed, there are reminiscences of Caccini's formulae.
In his opinion, ' L'esclamazione . . . è mezzo piu principale per
muovere l'affetto ', and he gives examples of two types of
exclamation :

---

[1] *A Pilgrimes Solace*, No. 11.

The first kind gains its effect from a *diminuendo*, followed by a *crescendo*. That is probably the way Dowland sang this exclamation :

The other type of exclamation, with its descent of a sixth, is recalled by Dowland's passionate outburst :

Robert Dowland's *Musical Banquet*, no. 10

Dowland's general style, however, is very different from the Italian recitative. He was not content with figured bass, relying on the solo voice for the effects and supporting it merely with chords here and there. In fact, he made the best of both worlds. He distilled passion from the declamation of the solo voice, and intensified it by weaving round it a contrapuntal structure that drew on the accumulated capital of the madrigal. The musical interest of his songs is as great as the literary. He justifies the monodists' insistence on the primacy of the text, and yet creates music of the highest quality. No better compromise has ever been reached between music and poetry. It was possible only at the moment when Dowland wrote, when the madrigal was dis-integrating under chromatic experiment, and the declamatory air was not yet standardized as an equivalent of passionate speech.

CHAPTER VIII

MUSICAL INFLUENCE ON POETRY

THE last two chapters have tried to show how both the chief vocal forms of the sixteenth century developed under pressure from literary ideas. The madrigal transformed the impersonal technique of late medieval polyphony into a medium of emotional expression, and its urge for dramatic illustration of the poetry to which it was set drove it to strain the traditional scheme of counterpoint with chromatic and harmonic innovations. The air, in spite of its roots in national song, tended towards recitative and the sacrifice of melody to 'natural' declamation of the verse in its efforts to attain the intimate union between music and poetry the Greek lyric was thought to have had.

The picture would be incomplete without some consideration of the influence on poetry of the expectation that lyrics would be sung. It is because they were prepared for singing rather than reading that sixteenth- and seventeenth-century lyrics differ from those of later periods. Their whole conception and technique were controlled by the requirements of music and by the idioms of the two chief vocal forms of the period, the madrigal and the air. The lyrics of Byron and Shelley, of Tennyson and Swinburne, are complete in themselves and can be read in the same way as any other kind of poetry. The Renaissance poet, however, aimed at something quite different. He had to create verses that were effective when sung. He worked not only within the literary conventions of his time but within the limitations of contemporary musical technique.

Any kind of musical setting imposes certain restrictions on the content and manner of verse. To begin with a practical and obvious point the poet has to remember, it is often difficult to hear the words and always more difficult to appreciate their full significance when they are sung than when they are read. This is truer of part-music than of solo song, but even in listening to a simple song for one voice the ear is preoccupied with the melody and cannot give undivided attention to the ideas conveyed by the words. The reader can go back to a phrase that is obscure. When the poem is recited the listener either takes the phrase in at once or misses it altogether : if he pauses to think it over, he misses the next part of the poem. He is even more apt to miss the full import of a phrase when it is sung. He can appreciate the general drift of the song more easily than any fine shades of meaning in particular parts of it. Verse for music should therefore keep to broad and simple emotions. Subtlety or verbal ingenuity are almost certain to be lost on the listener : they may be introduced sparingly, but will have to be carefully placed.

The intellectual appeal of music is quite different from that of poetry. It is more related to structure than to content. The ' thought' of poetry has no parallel in music. The two arts can meet only on the emotional plane. The atmosphere, mood, or tone of a piece of music may correspond to those of a poem, whether because of the natural emotional effect of particular combinations of notes or through past associations it is unnecessary to inquire. But the difficulty of ensuring music and verse should appear appropriate to each other is that music makes its impression much more slowly than poetry. A single word has associations ; a single note or chord hardly any, apart from its context. It is the melody as a whole, or the blending of the parts over a short period, that evokes an emotional response. Language is capable of more rapid transitions, more complex unions of diverse ideas and feelings. Music is, in a sense, more static than poetry. That is why in opera the action, which is communicated by the words, has every now and then to be suspended for set pieces—arias, duets, dances, &c.

Sixteenth-century poets were quite aware of these general limitations of verse intended for music. They did not attempt effects that would not be appreciated by the listener or for which the composer would have difficulty in creating suitable music. The Elizabethan lyric before Donne is always ' simple, sensuous and passionate '. Complex associations of idea, subtle play of wit, the poetic resources music cannot hope to copy, are almost absent from it. Indeed, the general quality of sixteenth-century poetic style is very suitable for music. It presents simple emotions, paints atmospheres and moods with a broad sweep. The diffuseness of the Spenserian style, to take one example, is full of possibilities for a musician. Spenser tends to make each stanza a sort of cameo, and many composers were able to compose madrigals on isolated stanzas of his. This stanza, for example, was the text of a madrigal by Kirbye :

Up then, Melpomene ! the mournfull'st Muse of nine
Such cause of mourning never hadst afore.
Up grisly ghosts ! and up, my rueful rhyme !
Matter of mirth now shalt thou have no more,
For dead she is that mirth thee made of yore.
Dido, my dear, alas, is dead,
Dead, and lieth wrapped in lead.
O heavy hearse !
Let streaming tears be poured out in store,
O careful verse ! [1]

There is a consistency of tone about this that leaves the composer free to construct a ' funeral note ', while the metrical form is sufficiently varied to prevent the periods of the music from becoming too monotonous.

Broad contrasts in mood are always effective in music, since the juxtaposition of different tones heightens each. Dryden's *Alexander's Feast* is a good specimen of a work written especially for music that exploits this principle. Timotheus knew an antidote for each passion he aroused in ' Philip's warlike son '. The sublimity of Jove was succeeded by the revelry of Bacchus, and when ' the master saw the madness rise ',

He chose a mournful Muse
Soft pity to infuse.

But when ' the tears began to flow '

Softly sweet, in Lydian measures,
Soon he soothed his soul to pleasures,

until ' a louder strain ' once more aroused the king. Dryden is offering the composer opportunities for contrasted movements. The Elizabethans often proved equally adaptable when they had no specific reason for considering a musician's requirements. A good example is a stanza by Drayton, set as a madrigal by Ward.

Upon a bank with roses set about,
Where pretty turtles, joining bill to bill,
And gentle springs steal softly murmuring out,
Washing the foot of pleasure's sacred hill,
There little love sore wounded lies,
His bow and arrows broken,
Bedewed with tears from Venus' eyes ;
O grievous to be spoken. [2]

---

[1] E. H. Fellowes, *English Madrigal Verse*, p. 115.
[2] ib., p. 205.

This stanza neatly divides into two sections, as the metre shows. The first section depicts a pleasant pastoral scene, and Ward finds gracious smooth-sliding phrases for it. The last four lines are pathetic, and Ward changes the movement of his music and clogs it with suspensions, in the approved manner of his school when describing painful emotions.

Spenser and Drayton were not writing lyrics for definite musicians in the instances cited. Their general style was suitable to music. Perhaps it is not too much of a stretch to seek an explanation in a conception of poetry influenced by the long traditional association of the two arts. The song lyrics that were written for music are even more clearly at the musician's service. When Shakespeare sings, ' Hark, hark, the lark ', he suggests a cheerful *aubade*, which the composer can easily translate into his own medium. When he sings, ' It was a lover and his lass ', he invites the composer to create a care-free spring-song. The general mood of each song is all the words try to communicate, and that the musician can translate into his own medium.

The temper of the time with its high opinion of wit encouraged the conceit, which is seldom appropriate to music ; but the good sense of lyric poets kept it within bounds. Campion compared his airs with epigrams because of their brevity ; but the epigrammatic quality of a few of his lyrics rather spoils their effect. The following song is all right to read ; the sudden *volte-face* in the concluding couplet is very amusing. But, as it is entirely different from the last couplet of the previous stanza, no strophic tune could be found to do it justice.

> Thou art not faire, for all thy red and white,
>   For all those rosie ornaments in thee.
> Thou art not sweet, though made of mere delight,
>   Nor faire, nor sweet, unlesse thou pitie me.
> I will not soothe thy fancies thou shalt prove
> That beauty is no beautie without love.
>
> Yet love not me, nor seeke thou to allure
>   My thoughts with beautie, were it more devine.
> Thy smiles and kisses I cannot endure,
>   I'le not be wrappt up in those armes of thine.
> Now show it, if thou be a woman right,
>   Embrace, and kiss, and love me in despight.[1]

The rhythms of the last couplets in the two stanzas confirm the impression that for once Campion had forgotten the strophic form of the air. On the other hand, an unexpected concluding phrase

[1] ib., p. 590 : Rosseter's *Booke of Ayres*, I, 12.

is often effective in a song. There is something epigrammatic about this song by Jones :

> Love is a babel ;
> No man is able
> To say 'tis this or 'tis that.
> 'Tis full of passions
> Of sundry fashions ;
> 'Tis like I cannot tell what.[1]

One can sense the pause in the last line after ' 'Tis like——', and the expectation of some comparison, disappointed by the non-committal ' I cannot tell what.' Jones increases the effect by repeating ' I cannot——', ' 'Tis like——'.

Jones's Second Booke, no. 17.

If this last phrase is half spoken, it makes an amusing climax to the song. All the other stanzas are equally suitable to such treatment.

Elizabethan critical theory was much concerned with the sound of verse. It was a natural result of the uncertainty that the early part of the century had felt about rhythm. The changes in the language had produced something like chaos in English verse at the beginning of the Tudor period. In the middle of the century a reaction against looseness threatened to confine verse to a monotonous jog-trot. Sidney and Spenser taught poets how to be free without anarchy. The ideal the critics held up to writers was rhythmical interest similar to that of music.

Our poeticall proportion holdeth of the Musical, because, as we sayd before, Poesie is a skill to speake and write harmonically : and verses or rime be a kind of Musicall utterance, by reason of a certaine congruitie in sounds pleasing the eare, though not perchance so exquisitely as the harmonicall concents of the artificiall Musicke, consisting in strained tunes, as is the vocall Musike or that of melodious instruments, as Lutes, Harpes, Regals, Records, and such like.[2]

The attractiveness of many sixteenth-century lyrics depends on

---

[1] ib., p. 509 : Jones, *Second Book of Ayres*, No. 17.
[2] Gregory Smith, *Elizabethan Critical Essays*, II, 68-9.

their rhythmical tunes. Even when the poets have little to say, they often give their verses an attractive lilt. Some of the lyrics almost translate themselves into tunes. Lines like these—

> What if I sped where I least expected,
> What shall I say ? Shall I lye ?
> What if I mist where I most affected ?
> What shall I do, Shall I dye ? [1]

have the slightest of content ; their effect is due to the reiterated rhythmical pattern ♩ ♪♪♩ ♪♪♩ with which each line begins. A composer has only to add pitch to this pattern to get for the first couplet a tune with a swing, which he can repeat for the second couplet. That is what Robert Jones does in his setting of the lines. The poet has gone half-way towards transforming the poem into a song. Sixteenth-century lyric writers often did that, because they were concerned less with saying something than with imagining their verses sung to rhythmical tunes. The rhythm is often more fundamental to the poet's conception than the sense, the form more fundamental than the idea.

Poets working in this way would regard the line as the rhythmical unit. The music they knew set the text line by line. At the end of each musical phrase in the air came a cadence, represented in the verse by a rime. The form of the tune or the stanza depended on the relationships of the lines. Spoken verse had freed itself from the tyranny of metre over rhythm. In the lyric the line remained the unit of rhythm. End-stopping was a necessity ; enjambment was exceptional. Variety came from the varied lengths of line, not from free counterpointing of speech rhythm on the metrical pattern, since the essence of the lyric was the pattern. In the seventeenth century, when poetry became more independent of music, poets sometimes took liberties that embarrassed the musician. An example occurs in a well-known song by Suckling :

> I am confirm'd a woman can
> Love this, or that, or any man !
> This day her love is melting hot ;
> To-morrow swears she knows you not ;
> If she but some new object find,
> Then straight she's of another mind.
> Then hang me, Ladies, at your door,
> If e'er I doat upon you more ! [2]

---

[1] Jones, *Third Booke of Ayres*, No. 5 (*English Madrigal Verse*, p. 515).
[2] *The Works of Sir John Suckling*, ed. A. H. Thompson, p. 73. The third line is there given as 'This day she's melting hot,' which cannot be what the poet intended.

This suggested to Henry Lawes a simple metrical tune :

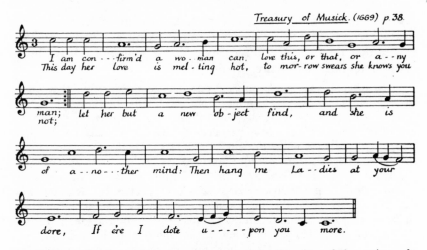

Treasury of Musick. (1669) *p.* 38.

I am con ‑ ‑ ‑ firm'd a wo ‑ man can. love this, or that, or a ‑ ‑ ny
This day her love is mel ‑ ting hot, to mor‑ row swears she knows you

man; let her but a new ob ‑ ject find, and she is
not;

of a ‑ ‑ no ‑ ‑ ‑ ther mind: Then hang 'me La ‑ ‑ dies at your

dore, If e're I dote u ‑ ‑ ‑ ‑ ‑ pon you more.

Unfortunately the cadence at the end of the first line falls on ' can ', which the sense requires to be run on to the next line. Lawes's long note and full close tend to make the word appear a noun, with ridiculous results. The singer must somehow minimize the composer's false emphasis. To avoid such disasters Elizabethan lyric poets usually treated the line as a unit, knowing that the rime at the end would fall on a cadence. Puttenham actually compares the rime with a cadence in music, remarking that

our maker by his measures and concordes of sundry proportions doth counterfait the harmonicall tunes of the vocall and instrumentall Musickes.

Therefore before all other things let his ryme and concordes be true, cleare, and audible, with no less delight then almost the strayned note of a Musicians mouth, and not darke or wrenched by wrong writing, as many do patch up their meetres, and so follow in their arte neither rule, reason, nor ryme.[1]

In longer lines the cadences had to coincide with the caesura. A certain flexibility was necessary here to avoid monotony, and Tudor music had not the rigid periods of some later music. But the cadences could not be too close or too far apart. Gascoigne recognizes that musical considerations must direct the placing of the caesura.

There are also certayne pauses or restes in a verse, which may be called Caesures, whereof I would be loth to stand long, since it is at the

---

[1] Gregory Smith, op. cit., II, 88, 78.

discretion of the wryter, and they have bene first devised (as should seem) by the Musicians.[1]

James I amplifies the point, and remarks that the chief need is to avoid breaking a word when the music requires a pause, and to ensure that the end of a musical period will fall on a syllable long enough to bear a cadence.

Bot specially tak heid, quhen your line is of fourtene, that your Sectioun in aucht be a lang monsyllable, or ellis the hinmest syllable of a word alwaies being lang, as I said before. The cause quhy it man be ane of thir twa is for the Musique, because that quhen your line is ather of xiiii or xij fete it wilbe drawin sa lang in the singing, as ye man rest in the middes of it, quilk is the Sectioun: sa as gif your Sectioun be nocht ather a monosyllable, or ellis the hinmest syllable of a word, as I said before, bot the first syllable of a polysyllable, the Musique sall mak yow sa to rest in the middes of that word, as it sall cut the ane half of the word from the uther, and sa sall mak it seme twa different wordis, that is bot ane. This aucht onely to be observit in thir foirsaid lang lynis: for the shortnes of all shorter lynis then thir before mentionat is the cause that the Musique makis na rest in the middes of thame, and thairfore thir observationis servis nocht for thame.[2]

In strophic lyrics it is often possible to detect a careful placing of the caesura so that all stanzas correspond. The following poem by Wyatt has been planned so that the second line runs on to the third, in the middle of which there is a pause dictated by the sense. The last stanza is the only one that is not quite to pattern, but no word would be interrupted by the pause in the third line.

> Farewell, the rayn of crueltie:
>   Though that with pain my libertie
> Dere have I boght: yet shall suretie
>   Conduyt my thoght of Joyes nede.
>
> Of force I must forsake pleasure:
>   A goode cause iust syns I endure
> Therby my woo: which be ye sure
>   Shall therewith goo me to recure.
>
> I fare as oon escaped that fleith:
>   Glad that is gone, yet stille fereth
> Spied to be cawght: and so dredeth
>   That he for noght his pain leseth.
>
> In joyfull pain reioyse myn hert
>   Thus to sustain of eche apart;
> Let not this song from the estert;
>   Welcome emong my plaisaunt smert.[3]

---

[1] Gregory Smith, op. cit., I, 54.   [2] ib., I, 214.
[3] *The Poems of Sir Thomas Wiat*, ed. Foxwell, p. 42.

The madrigal always remained an Italian form and influenced English poetry only incidentally. Most of the poetry of the period was strophic and intended to be set as airs. The fact that one tune was sung to all the stanzas imposed a certain regularity on the structure of lyrics. The minimum requirement of a strophic tune is that all the stanzas should have rhythmical uniformity, especially as Tudor composers were very particular about their declamation. The skill of different poets in meeting this requirement varied considerably, but generally speaking one can see them trying hard to attain it. Corresponding lines in different stanzas usually have the same rhythmical features. The easiest test is when a stop occurs somewhere in the line. It will almost always be reproduced in the same place in all the succeeding stanzas. A few examples are here chosen at random.

> Go christall teares, like to the morning showers.
> Hast haplesse sighs, and let your burning breath.[1]

> Farewell too faire, too chaste, but too too cruell.
> Farewell too dear, and too too much desired.[2]

> Up merry mates, To Neptunes prayse.
> Stay merry mates, Proud Neptune lowres.[3]

> Author of light, revive my dying spright.
> Fountaine of health, my soules deep wounds recure.[4]

> Sunne and Moon, Starres and underlights I see.
> Sinne and Death, Hell and tempting Fiends may rage.[5]

> Awake, awake, thou heavy spright.
> Get up, get up, thou leaden man.[6]

> Come away, come away, death.
> Not a flower, not a flower sweet.[7]

> Mercy ! madame alas, I dy ! I dy !
> To here my plaint, dere hert, awake ! awake !
> To breke your slepe crieng alas ! alas !
> For in dispere alas I faint ! I faint ![8]

There is much more irregularity when poets have set verses to existing tunes. Campion, who worked out poem and tune

[1] Dowland, I, 9.   [2] Dowland, III, 1.   [3] Dowland, IV, 19.
[4] Campion, I, 1.   [5] ib.   [6] Campion, I, 16.
[7] Twelfth Night, II, iv.
[8] Poems of Sir Thomas Wiat, ed. cit., p. 77.

together, often has lines which, apart from their context, do not seem to correspond at all. They all fit the music perfectly, however. The tune often suggests different rhythms in different stanzas. But the poet who prepared his verses for a musician could not know what differences might be troublesome to the composer, and he tended to simplify the musician's task by an obvious correspondence. In transcribing airs it is amazing how the correspondence goes down to the smallest details.

Not only in individual lines is this trait noticeable. The stanza often consists of several sections, and the sentiment of each section is paralleled in succeeding stanzas. A good example occurs in *The Passionate Pilgrim* and in Weelkes's 1597 *Madrigals*. The metrical scheme marks the sections of the stanza clearly. The first section is a lament ; the second recalls the pleasures now lost ; and the third refers the present mourning to the lady who caused it.

> My flocks feed not,
> My ewes breed not,
> My rams speed not,
>   All is amiss.
> Love is dying,
> Faith's defying,
> Heart's denying,
>   Causer of this.
>
> All our merry jigs are quite forgot ;
> All my lady's love is lost, God wot ;
> Where our faith was firmly fixed in love,
> There annoy is placed without remove.
>
>   One seely cross
>   Wrought all my loss,
> O frowning Fortune, cursed fickle dame !
>   For now I see
>   Inconstancy
> More in women than in many men to be.

The two following stanzas follow exactly the same plan. In each the middle section is reminiscent, a contrast to the first section, which depicts general dissatisfaction, and the last section, which refers the pathetic fallacies of the first section to the feelings of the rejected lover.

>   In black mourn I,
>   All fear scorn I,
>   Love hath forlorn me,
>   Living in thrall.

Heart is bleeding,
All help needing,
O cruel speeding
  Fraught with gall !

My shepherd's pipe will sound no deal ;
My wether's bell rings doleful knell ;
My curtall dog that wont to have played,
Plays not at all, but seems afraid.

  My sighs so deep
  Procures to weep
With howling noise to see my doleful plight.
  How sighs resound
  Through harkless ground,
Like thousand vanquished men in bloody fight.

Clear wells spring not,
Sweet birds sing not,
Loud bells ring not
  Cheerfully.
Herds stand weeping,
Flocks all sleeping,
Nymphs back creeping
  Fearfully.

All our pleasures known to us poor swains,
All our merry meetings on the plains,
All our evening sports from us are fled,
All our loves are lost, for Love is dead.

  Farewell, sweet lass,
  The like ne'er was
For sweet content, the cause of all my woe.
  Poor Corydon
  Must live alone,
Other help for him I know there's none.[1]

Weelkes set this as three madrigals parallel in general design. In
all three the short lines of the first section are telescoped, each of the
voices singing one line only. The second section of each madrigal
introduces triple time, the ordinary rhythm for dancing in madrigals,
to suggest a reminiscence of former pleasure running through
contemplation of present grief. In the first madrigal the triple time
on 'All our merry jigs' drags into slow minim movements in
common time at 'are quite forgot'. In the second the triple time
at 'My shepherd's pipe' changes to common time at 'My wether's
bell rings doleful knell' ; and in the third energetic quaver runs on
'All our evening sports' tail off into slow suspensions at 'from

[1] *English Madrigal Verse*, p. 208.

us are fled '. The third section of each madrigal is highly pictorial. This poem was not intended to be set as a madrigal, but Weelkes's treatment extends the parallelism of the stanzas into a series of madrigals. A strophic tune, for which the poem was obviously intended, would inevitably take advantage of the parallelism in form and content which Weelkes observes in his more elaborate treatment.

Another good example is a poem by Campion. Here the first two sections, of three lines each, are sung to a repeated part of the tune. They both contain an entreaty. The last two lines, in a different rhythm, express a resolution.

> Faire, if you expect admiring,
> Sweete, if you provoke desiring,
> Grace deere love with kind requiting.
> Fond, but if thy sight be blindnes,
> False, if thou affect unkindnes,
> Flie both love and loves requiting.
> Then when hope is lost and love is scorned,
> I'le bury my desires, and quench the fires that ever yet in vaine have burned.[1]

The second stanza preserves the same general disposition. The entreaty is this time addressed to the Fates, instead of to the mistress, and the resolution in the last two lines is the exact opposite of the one in the previous stanza ; but the characters of the sections are much the same.

> Fates, if you rule lovers fortune,
> Stars, if men your powers importune,
> Yield relief by your relenting :
> Time, if sorrow be not endles,
> Hope made vaine, and pitie friendles,
> Helpe to ease my long lamenting.
> But if griefes remaine still unredressed,
> I'le flie to her againe, and sue for pitie to reneue my hopes distressed.

It is worth noticing that in the first section of each stanza each line begins with a long monosyllable—a further instance of the correspondence between lines occupying similar positions in different stanzas. The last two lines obviously owe their rhythm to the tune.

It was common to write poems of two stanzas, in which the situation described by the first stanza was paralleled point by point in the second. An air in Jones's *First Booke* illustrates the device.

> Sweet Philomell in groaves and desarts haunting,
> Oft glads my hart and eares with her sweet chaunting.

---

[1] ib., p. 589 ; Rosseter's *Booke of Ayres*, I, 11.

But then her tunes delight me best
When pearcht with prick against her breast,
Shee sings, fie, fie, as if shee suffred wrong,
Till seeming pleas'd, sweete, sweete, concludes her song.

Sweet Jinny singes and talkes and sweetly smileth,
And with her wanton mirth my griefes beguileth.
But then methinkes shee pleaseth best
When, while my hands move loves request,
Shee cries phi, phi, and seeming loath gainsaies,
Till better pleas'd, sweete, sweete, content betraies.[1]

A popular extension of this idea was the writing of replies to poems, using the same rhythm and, as far as possible, the same phraseology. Both could, of course, be sung to the same tune ; as in this case, from Daniel's *Songs* :

Coy Daphne fled from Phoebus' hot pursuit,
    Carelesse of Passion, senseless of Remorse ;
While hee complain'd his griefs shee rested mute ;
    He beg'd her stay, shee still kept on her course.
But what reward shee had for this you see,
She rests transform'd, a winter-beaten tree.

The Answer.

Chaste Daphne fled from Phoebus' hot pursuit,
    Knowing mens passions Idle and of course ;
And though he plain'd 'twas fit shee should be mute,
    And honour would shee should keepe on her course.
For which faire deede her Glory still wee see :
She rests still Greene, and so I wish to bee.[2]

A more difficult situation presents itself when words of strong emotional connotation occur in the first stanza of a poem. Such words as ' sigh ' or ' weep ' both madrigal and lutanist composers illustrated by detaching them from the preceding words and following them with rests. In the airs a two-note figure in the accompaniment generally filled in the pause of the voice part.

Dowland, *Second Booke of Ayres*, no. 2.

and teares,   and sighes,   and grones.

---

[1] No. 16 (*English Madrigal Verse*, p. 496).   [2] No. 1 (ib., p. 401).

This idiom threw the word so treated into great prominence, and similar words had to be supplied in succeeding stanzas to fit the musical figure. The penultimate line of a lyric, which may be by Lodge [1] and was set to music by Dowland, is entirely composed of emotional words of the kind under consideration, and there is a stop after every other syllable. The crescendo of feeling in the line invites the composer to treat it as the climax of the stanza. In the later stanzas the punctuation is not so clearly marked, but the poet has been careful that the rests should occur always at the ends of words, and that the emotional quality of the words should justify their being set to the same sort of phrase as that used for the first stanza.

Dowland, *First Book*, no. 17.

to see,	to heare,	to touch,	to kisse,	to die.
I sit,	I sigh,	I weepe,	I faind,	I die
Her smiles,	my springs	that makes	my ioyes	to grow
To see	the fruits	and ioyes	that some	do find
Her eies	of fire	her hart	of flint	is made
By sighs	and teares	more hote	than are	thy shafts

A similar figure on the word 'sigh' in the last line of one of Campion's songs is equally happily fitted to the word 'heart' in the second stanza.

Rosseter's *Booke of Ayres*, I.6.

ev'n with her sighes,	her sighes,	her sighes, the strings do breake, the	strings do breake.
Ev'n from my hart,	my hart,	my hart, the strings doe breake, the	strings doe breake.

In another place Campion's employment of a chromatic passage necessitates similar words for all stanzas, since chromaticism always accompanied poignant emotional phrases in the text.

Though thou be	blacke as	night	and	she	made	all	of	light
Though here thou	liv'st dis-	grac't,	and	she	in	heaven	is	plac't,
That so have	scor-	ched	thee,	As	thou	still	black must	bee,
There comes a	luck-	les	night,	That	will	dim	all	her	light.
The Sunne must	have his	shade,	Till	both	at	once	doe	fade.

---

[1] In *The Phoenix Nest* (1593 ed., p. 49) there is a poem by Lodge in the same metre, which is not found elsewhere, as far as I know. Dowland's text would fit on to the end of Lodge's poem very well.

The air was too simple a form to allow any extensive exploitation of the voice as a musical instrument. Nevertheless, in the simplest song, the composer may fairly seek some freedom from a too nice declamation of the words and an opportunity for some slight development of his musical ideas. The refrain is one of the oldest and most universal concessions of the poet to the composer. Its very recurrence at the same point in every stanza removes it from the plane of the rest of the stanza, which has to communicate a sense meaning, whatever else it does ; for repetition is an element of musical rather than of literary form (when it is used in literature it is the reiteration of the sound as much as that of the sense that is effective). The composer can therefore handle the words of the refrain with less regard for their pronunciation and significance in ordinary speech. Wyatt often provides as refrain a short line, which the composer can either set to a slower movement than the rest of the stanza or else repeat as many times as he likes to form a coda.

> The knot which fyrst my hert did strayn,
> When that your servant I becam,
> Doth bynd me still for to remain
> Allwayes your owne, as now I am ;
> And if you fynd that I do fayne,
> With just judgement my selfe I dam
> *To have dysdain.*[1]

When the refrain is longer it generally summarizes the theme of the poem, each stanza leading to the one conclusion, which the composer can repeat, because of its importance in the sentiment of the song, or else can treat freely because its recurrence will ensure the words will be grasped eventually by the listeners.

> And if an Iye may save or sleye
>   And streke more diepe than wepon longe ;
> And if an Iye by subtil play,
>   May move oon more then any tonge ;
>   How can ye say that I do wronge
> Thus to suspect without deserte ?
> *For the Iye is traitor of the herte.*[2]

Nonsense syllables were popular refrains : obviously they left the composer much more complete freedom than actual words. It is rather difficult to discuss them, however, because composers often inserted them, and, as many of the extant lyrics have almost certainly been copied from musical score, it is impossible to determine what the poet and what the composer contributed to the

[1] *The Poems of Sir Thomas Wiat*, ed. cit., p. 186. [2] op. cit., p. 111.

final result.   Occasionally one may guess the poet offered a refrain to the composer.   In the following famous lyric by Chettle, for instance, the internal refrain of the third line seems part of the essential structure of the stanza :

> Diaphenia like the Daffadowndillie,
> White as the Sunne, faire as the Lillie,
> heigh ho, how I doo love thee !
> I doo love thee as my Lambs
> Are beloved of their Dams ;
> how blest were I if thou would'st proove me.[1]

This is confirmed by the substitution of fresh words for the ' Heigh ho ' in the succeeding stanzas :

> Diaphenia like the spreading Roses,
> That in thy sweetes all sweetes incloses,
> fair sweete, how I doo love thee !
> I doo love thee as each flower
> Loves the Sunnes life-giving power ;
> For dead, thy breath to life might moove me.
>
> Diaphenia like to all things blessed
> When all thy praises are expressed,
> deare Ioy, how I doo love thee !
> As the birds doo love the Spring,
> Or the Bees their careful King :
> then in requite, sweet Virgin, love me !

It is probable, too, that the third line should be symmetrical with the sixth and that the poet always intended the first two words of the third line in each stanza to be repeated : he must have known the composer would be almost certain to want to do that. Pilkington repeats them in his setting of the poem.[2]

Several of Shakespeare's songs have refrains that one would judge to be integral parts of the poem.   The rime in the final couplet of this one, for example, suggests the last line was the work of the poet : it is clearly suitable for a choral refrain :

> Full fathom five thy father lies ;
> Of his bones are coral made ;
> Those are pearls that were his eyes :
> Nothing of him that doth fade,
> But doth suffer a sea-change
> Into something rich and strange.
> Sea-nymphs hourly ring his knell :
> [Burden, ding-dong.
> Hark ! now I hear them,—ding-dong bell.[3]

---

[1] *Englands Helicon*, ed. Rollins, I, 96.
[2] *First Booke of Songes or Ayres*, No. 17.   [3] *The Tempest*, I, ii.

Phrases like ' heigh ho ' and ' ding-dong bell ' can readily be set to little sequential figures. Couplets of short lines often serve the same purpose, and that is probably why they are so common in sixteenth-century lyrics :

Jones, *Second Booke*, no. 12.

not too fast, too much haste : ma·keth waste, but if thou wilt needes be· gone, take my love with thee.

Often the short lines make a kind of bridge passage between two parts of a stanza. In madrigals they could be set homophonically as a transition between two contrapuntal sections.

It has been said that repetition is a normal element of musical form. A kind of repetition that became very popular was the echo. It must be remembered that *crescendo* and *diminuendo* did not really enter musical conceptions until the late eighteenth century, probably because of the limitations of instruments, although there is some evidence singers knew how to use such effects to bring out the emotional force of the words. In any case, the alternation of loud and soft passages is always striking : it is common in the music of Bach and Handel. The echo is in practice merely a repetition of a *forte* passage *piano*. On the stage the voices of the echo would be behind the scenes. Peele's *Araygnment of Paris* (1584) contains a song for which the boy singers are divided into ' a quire within and without '.[1] Here the two choirs sing different words, and the double chorus is concluded by a solo from Pan. Generally, however, the echo sings the same words as the original statement. The effect was especially popular in masques because of the disposition of the musical forces in several choirs and consorts. In Jonson's *Masque of Beauty* the song ' When Love at first did move ' was to be sung by all the musicians ' iterated in the closes by two Echoes ', and ' Come away ' in the *Masque of Blackness* was to be sung by two trebles ' whose cadences were iterated by a double echo from several parts of the land '.

Among specific classes of lyric that gained favour through their musical adaptability the dialogue was one of the most widespread. ' Airs and Dialogues ' became a common title for songbooks in the seventeenth century. In the plays and masques duets

[1] *Works*, ed. Bullen, I, 14–15.

are frequent, and the text is arranged so as to make them relevant to the plot. In Jonson's *Poetaster* Hermogenes and Crispinus, the rival singers, ' contend to please and revive [the gods] senses ', and their lines reply to each other's, with couplets interspersed in which both can join.[1] Often the dialogue is broken by sections for a full chorus. This is clearly the purpose of the short lines in the middle and at the end of Shakespeare's famous song, ' Tell me where is fancy bred?'

[1st singer]	Tell me where is fancy bred,
	Or in the heart or in the head ?
	How begot, how nourished ?
[Chorus]	Reply, reply.
[2nd singer]	It is engendered in the eyes,
	With gazing fed ; and Fancy dies
	In the cradle where it lies.
	Let us all ring Fancy's knell :
	I'll begin it—Ding, dong, bell.
[Chorus]	Ding, dong, bell.[2]

Songs like this, however, come near to being libretti for choral works, and it is not easy to decide what Shakespeare wrote and what the composer added to suit the musical forces at his command. In the drama lyrics were prepared for definite voices, and the texts extant are often transcribed from the score. Other lyrics written for special occasions, or even for private circles, may equally have been intended for specific voices.

It would be tedious to enumerate some of the smaller devices of poets to adapt their verses to music. If the Elizabethan lyrics have a singing quality, it is because' their authors deliberately set out to prepare them for the composer. They knew how to make his task easier, and they also knew what to leave to him. Suggestions they provided in plenty, but they left the musicians to illustrate them. The lyrics of Shelley, Tennyson and Swinburne do not need music ; they provide their own. complete effect, of sound as well as content. The Elizabethans were content to leave the musician with a few words of emotional connotation : they knew he would secure the right atmosphere better than the poet could. A few open vowels were more useful than the titillation of consonants with which some later poets have sought to make the sound echo the sense. Jonson has left a picture of two amateurs

---

[1] IV, iii.

[2] *Merchant of Venice*, III, ii. Mr. Noble argues the song was a solo. Whether it were solo or duet, provision has been made deliberately for a chorus.

discussing the setting of a poem, in *Cynthia's Revels*.[1] Hedon sings a ditty of his own, set to his own music, and ending with the couplet :

> It should bee my wishing
> That I might dye, kissing.

He asks Amorphus's opinion of it, and is told :

A pretty ayre ! in generall, I like it well : but in particular, your long *die*-note did arride me most, but it was somwhat too long. I can shew one, almost of the same nature, but much before it, and not so long, in a composition of mine owne. I thinke I have both the note, and dittie about me.

A poet who was aware that musicians liked to treat the word ' die ' with a long note, probably accompanied with *crescendo* or *diminuendo*, would be quite capable of putting the word into a line deliberately to secure a climax. The conventions of contemporary musical style were always giving poets hints of this kind, and nearly all the poets were knowledgeable about musical requirements. There was a very general ability to imagine what lyrics would sound like when they received their musical setting. This is one of the distinguishing marks of the Renaissance lyric, and in criticizing it standards suitable for later poetry are quite inappropriate, for, without music, only half of the poets' intentions are realized.

[1] IV, iii.

CHAPTER IX

BALLAD AND DANCE

IN the last chapter some attempt was made to indicate the influence on the lyric of the expectation it would be set to music and sung. A good deal of Renaissance verse was even more directly controlled by music, for it was actually written to existing tunes. This was far from being a new thing. The middle ages had produced much literature adapted to music : ecclesiastical *proses* and *tropes* had been fitted to vocalizations on ' Alleluia ' and in the Gospels and Epistles, and secular poetry had often obeyed the rhythms of the dance. The New Poetry of the sixteenth century was more purely literary than any European school of verse that had preceded it ; but the period had not outgrown a primitive and universal way of creating poetry, that of letting a tune serve as metrical framework. In folk-song there is often a very subtle interchange between traditional tunes and stock poetic phrases, and verse and air modify each other. The sixteenth century had not lost touch with folk-lore. Moreover, it had a type of popular journalism that was sung rather than read. This was the much-despised broadside ballad. Its vitality and popularity largely depended on the tunes to which it was sung.

An adequate account of the broadside ballad would require a whole volume and would lead too far from the present subject. Its importance has been recognized by most recent students of the Renaissance. Many collections of ballads have been re-edited ; their social background has been explored, and the vulgar erudition stored in them has been applied to the illumination of higher orders of literature. Their tunes have received less attention. Every student of the period is grateful to William Chappell and to Prof. Wooldridge for *Old English Popular Music* ; but the development of popular music still needs more scientific scrutiny, and until that is done a chapter in the history of popular poetry will remain unwritten. This is no place to attempt anything so ambitious : we are concerned rather with the way popular tunes affected the writing of poetry for educated people. Many poets went through the same operations as the ballad-writers and fitted their verses to music already in existence ; moreover, many quite respectable poems became associated with ballad tunes.

The word ballad is rather loosely used in English. It is often applied to the narrative poetry found in Child's great collection, to verse of the type of *Chevy Chase* or *The Battle of Otterburn*. It might be better to call this simply folk-song. At any rate, the broadside ballad had nothing to do with it, though it sometimes did draw on folk-material and though it did to some extent corrupt folk-song in parts of the country. It can claim none of the doubtful mysteries of communal authorship, for many of its writers are well known. It began its career in the office of a London printer who issued it on a single sheet of paper in crude black-letter type.

The name ' ballad ' obviously comes from ' ballare ', to dance. The application of it to narrative verse of the Child type has led to extraordinary theories about the communal authorship of these pieces, which seem to have absolutely none of the features generally found in poetry of dance origin. The word came into English in connexion with a highly artificial kind of French verse that had once been associated with the dance but had long since lost that association. Chaucer's *ballades* are inspired by the very elaborate music of de Machaut. The word may sometimes have been used in England for courtly dance poems : in the fifteenth century Dunbar mentions a company that

> . . . sang ballettes with mighty notes clere,
> Ladyes to daunce full sobirly assayit.[1]

But the connexion with dancing must already have become tenuous. The refrain of the *ballade* had already been practically absorbed into the stanza, and de Machaut's music is as unlike dance music as anything possibly could be. Hence any courtly lyric seems to have come to be called a ballad. Woodville's complaint of his imprisonment in 1483 is described as a ' Balet ', and at the end of Medwall's interlude *Nature* ' some goodly ballet ' is sung. Henry VIII is said by Holinshed to have spent part of his time ' in setting of songs, and making of ballads '.[2] Skelton's lyrics were printed as ' Dyuers Balettys and Dyties solacyous '. Copland in 1525 asks

> Haue ye the balade called maugh murre
> Or bony wench, or els go from my durre
> Col to me, or hey downe dery dery
> Or a my hert, or I pray you be mery.[3]

---

[1] Quoted by L. Pound, *Poetic Origins and the Ballad*, . 44.
[2] Quoted by Chappell, op. cit., I, 41.
[3] Prologue to *The seuen sorowes that women haue.*

These would all seem to have been popular songs, yet to have had courtly associations. ' Col to me ' is probably ' Cull to me the rushes green ', which is mentioned among ' sucit sangis ' of the time in *The Complaynt of Scotland* and is set to music in one of Henry VIII's manuscripts, Royal Appendix 58. ' A my hert ' is included in the same list of popular songs, but it was probably used by Wyatt, as we shall see in a moment. By this time ballad would seem to have been applied to courtly songs of popular character, that is to say, songs with simple metrical tunes set to poetry of courtly style. Prof. Baskervill rather inclines to emphasize the courtly nature of the ballad at the beginning of the sixteenth century.[1] He points out that in *The Four Elements* (c. 1525) Ignorance refuses to sing ' some lusty balet ' because he scorns the subtleties of ' pricksong '—i.e. contrapuntal music. But Ignorance is a clown, and he actually produces a nonsense song. The joke probably is that a ballad was not pricksong at all but a simple tune with a strong swing about it. This would account for the degeneration of the term later in the century.

When printing had become general enough to stimulate journalism it was not surprising that the name ballad should have been usurped by catch-penny printers anxious to reach a semiliterate audience. The term sonnet suffered the same fate : many of the more lyrical broadsides are called sonnets. At first rough copies of poems printed in the miscellanies were hawked round to popular tunes. Classical subjects predominate among the ballads entered in the Stationers' Register between 1560 and 1580, and most of them probably had an educated origin. Clement Robinson's *Handeful of pleasant delites* (1566) is nothing more than a collection of broadsides, though its title-page describes the contents as ' sonets ' and ' histories ' and it was intended to look like a miscellany of the type of Tottel's. Gradually stratification of the public began. A special class of hack-writers concentrated on sensational matter for the credulous. Elderton, Deloney, and Martin Parker became household names, never mentioned by the learned without contempt, but immensely popular among the people as a whole. Their productions were on everybody's lips. Without them ' the maidens shall want sonnets at there pales, and the cuntrey striplings ditties to sing at the maydes windowes ; the cart-horses will grow discontented for want of them '.[2] Autolycus and Nightingale and their fellows spread the ballads at fairs, singing them to a fiddle. Yet the early connexion of the

[1] *The Elizabethan Jig*, p. 29. [2] *Pilgrimage to Parnassus*, ll. 1530 ff.

ballad with courtly poetry did not entirely disappear. Broadsides often borrow the work of superior poets. The gap between genuine poetry and the hack-work of the broadside widens, but there are reminiscences of the fact that the early printers of ballads had started from material that educated people did not disdain.

The tunes, too, forbid any rigid separation between popular and cultured. The tune is the essence of the ballad. Without the lilt of the music the rough versifiers would have been unable to impart any semblance of verse to their effusions. These tunes did not come from the people : they have no characteristic of folk-music about them. Occasionally a ballad is to be sung to a ' new northern tune ' or a ' new Scotch tune ', which may imply an origin remote from the metropolis. But generally there is no doubt that the tunes were by London composers. In the seventeenth century it became common to commend tunes as ' new playhouse tunes ', and this may account for some of the sixteenth-century tunes too. In *The Return from Parnassus* (1606) a fiddler is asked, ' Have you never a song of maister Dowlands making ? '[1] Dowland's ' Frog Galliard ' became a great favourite to which many ballads were set. Another popular tune was Tarleton's Medley, apparently either composed by or sung by the famous comedian. Judge Whitelock tells how he composed a coranto and was surprised to hear it taken up in the playhouses.[2] *Basse's Career*, by the early seventeenth-century poet, William Basse, was another tune much used for ballads. The ballads were written to the tunes the virginals composers employed as themes for their variations.

The name ballad earned an opprobrious connotation because printers used it to cover the functions of sensational journalism and fiction. All sorts of people tried their hands at ballad-making, and the results could not be very polished. Bottom intended to get Peter Quince to write about his adventures in the wood, and Falstaff threatened to pay back those who had played a trick on him by having ballads about them sung to ' scurvy tunes '. A society in which folk-song was still active was full of creative energy, and all conditions felt qualified to turn out rough verses. ' I thinke there be never an Ale-house in England nor yet so base a Maypole on a country greene, but sets forth some poets petter-nels or demilances to the paper warres in Paules Churchyard.'[3]

[1] fol. Hv.
[2] *Liber Famelicus of Sir J. Whitelock*, Camden Society Publications, p. 66.
[3] *Return from Parnassus*, fol. B.

But it was not only the ignorant who read and sang ballads. Nor was it only they who performed the same operation as a ballad-writer. The educated also wrote verses to tunes. In Lyly's *Endimion* Sir Thopas is said by his page, Epiton, to do nothing but write sonnets, and the page quotes one with the comment : ' It is set to the tune of the black Saunce, *ratio est*, because Dipsas is a black saint.' [1] The poem is obviously a satire of an Italianate love lyric. In Jonson's *Staple of News* Madrigal composes a madrigal to the tune the fiddlers played.[2] Neither Lyly nor Jonson were satirizing hack-writers of broadsides. Amateurs of higher social station than the Eldertons and Deloneys wrote verses to tunes, often to popular tunes of the kind the ballad-writers used. It was also common to press one of these tunes into service to sing a lyric that had no music provided for it. The publisher of *The Paradise of daynty devises* says that his poems ' are so aptly made to be set to any song in .5. partes, or song to instrument '. The buyer of the book was expected to cast round for a suitable tune for each poem, just as users of a modern hymn-book find a tune they already know to fit the metre of an unfamiliar hymn. Thus many lyrics became associated with popular tunes, although they were not written to them.

Wyatt's lyrics obviously owe a great deal to the musical background against which he worked, and several of his poems appear either to have been written to tunes by court composers or suggested by tunes on which court composers based part-music. The rhythm and the refrain of this song are found in others of the time :

> A ! my herte, a ! what aileth the
> To sett so light my libertye,
> Making me bonde when I was fre.
> A my herte a ! what aileth thee.[3]

In the Bodleian MS. Ashmole 176 there is a song very similar and probably to the same tune :

> Ah my hart ah this ys my Songe
> with weping eeis nowe and then among
> opprest with paynfull Sighes stronge
> that ah my hart ah . . .[4]

A song bearing some resemblance to these occurs with music in the Fairfax Book. The popularity of the original tune is

---

[1] IV, ii.   [2] IV, i.
[3] ed. cit., I. 323.   [4] fol. 100.

suggested by its inclusion in a list of contemporary songs in *The Complaynt of Scotland*, and by its being moralized into one of the *Gude and Godlie Ballatis* : there would be no point in replacing secular words by edifying ones if the tune were not already on everybody's lips.

> All my hart ay this is my sang
> > With doubill myrth and ioy amang,
> Sa blyith as byrd my God to fang,
> > Christ his my hart ay.[1]

In the texts of this song and the last one quoted some repetition would be necessary in the last line to fill out the metre as Wyatt's version gives it ; but it is quite usual only to indicate the refrain, which would be well known.

Two of Wyatt's poems, ' Blame not my lute ' and ' My lute awake ',[2] were moralized by John Hall in his *Courte of Vertue* (1565).[3] Hall supplied his own tunes, perhaps thinking the common ones too frivolous ; but the mere fact of his composing imitations points to the frequency with which the original poems were sung.

Many of the poems in the miscellanies were associated with popular tunes down to the late seventeenth century. A poem in Tottel's Miscellany, ' If care do cause men cry ', is found in John Forbes's *Cantus, Songs and Fancies* (1666), which contains many lutanist airs and ballads of the early seventeenth century. It also appears in the *Melvill Book of Roundels*.[4] There is therefore every reason to believe that the Tottel poem continued to be sung to this tune for almost a century.

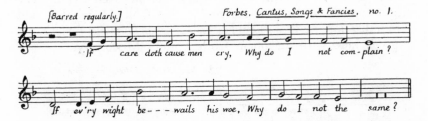

The same two collections of tunes contain settings of another poem in Tottel's Miscellany ' Like as the lark '. Of this a moralization was included in *The Courte of Vertue*.[5]

[1] op. cit., p. 139.   [2] Wyatt, ed. cit., I, 303, 117.   [3] pp. 74 and 76.
[4] ed. Bantock and Anderton, p. 199.   [5] p. 108.

'Who loves to live in peace' appears not only in Tottel but in three manuscripts—Ashmole 48,[1] Sloane 1896 (fol. 35v), and Additional 15225 (fol. 56). The last manuscript is composed mainly of broadsides, and this poem, like its companions, is marked to be sung to a tune—to either 'The Rich Merchantman' or 'John, come kiss me now'. This must mean that no particular tune was generally associated with the poem: it was left to the singer's fancy which tune in the appropriate metre he chose. Both were popular and employed for innumerable ballads. 'The Rich Merchantman' was still sung after the Restoration: three ballads in the Pepysian collection, all dating from the 1680's, are directed to be sung to it.[2] 'John, come kiss me now' was chiefly famous as a dance. Burton tells us that 'Yea, many times this *love* will make old men and women, that have more toes than teeth, dance *John, come kiss me now.*' It is called an old dance in Rowland's *'Tis merry when Gossips meet,*[3] but it was still known after the Restoration, being mentioned in Ward's *London Spy.*[4] There are variations on it in the *Fitzwilliam Virginals Book,* and it is printed in Playford's volumes for the cither and treble viol. The original poem to it survives in Trinity College, Dublin, and a moralization of it is included in *Gude and Godlie Ballatis.* It is given here with the poem from Tottel's Miscellany.

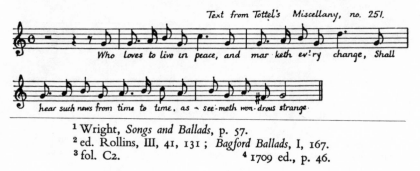

Text from Tottel's Miscellany, no. 251.

[1] Wright, *Songs and Ballads,* p. 57.
[2] ed. Rollins, III, 41, 131; *Bagford Ballads,* I, 167.
[3] fol. C2.   [4] 1709 ed., p. 46.

It was common for a very popular poem to give a new name to the tune to which it was sung. This has apparently happened with one of the poems in Tottel's Miscellany. 'Apelles and Pygmalion' is also found in the Huth collection of ballads,[1] and a ballad of that name was licensed in 1555–6 by William Griffith and Alexander Lacey, and in 1568–9 by Richard Jones.[2] In the Huth collection a ballad by John Barker, 'The Plagues of Northumberland', is to be sung to the tune of 'Apelles'.[3] It was entered in the Stationers' Register in 1569–70. Howell wrote to the tune of Apelles 'the lamentable historie of Sephalus with the Unfortunate end of Procris', which is printed in his *Newe Sonets, and pretie Pamphlets* (1567–8).[4] Another poem to the tune appears in *A Handeful of pleasant delites*.[5] The tune itself has not been identified. Its vogue seems to have lasted from about 1560 to about 1580.

Two poems by Lord Vaux, a contributor to Tottel's Miscellany, gave their names to tunes. 'I loth that I did love' is found in two versions, in Additional MSS. 4900 and 38599.

It was registered as a ballad by Richard Serle in 1563–4, and by John Alde on 19 October 1597, and soon won popularity. Two other poems in the Miscellany have the same metre and may have been sung to the tune (Nos. 210 and 212 in Rollins's edition) : on the other hand, there are other tunes of the period that would suit the metre. 'I loth that I did love' is mentioned as a tune in *The gorgious Gallery*,[6] and ballads to it are found in the Roxburgh, Britwell Court, and Society of Antiquaries collections. The original song by Lord Vaux is sung by the grave-diggers in Hamlet (Act V, scene i).

---

[1] No. 43. [2] Rollins, *Index*, 90, 91, 2887. [3] No. 16.
[4] fol. Fiv. [5] ed. Kershaw, p. 91. [6] ed. Rollins, p. 35.

A tune for 'How can the tree', another poem by Lord Vaux, is found in several contemporary sources. The poem first appeared in *The Paradise of dayntie devises*. An imitation in a slightly different metre was written by George Peele in *Sir Clyomon and Sir Clamydes*,[1] and Deloney has a ballad to the tune in his *Strange Histories* (No. VII).

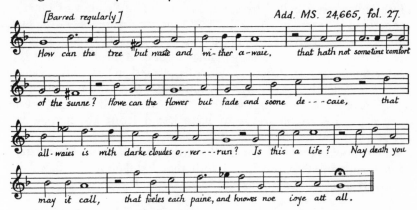

[Barred regularly]

Add. MS. 24,665, fol. 27.

How can the tree but waste and wi-ther a-waie, that hath not sometime comfort of the sunne? Howe can the flower but fade and soone de---caie, that all-waies is with darke cloudes o--ver---run? Is this a life? Nay death you may it call, that feeles each paine, and knowes noe ioye att all.

Other poems in the *Paradise*, as in Tottel's Miscellany, were sung to popular tunes. 'O heavenly God', by Francis Kinwelmarch, is set for voice and lute in Additional MS. 15117, but Prof. Rollins notes that an old hand in the 1596 edition of the *Paradise* (second impression), of which the unique copy is now in America, has added 'To the tune of Rogero', and this may be the one most favoured for it.

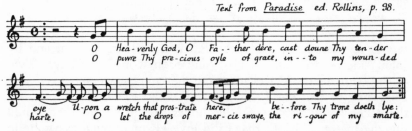

Text from *Paradise* ed. Rollins, p. 98.

O   Hea-venly God, O   Fa--ther dere, cast doune Thy ten-der
O   puwre Thy pre-cious oyle   of grace, in--to   my woun-ded

eye   u-pon a wretch that pros-trate here,   be--fore Thy trone doeth lye:
harte,   O   let the drops of   mer-cie swaye, the ri-gour of my smarte.

The same author's 'Rejoice, rejoice', also in the *Paradise* (No. 9), was set by Byrd, but it is included in Additional MS. 15225 among a number of ballads, and was probably sung to a ballad tune.

The largest contributor to the *Paradise* was Richard Edwards. His classical play *Damon and Pithias* inspired a ballad to whose tune many poems were set. There is one in *A Handeful of pleasant*

[1] ed. Bullen, II, 153.

delites,[1] one among the Huth Ballads (No. 7) and one in John Phillips's interlude *Patient Grissell* (ll. 493 ff.).

The gorgious *Gallery of Gallant Inventions*, the next important miscellany, specifies a number of tunes to which poems had been composed. One is to be sung to the tune of 'Lusty Gallant'.[2] This again was a dance tune, and a poem to it with a very attractive lilt is included in *A Handeful of pleasant delites*.[3]

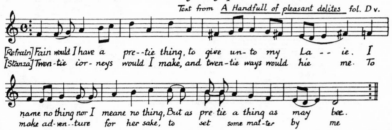

More stately music served another poem in the *Gallery*. It is clearly to be sung to the famous 'Willow song', which Desdemona sings in the last act of *Othello*. The original words for the tune are found in Additional MS. 15117, where it is arranged for solo voice and lute. It is an air rather than a ballad, but the words are reproduced in many ballad collections. Another poem to the tune was written by Howell.[4]

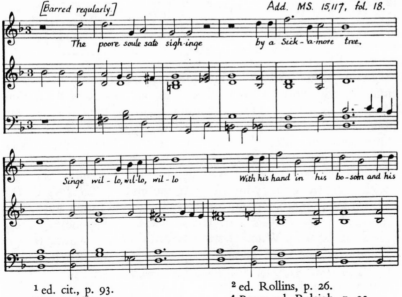

1 ed. cit., p. 93.   2 ed. Rollins, p. 26.
3 ed. Kershaw, p. 95.   4 *Poems*, ed. Raleigh, p. 23.

heade upon his knee O wil-lo, wil-lo, wil-lo, wil-lo, O wil-lo, wil-lo, wil-lo, wil-lo shal

be my gare-land. Singe all a greene wil-lo,   wil--lo, wil-lo, wil-lo,

Aye me the greene wil--lo must be my gare-land.

Many of the early Elizabethan court poets wrote to popular tunes. Lord Oxford is credited with the authorship of the famous 'In peascod time'.[1] This gave a new name to the old tune 'The hunt is up', which dates from the early years of the century. Puttenham attributed the original poem to 'one Gray',[2] who was a contemporary of Henry VIII. In 1537 a certain John Hogan offended the authorities by singing a political song to the tune 'with a crowd or a fyddyll'.[3] At the end of *The Play of Wit and Science* is another poem to it, and a moralization appears in *Gude and Godlie Ballatis*. To it also was sung Deloney's famous ballad of Shore's Wife. Lord Oxford's poem, which is here quoted with the tune, became so popular that its first line came

[1] Harleian MS. 7392, fol. 51 ; *Englands Helicon*, No. 134.
[2] Gregory Smith, op. cit., II, 17.
[3] Collier, *Shakespeare*, I, cclxxxviii, quoted Chappell (Wooldridge), I, 87.

Text from *England's Helicon*, no. 134.

In Peas-cod time, when Hound to horne, gives eare till Buck be kild. And
lit--tle Lads with pipes of corne, sate kee-ping beasts a---field.

to designate the tune. Later the title 'The Lady's Fall' replaced
'In peascod time', and to it innumerable ballads were set. In a
Dutch collection it appears as 'O sweet Oliver', a fragment of which
is carolled by Touchstone.[1] A variant of the tune is 'The
Queenes Maiesties new Hunt is up', to which Anthony Munday
wrote a poem in *The Banquet of daintie Conceits*.

If nei--ther is the migh-ty King, nor a---ny men be--side.
Nor wine that may be stron-gest namde, a---las you are too wide

During the sixteenth and seventeenth centuries 'The hunt is up'
was the tune used for 'Chevy Chase'. It must therefore be the
tune that stirred Sidney like the sound of a trumpet.[2]

Sir Edward Dyer's best-known poem, 'My mind to me a
kingdom is', had a tremendous vogue to the tune of 'In Crete
when Daedalus'. The Shirburn and Pepysian collections and
Additional MS. 15225 all mark the poem to be sung to this tune,
which derived its name from a ballad by Deloney. Howell
had set a poem to it in *Newe Sonets*.[3] The tune, which is very
dull, is in Harleian MS. 7578 (fol. 103).

Two poems assigned to Nicholas Breton were written to tunes.
In *Brittons Bowre of Delights* (1591) there is 'A Sonet to the tune
of a hone a hone'.[4] This would seem to refer to 'The Irish
Ho-hone', on which there are anonymous variations in the
Fitzwilliam Virginals Book. It long remained popular, and there
is a song to it in *Wits Restored* (1658). The version given here

---

[1] *As You Like It*, III, iii.
[2] Gregory Smith, op. cit., I, 178.   [3] fol. Fiv.
[4] ed. Rollins, p. 36.

is very conjectural and omits part of the tune as given in the *Fitzwilliam Virginals Book*, in order to fit Breton's four-line stanza.

Breton's 'Pastoral of Phillis and Coridon' in *Englands Helicon* (No. 17) is extant also in the Roxburgh and Ewing collections of ballads, where it is to be sung to 'The Frog Galliard'. This would explain the trochaic movement of the verse, though the stanza is too short to provide words for the whole tune. Dowland was the composer of the tune, and it is provided with different words in his *First Booke of Ayres*. It had wide popularity as an instrumental galliard, and was printed in Morley's *Consort Lessons*, Robinson's *New Cithern Lessons*, and, on the Continent, in the *Neder-Landtsche Gedenck-Clancke* of Adriaen Valerius (1626). Another ballad to it is found in the Ewing collection.

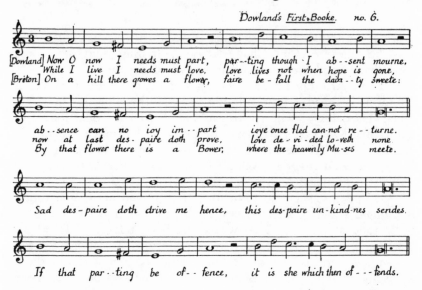

Munday wrote another poem ' to Dowlands Galliard ' in *A Banquet of daintie Conceits*, but the rhythm of the verse shows that he did not mean this particular galliard.

Two successive poems in *Englands Helicon* are marked by an old hand in the British Museum copy to be sung to ' Crimson Velvet '. One is ' Faire Phillis and her Sheepheard ' by I. G. (John Grange ?), and the other ' Venus and Adonis ' by Henry Chettle. The first occurs in Forbes's *Cantus, Songs and Fancies* with the tune, and the second, with the name of the tune at its head, in Deloney's *Strange Histories*. The tune is given here with the more famous poem by Chettle.

The apostles of the New Poetry, although more indebted to foreign models than the early court poets, and though anxious to remove any stain of balladry from English verse, occasionally wrote to popular tunes. In the August eclogue of *The Shepheardes Calender* Willye and Perigot maintain in song ' a delectable controuersi, made in imitation of that in Theocritus : whereto also Virgile fashioned his third and seuenth Æclogue '. Their contest takes the traditional form of a roundelay. Perigot and Willye sing alternate lines, the former telling the story and the latter replying with a sort of impromptu commentary. Now Perigot's second line,

> When holly fathers wont to shrieue,

carries the mind back to pre-Reformation days. It is quite common for new poems to old tunes to retain traces of the original words sung to the tunes ; and this, together with the rough rhythm of the roundelay, so unlike Spenser's usual smoothness, induces the suspicion that Spenser was working with an old tune in mind. There actually was a tune called 'Heigh ho, holiday', the very refrain with which Willye begins his under-song. It is noted down in an early seventeenth-century commonplace-book, now Additional MS. 4338 in the British Museum, but unfortunately the part of the book in which it occurs is a mere collection of fragments, and the notation of the tune has been so careless that it is unintelligible. Other poems, however, were written to it, and they are all in the same metre as Spenser's roundelay. Deloney heads one of his ballads 'To the tune of Heigh ho Holiday,'[1] and the refrain occurs in another of his.[2] A ballad called 'The Sailor's Joy' to the tune was licensed to Thomas Creede on 14 January 1595.[3] Lodge wrote to the same tune a poem [4] which mentions 'Bonibell', a figure that comes into the Spenser roundelay and is probably a relic of the original song that supplied the name of the tune. Another song in *Englands Helicon* (No. 126) has the same under-song and the same metre and is almost certainly written to the tune.

The use of a popular tune was perhaps an attempt by Spenser to suggest the rustic character of his singers, especially as the round-elay is contrasted with an elaborate song by Colin Clout later in the eclogue. Drayton seems to have had the same idea, for one of the songs in the ninth eclogue of his *Pastorals* goes very well to the tune of Walsingham. He does not mention any tune, but again there seem to be reminiscences of the original 'Walsingham' in his text, and the lilt of the verse agrees very well with the tune.

Text from Drayton's Works. ed J.W. Hebel. II 566

Sidney's metres are generally very Italianate, and we shall see presently that he wrote verses to several Italian tunes, but he has left one song to a popular dance tune. He contributed it to William Percy's *Fairy Pastorals,* and the tune is called 'Greensleeves'. The lively 6/8 time imparts a sprightliness to the verse, as it often does to even the crudest of the many ballads the tune graced.

[1] *Works*, ed. Mann, p. 90. [2] ib., p. 344.
[3] Rollins, *Index*, 2357. [4] *Englands Helicon*, No. 81.

Text in Works of Sidney, ed. Feuillerat, II. 342

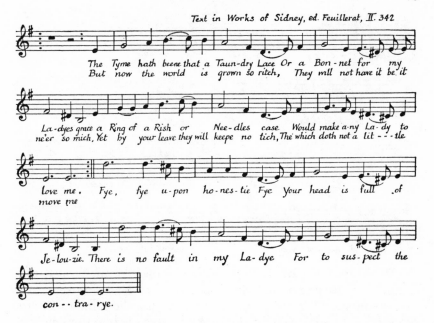

The Tyme hath beene that a Taun-dry Lace Or a Bon-net for my
But now the world is grown so ritch, They will not have it be it

La-dyes grace a Ring of a Rish or Nee-dles case Would make a-ny La-dy to
ne'er so mich, Yet by your leave they will keepe no tich, The which doth not a lit - - - tle

love me. Fye, fye u-pon ho-nes-tie Fye Your head is full of
move me

Je-lou-zie. There is no fault in my La-dye For to sus-pect the

con - - tra - rye.

The earliest ballad to the tune was registered by Richard Jones in 1580, and an answer was entered by Edward White in the same year.[1] 'A New Courtly Sonet of the Lady Greensleeves,' in *A Handeful of pleasant delites*, may be the original poem after which the tune was named.[2] Among the more famous to it is 'The Blacksmith', which has a refrain often given as a name for the tune—'Which nobody can deny'.[3] Prof. Wooldridge says that this catchy phrase continued to figure in popular songs down to the nineteenth century.

A poem of Sidney, 'Only joy now here you are', is marked in the Rylands Library copy of *Englands Helicon* as sung to 'Shall I wrastle in disp.'[4] This note cannot be contemporary with the poem, for 'Shall I wrastle [or wasting] in dispair' is named from a poem in George Wither's *Faire-Virtue*, which is found in a ballad copy printed in 1615.[5] The tune is quite likely to be older than Wither's poem, which probably only gave it a new name. It is here given with both the Sidney and the Wither verses.

---

[1] Rollins, *Index*, 1742, 1049.　　[2] ed. Kershaw, p. 37.
[3] *Roxburgh Ballads*, II, 127, and elsewhere.
[4] No. 1. *Works of Sidney*, ed. Feuillerat, II, 288.
[5] *Pepys' Ballads*, I, 230.

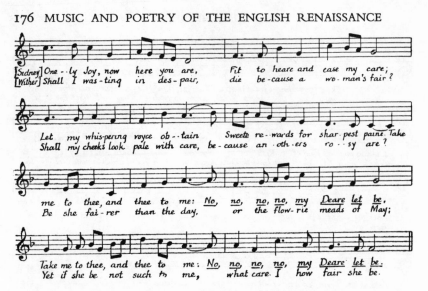

[Sidney] One--ly Joy, now here you are, Fit to heare and ease my care;
[Wither] Shall I was-ting in des-pair, die be-cause a wo-man's fair?

Let my whispering voyce ob--tain Sweete re-wards for shar-pest paine. Take
Shall my cheeks look pale with care, be-cause an-oth-ers ro--sy are?

me to thee, and thee to me: No, no, no, no, my Deare let be,
Be she fai-rer than the day, or the flow-rie meads of May;

Take me to thee, and thee to me: No, no, no, no, my Deare let be:
Yet if she be not such to me, what care. I how fair she be.

While speaking of George Wither it may be mentioned that another of his poems has the appearance of being written to a current tune. 'I loved a lass, a fair one' has the refrain 'Falero, lero, lo'. This is given for the tune of two ballads in the Pepysian collection. Neither preserves the refrain, but both could well be sung to the tune. Wither has worked the refrain into the body of the poem. Its recurrence is like a reiterated sigh of nostalgic regret.

> I loved a lass, a fair one,
>   As fair as e'er was seen ;
> She was indeed a rare one,
>   Another Sheba queen.
> But fool as I then was,
>   I thought she loved me too ;
> But now alas ! sh'as left me,
>   Falero, lero, loo.[1]

Marlowe contributed to popular song the famous 'Come, live with me and be my love'. It was published in both *The Passionate Pilgrim* and *Englands Helicon*. Isaak Walton had it sung to him by a milkmaid, for it was by then an old favourite.[2] It gave its name to a tune that served innumerable ballads, and which was probably already old when Marlowe wrote. A passage in *The World's Folly* (1609) reads : 'But there sat he, hanging his head, lifting up the eyes, and with a deep sigh, singing the ballad of

---

[1] ib., I, 72, and Rollins, *Pepysian Garland*, p. 132.
[2] *Compleat Angler*, ed. Buchan, p. 71.

Come live with me, and be my love, to the tune of Adew, my deere.'[1] No tune of this name is known, and the broadside edition of Marlowe's song advertises it as sung to a new tune.[2] But strict veracity is not always a trait of ballad printers : this may mean only that the printer did not know the tune intended for the poem. Not only ballads but serious poems were written to the tune under its new name. Raleigh is accredited with a reply, and Donne wrote an imitation that has every appearance of being set to the tune.[3]

It would be possible to go on for a considerable time citing instances of poets writing to popular tunes and of poems that became associated with popular tunes. Right down to the Restoration there was constant interchange between popular music and poetry. Many of Herrick's lyrics suggest a background of popular song and dance. Bishop Corbet wrote a number of popular ballads, and Patrick Carey set a whole volume of ballads to popular tunes. Sometimes poets of reputation had settings composed by eminent musicians, and these settings passed into the popular repertoire. Sir John Suckling wrote a Ballad upon a Wedding for the marriage of Roger Boyle, Earl of Orrery, and it was set to music by one of his friends.

Pills to Purge Melancholy (1719), III, 132.

I tell thee Dick where I have been, Where I the ra--rest things have seen, O things be-yond com-pare; Such sights a-gain can-not be found, In a-ny place on En-glish ground, Be it at Wake or Fair.

The catchiness of the tune soon won it a wide public, and many other songs were fitted to it. In Carey's *Trivia* (1651) is a poem ' To the tune of I tell thee, Dick that I have been ',[4] and *Folly in Print* (1667) contains ' Three merry boys of Kent, to the tune of

[1] Quoted by Wooldridge, I, 123.

[2] *Roxburgh Ballads*, II, 3.

[3] Donne's *Songs and Sonets*. Raleigh's reply is appended to the copy cited in n. 2.

[4] Saintsbury, *Caroline Poets*, II, 458.

an old song beginning thus "I rode from England into France" or the tune of Sir John Suckling's ballad.' Another poem that gave its name to a tune used for ballads was Lovelace's 'When Love with unconfined wings'.[1] The music for it was composed by John Wilson.[2]

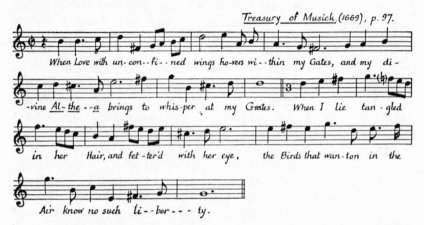

Treasury of Musick, (1669), p. 97.

When Love with un-con--fi--ned wings ho-vers wi--thin my Gates, and my di--vine Al-the--a brings to whis-per at my Grates. When I lie tan-gled in her Hair, and fet-ter'd with her eye, the Birds that wan-ton in the Air know no such li--ber--ty.

'Love with unconfined wings' is given as the tune of a ballad called 'The Pensive Prisoner's Apology', extant in the Huth and Pepysian collections.

One of the most important aspects of the poetic revival in the last two decades of the sixteenth century is the enrichment of form. Lyric stanzas became more varied; there was greater sureness in handling the rhythm of the line. In the early miscellanies and among the early court poets the metres are very few. Four-teeners, 'poulter's measure', pentameters either in pairs or cross-rimed, various combinations of six-syllable and octosyllabic lines—these are practically all. A jog-trot stress-iambic is the only rhythm in which these poets feel safe. But after Spenser and Sidney the variety of pattern is amazing. To some extent the change is due to Italian and French influence. But part of the foreign influence came by way of foreign music. The madrigal translations did a good deal to make English verse more flexible. Trochaic rhythms, lines of seven and eleven syllables, and feminine endings are all signs of Italian influence. The madrigal was particularly noted for the variety in the lengths of its lines: the lines ' vanno crescendo e sminuendo' (see p. 93). This distinctive quality was satirized by several English dramatists and poets when madrigals had

---

[1] *Lucasta*, Oxford ed., p. 78.   [2] *Cheerful Ayres* (1660).

become fashionable in England. In Lyly's *Endimion* Epiton repeats a sonnet Sir Thopas has written :

> The beggar Loue that knows not where to lodge :
> At last within my hart when I slept,
> He crept.
> I wakt, and so my fancies began to fodge.

Samias comments : ' That's a verie long verse.' To which Epiton replies : ' Why, the other was shorte, the first is called from the thombe to the little finger, the second from the little finger to the elbowe, and some hee made to reach to the crowne of his head, and downe again to the sole of his foote.' [1] In Jonson's *Epicoene* Daw composes a madrigal that has the same characteristics.

> Modest and fair, for faire and good are neere
> Neighbours, howe'er.
> No noble vertue ever was alone,
> But two in one.
> Then, when I praise sweet modestie, I praise
> Bright beauties raies :
> And having prais'd both beauty and modestie,
> I have prais'd thee. [2]

The madrigal, therefore, by its variety of rhythms and lengths of line, helped to relieve the monotony of English verse. But simpler kinds of Italian music were also well known here. Sidney wrote a number of lyrics to the tunes of Neapolitan *villanelle*. Two—' The Nightingale ' and ' The fire to see my woes ' [3]—are to the tune *Non credo gia piu infelice amante*. Another is ' to the tune of a Neapolitan song, which beginneth : *No, no, no, no* '. [4] Another is headed merely ' to the tune of a Neapolitan Villanell '. [5] I have not been able to identify these. ' Sleep, baby mine ', [6] however, is said to be written to the tune of *Basciami vita mia*, and this tune is to be found in *Il Secundo Libro Delle Villotte alle Napoletana*, printed by Gardano of Venice in 1571. Lord Herbert of Cherbury has also left a record of two Italian tunes to which he wrote verses— ' *Cose ferite*, made by Lorenzo Allegre to one sleeping to be sung ', and ' *A che del Quantomio* of Pesarino '. [7] Spanish airs, too, were well known in England, and Sidney wrote a poem ' to the tune of the Spanish song, *Se tu senora no ducles di me* '. [8] Another of

---

[1] IV, ii.   [2] II, iii.
[3] *Works*, ed. Feuillerat, II, 302–3.   [4] ib., 317.
[5] ib., 318.   [6] ib., 304.   [7] *Poems*, Oxford ed., 26, 29.
[8] op. cit., p. 304.

Sidney's poems is to *Wilhelmus van Nassau,* which has become the Dutch national anthem.[1]

While foreign music had much to do with the increasing variety and flexibility of English verse, there was a parallel development in popular tunes that cannot have been without influence on poetry. The early tunes quoted in the course of this chapter are much simpler than the popular tunes of the seventeenth century. The fourteener and lines of six and eight syllables are the common metres of poems set to these early tunes : they correspond to the long and short metres in which a great part of English folk-song is written. While it is dangerous to generalize where the documentation is incomplete, there seems to be some evidence of freer melodic invention and a growing complexity of structure in the popular tunes. Many of the early seventeenth-century ballads have an attractive lilt, very different from the rather four-square character of the early miscellany poems. Instead of a few strains, the tunes have usually several sections, often repeating, and quite long stanzas written to them manage to have rhythmical unity. The heightened vitality of the popular tunes has obviously something to do with the improvement in lyric poetry.

Not only are the stanza patterns more varied but the individual line achieves greater freedom. The early miscellanies use practically no other metre than a rigid stress-iambic. Gascoigne deplores the lack of variety but cannot see how it is to be avoided in the current insecurity of control over rhythm.

Note you [he remarks] that commonly now a dayes in English rimes (for I dare not cal them English verses) we use none other but a foote of two sillables, whereof the first is depressed or made short, and the second is elevate or made long ; and that sound in scanning continuate throughout the verse.[2]

Trochaic rhythms crept in with the madrigal and other Italian forms, but the predominating measure in all Elizabethan verse continued to be the stress-iambic. In the early seventeenth century, however, triple resolutions become more and more frequent, until after the Restoration triple rhythms were very common indeed in lyric verse. We recognize the typical Dryden lyric in a stanza like :

> Wherever I am, and whatever I doe,
>   My *Phillis* is still in my mind :
> When angry, I mean not to *Phillis* to goe,
>   My Feet of themselves the way find :

---

[1] op. cit., 314.   [2] Gregory Smith, op. cit., I, 49.

Unknown to myself I am just at her door,
And, when I would raile, I can bring out no more,
Than, *Phillis*, too fair and unkind ! [1]

This increased fondness for triple rhythms appears to be connected with developments in the dance.   In describing the common English metres of his time Webbe soon exhausts the stock of purely literary ones and comprehends all further metres under the tunes to which they might be set.

Neither is there anie tune or stroke which may be sung or plaide on instruments which hath not some poetical ditties framed according to the numbers thereof, some to Rogero, some to Trenchmore, to downe right Squire, to Galliardes, to Pauines, to Iygges, to Brawles, to all manner of tunes which euerie Fidler knows better then my selfe. [2]

It is notable that all the instances he gives are dance tunes.   Although there were plenty of ballad tunes that were not danced—we have just been discussing some—dance songs were always the most popular.   Nor was it only country dances that found their way into the fiddlers' repertoires.   Pavans and galliards were court dances. But there was constant interchange between the two classes of dance.   It was therefore only to be expected that both popular and courtly poetry would be influenced by changes in dance fashions ; and there was actually a considerable evolution in the general character of court dancing during the sixteenth and early seventeenth centuries.

Throughout the variations in the individual dances chosen it was always customary to start the programme with the slow and stately figures and progress towards the quicker and more acrobatic ones.   The stately dances of the first half of the sixteenth century were the base dance and the pavan.   According to Arbeau, the French authority, the base dance required a *chanson* of three parts—an opening of sixteen bars, repeated, a ' mediation ' of sixteen bars, and a close of sixteen bars repeated.   The rhythm of each bar is given by the drum-taps 3 ♩ ♫ ♫.   By the time of Elizabeth, however, the base dance had gone out of fashion. Writing in 1588, Arbeau says that it has been neglected for forty or fifty years in France, and probably its decline in England dates from the same time.   It was replaced by the ' measures ', which must have been very much what the particular dancer cared to make them, for Davies in his *Orchestra* describes them as ' full of

---

[1] *Conquest of Granada* (Poetical Works, p. 375).
[2] Gregory Smith, op. cit., I, 272.

change and rare varieties'. Their movement he pictures as
spondaic, grave, and slow, from which we may surmise that the
music was similar to that of the pavan. By the end of the century
the measures were becoming old-fashioned. Beatrice in *Much
Ado About Nothing* says they are 'full of state and ancientry'.[1]
The pavan held its ground better. It, too, was a slow and stately
dance. Arbeau gives its rhythm as ♩ ♫, running to sixteen bars.
It suffered from a certain amount of license. Morley defines it as

a kind of staide musicke, ordained for graue dauncing, and most commonlie made of three straines, whereof euerie straine is plaid or sung
twice, a straine they make to containe 8. 12. or 16 semibreues as they
list, yet fewer then eight I haue not seene in any pavan. . . . Also in
this you must cast your musicke by foure, so that if you keepe that rule
it is no matter howe many foures you put in the straine, for it will fall
out well enough in the ende, the arte of dauncing being come to that
perfection that euerie dauncer will make measure of no measure.[2]

Consequently there is great diversity in the 'ditties' set to pavans.
An early one, 'the Cicilia Pavan', has a poem written to it in
A Handeful of pleasant delites : [3]

> Heart, what makes thee thus to be,
>   in extreame heauinesse ?
> If care do cause al thy distresse,
> Why seekest thou not some redresse,
>   to ease thy carefulnesse ?
> Hath *Cupid* stroke in Venerie,
> Thy wofull corps in ieoperdie :
>   right wel then may I sob and crie,
> Till that my Mistresse deer,
>   my faith may trie
> Why would I cloake from her presence,
> My loue and faithfull diligence ?
>   And cowardly thus to die,
>   And cowardly thus to die.

Dowland's celebrated *Lachrimae* pavan was fitted with words and
published in his *Second Booke of Ayres*. The verses follow the
three repeated sections characteristic of the dance, the same text
serving for both times the last section is sung : this is because the
air, like the madrigal, had a conventional repeat at the end of
the stanza. The divisions of the tune determine not only the form
but the sentiments of the text.

[1] II, i.   [2] *Introduction*, p. 181.
[3] ed. Kersham, p. 53.

Flow my teares, fall from your springs,
    Exilde, for ever let me morne   A
Where nights black bird her sad infamy sings,
    There let me live forlorne.

Downe, vain lights, shine you no more,
    No nights are dark enough for those   A
That in dispaire their last fortuns deplore.
    Light doth but shame disclose.

    Never may my woes be relieved,
        Since pitie is fled,   B
    And teares, and sighes, and groans my wearie dayes
        Of all ioyes have deprived.

    From the highest spire of contentment
        My fortune is throwne,   B
    And feare, and griefe, and paine for my deserts
        Are my hopes, since hope is gone.

Harke you shadowes that in darknesse dwell,
Learn to contemne light.   C
Happie, happie they that in hell   (bis)
    Feele not the worlds despite.[1]

A poem like this scarcely exists apart from its music. Its content is inspired by the intense passion at which Dowland excelled, and its form is that of a pavan.

The pavan was always followed by the galliard, composed on the same theme as the pavan but in triple instead of duple time. Its rhythm was composed of five drum-taps 3 ♩♩♩|♩.♩| whence it gained the alternative title 'cinquepace'.

This is a lighter and more stirring kinde of dauncing then the pauane consisting of the same number of straines, and looke howe manie foures of semibreues, you put in the straine of your pauane, so many times sixe minimes must you put in the straine of your galliard.[2]

Four of the airs in Dowland's *First Booke of Ayres* were known as instrumental galliards. The Frog Galliard has already been quoted. 'My thoughts are winged with hope', set to 'Sir John Souch his Galliard,'[3] has merely the familiar stanza of pentameter lines riming ababcc. The other two, Captain Piper's Galliard and

---

[1] *Second Booke of Songs or Ayres*, No. 2 ; Fellowes, *English Madrigal Verse*, p. 421.
[2] Morley, op. cit., p. 181.   [3] *Lachrimae*.

the Earl of Essex Galliard, show the three repeated sections customary in the dance. Captain Piper's Galliard runs as follows :

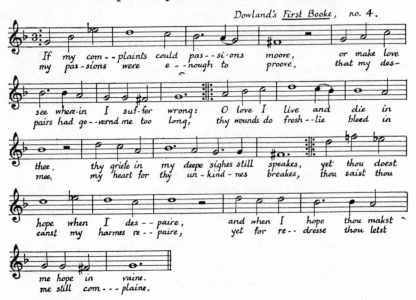

Dowland's First Booke, no. 4.

If my com--plaints could pas--si-ons moove, or make love
my pas-sions were e---nough to proove, that my des-

see where-in I suf-fer wrong: O love I live and die in
pairs had go--vernd me too long, thy wounds do fresh--lie bleed in

thee, thy griefe in my deepe sighes still speakes, yet thou doest
mee, my heart for thy un-kind-nes breakes, thou saist thou

hope when I des--paire, and when I hope thou makst
canst my harmes re--paire, yet for re--dresse thou letst

me hope in vaine.
me still com---plaine.

The *Alman* is a more heauie daunce then this (fitlie representing the nature of the people, whose name it carieth) so that no extraordinarie motions are vsed in daunceing of it. It is made of straines, somtimes two, sometimes three, and euerie straine is made by foure, but you must marke that the foure of the pauan measure is in *dupla* proportion to the foure of the *Alman* measure, so that as the vsuall Pauane conteineth a straine the time of sixteene semibreues, so the vsuall *Almaine* conteineth the time of eight, and most commonlie in short notes.[1]

Arbeau confirms the common time of the almain, contrasted with the duple time of the pavan, and says it consists of three sections, the first of five bars, to the rhythm ₵♩♫♩♪, the second of two bars, and the third of four bars to the rhythm ₵♩♩♩♩. It was danced throughout the century, and occurs in the list of dances at the end of *The Complaynt of Scotland*, and Nashe and Jonson mention it at the turn of the century. A poem to the Black Almain is printed in *A Handeful of pleasant delites* :

> Maid, wil you marie ? I pray sir tarie,
> I am not disposed to wed a :
> For he yt shal haue me, will neuer deny me
> he shal haue my maidenhed a.

---

[1] Morley, op. cit., p. 181.

Why then you will not wed me?
 No sure sir I haue sped me,
 You must go seeke some other wight,
 That better may your heart delight.
For I am sped I tell you true,
 beleeu me it greeues me, I may not haue you,
 To wed you & bed you as a woman shold be.[1]

The branle too covers the whole period.   There were a number
of varieties of it.   Most of them were in common time, but
Arbeau gives the *branle gai* as 4 bars of 6/4 rhythm 3 ♩♩♩♩ ♩.   This
agrees with Morley's *branle de poictu* or *branle double*.   'The
bransle de poictou or *bransle double* is more quick in time, (as being
in a rounde Tripla) but the straine is longer, containing more
vsually twelue whole strokes.' [2]   All the varieties seem to have
been danced in a line or in a ring, which assimilates them to folk-
dance, and, whereas the other dances mentioned by Morley were
chiefly accompanied by instruments, the branle was often accompanied by singing.   In the pastorals at the end of Book I in Sidney's
Arcadia two groups of shepherds dance to their own song 'as it
were in a branle'.   Moth, in *Love's Labours Lost* (III, i), asks,
'Master, will you win your love with a French brawl?' and
proceeds to give a satirical account of a wooing by dancing and
singing a love song.   A poem to the 'Quarter Brawles' is printed
in *A Handeful of pleasant delites*.

Diana and her darlings deare,
Walkt once as you shall heare:
Through woods and waters cleare,
   themselues to play:
The leaues were gay and green,
And pleasant to be seen:
They went the trees between,
   in cool aray,
So long that at the last they found a place,
   of waters full cleare:
So pure and faire a Bath neuer was
   found many a yeare.
There shee went faire and gent,
Her to sport, as was her wonted sort:
   In such desirous sort;
   Thus goeth the report:
Diana dainteously began herselfe therein to bathe
And her body for to laue
   So curious and braue.[3]

---

[1] ed. Kershaw, p. 65.   [2] Morley, op. cit., p. 181.
[3] ed. Kershaw, p. 47.

A very lively dance of the same period is the canaries. This consisted of four bars to the rhythm ¢ ♩ ♫♩ ♫. The tordion, contemporary with the dances just mentioned, requires no special comment, for it was equivalent in purpose to the galliard and consisted of the same number of measures as the pavan, only in triple time.

Now the dances we have just been discussing may all be said to belong to the dignified tradition of early court dancing. But as the century advanced a greater freedom and liveliness replaced the old stateliness. Agile steps came into fashion in place of figures. Ravenscroft expresses this revolt against formalism and preference for individual exhibitionism. He recommends dancing

not grounded on the *Dauncing of the Measures,* and accordingly bound to some particular *Rules and Numbers,* proper to the *Nature* of that *Daunce* onely, which is then afoot : But fashioned like those *Antique Daunces,* which the Poets would haue vs beleeue, the *Fayries,* and the *Satyres,* and those other *Rurall Natures* frequented, and hauing in them, much more *variety* and *change* then an other *Composition.*[1]

The galliard maintained its position fairly well, because it allowed of the introduction of new tricks at will. The pavan, however, succumbed to its more lively descendant, the Spanish pavan, which bore some resemblance to the canaries.

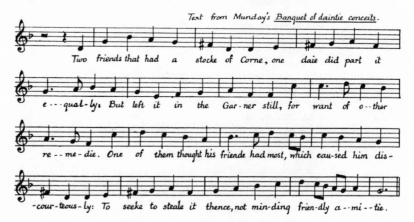

Text from Munday's *Banquet of daintie conceits.*

Two friends that had a stocke of Corne, one daie did part it
e---qual-ly. But left it in the Gar-ner still, for want of o--ther
re--me-die. One of them thought his friende had most, which cau-sed him dis-
-cour-teous-ly: To seeke to steale it thence, not min-ding frien-dly a--mi--tie.

The measures and the almain seem to have gradually passed out of the repertoire altogether. But new dances of more lively character crept in. Of these the chief during Elizabeth's reign

[1] *Briefe Discovrse* (1614). Prof. Baskervill gives an interesting account of Elizabethan dancing in *The Elizabethan Jig.*

were the coranto and the volta.   In France Arbeau gives common
time for the former, but in England both were in quick triple time.
Davies's descriptions of them show that they were both exceedingly
violent, and it is said that the volta caused dancers to perspire so
much that ladies at the French court used to change their linen
after it.   Moreover, country dances became very popular at court,
and the most popular of them were very close to the new court
dances, as far as the music was concerned.   Morley compares the
branle de poictu with the volta and coranto, and with the country
dances.

Like vnto this (but more light) be the *voltes* and *courantes* which
being both of a measure, are notwithstanding daunced after sundrie
fashions, the *volte* rising and leaping, the *courante* trauising and running,
in which measure also our countrey daunce is made, though it be daunced
after another forme then any of the former.   All these be made in straines,
either two or three as shall seeme best to the maker, but the *courant* hath
twice so much in a straine, as the English country daunce.[1]

In the time of Elizabeth and James the new dances existed side
by side with the old ; but in the seventeenth century the more
lively dances ousted the older and more stately ones.   Selden
describes the change rather regretfully.

The court of England is much altered.   At a solemn dancing, first
you had the grave measures, then the corantoes, and the galliards, and
all this is kept up with ceremony ; at length they fall to Trenchmore,
and so to the cushion dance, and then all the company dance, lord and
groom, lady and kitchin-maid, no distinction.   So in our court in Queen
Elizabeth's time, gravity and state was kept up ; in King James's time
things went pretty well ; but in King Charles's time, there has been
nothing but Trenchmore and the cushion dance, *omnium gatherum*, tolly
polly, *hoyte cum toyte*.[2]

The culmination of the country dance vogue is the volumes of
Playford in the Restoration period.   Here country dances are
collected by a London publisher for fashionable society.

We are concerned here not so much with the steps as with
the music to these dances and the words fitted to it.   Webbe's
remarks leave no doubt that a large proportion of the popular
ballad tunes were dance tunes, and therefore the history of popular
poetry is affected by the change of fashion in dancing.   A large
proportion of the older dances are in duple time.   The verses set

[1] op. cit., p. 181.   [2] *Table-Talk*, ed. Reynolds, pp. 93–4.

to them would generally have an iambic metre. The galliard and one variety of branle are in triple time, but it will be noticed that every other bar contains only two notes. Morley draws attention to the trochaic rhythm of the galliard. It goes

by a measure, which the learned cal *trochaieam rationem*, consisting of a long and short stroke successiuelie, for as the foote *trochaeus* consisteth of one sillable of two times, and another of one time, so is the first of these two strokes double to the latter : the first beeing in time of a semibrefe, and the latter of a minime.[1]

The consequence is that a poem set to such a measure will again tend to have feet of two elements predominating. The Dowland galliard quoted is an example.

The new dances of the seventeenth century were all in triple rhythm—the volta, the coranto, and the saraband. A large percentage of the country dances in Playford are also in 6/8 time. These triple measures did not necessarily produce feet of three syllables in the poetry set to them, but triple resolutions of two-syllable feet would be encouraged by them. The first to write a ballad now extant to the volta had obvious difficulties with the new rhythm. Davies in his *Orchestra* describes the movement of the dance as anapaestic, and the tune would confirm that ; but the ballad writer has had to add an extra note at the beginning to make his verses fit. The movement is in triple rhythm throughout.

Text from *Shirburn Ballads*, no. 51.

Hen-ry our roy-all Kinge, would go a---hun---ting to the greene
To have the hart cha-sed the mer--ry Does trip - -pinge, un-to mer--ry

for-rest most plea-sant and fayre.
Shere-wood his no--bles re---payre Hawke and hound was un-bound; all things pre-

-pard for the same to the game, with good re---gard.

The tune known as ' the corranto ', probably the first to which the dance was performed on its arrival in England, was fitted to a stanza that begins in the common iambic metre, but whose second half is full of triple resolutions.

[1] op. cit., p. 181.

A Prince dothe sit a slippery seate,
   and beares a carefull minde :
The Nobles, which in silkes do iet,
   do little leasure finde.
Our safeguard and safetie, with many great matters, they scan ;
and none liues merrier, in my mynde,
    than dothe the plaine countryman.[1]

A free stanza form seems to have characterized the poems written to the coranto. Lovelace has a poem to ' Courante Monsieur ' with the following metre :

That frown, Aminta, now hath drowned
Thy bright fronts power, and crown'd
   Me that was bound.
No, no, deceived Cruel, no,
   Loves fiery darts
Till tipt with kisses, never kindle Hearts.[2]

The saraband, too, seems to have been very free in form. Lovelace has a poem ' to a loose Saraband ' with a very attractive lilt, to which the feminine endings of the second and fourth line contribute much.

Ah me ! the little Tyrant Theefe !
   As once my heart was playing,
He snatcht it up and flew away,
   Laughing at all my praying.[3]

Waller has a saraband that takes a rather different form and shows the triple movement of the dance better.

Hylas, oh Hylas ! why sit we mute,
Now that each bird saluteth the spring.
Wind up the slack'ned strings of thy lute,
Never canst thou want matter to sing ;
For love thy breast does fill with such a fire,
That whatsoe'er is fair moves thy desire.[4]

The growth of triple rhythms in the lyric belongs properly to the seventeenth century, and the full story is rather outside the scope of the present work. The livelier style of dancing and the increase in definitely triple rhythms in the court and country dances in vogue in London society have undoubtedly something to do with it. But the popular songs, too, lose some of the square-ness of the early sixteenth-century tunes. A shapely tune in triple measure, like the following, is very typical of the early seventeenth century.

[1] Clark, *Shirburn Ballads*, p. 361.   [2] ed. Wilkinson, I, 129.
[3] ib., I, 30.   [4] *Poems*, ed. G. Thorn Drury, p. 114.

The contacts between popular music and poetry need further investigation, and it would be dangerous to dogmatize on what was cause and what effect. That there was a parallel development in both, and that they were connected, is evident.

CHAPTER X

DIVERGENCE

IN the preceding chapters we have traced some of the ways in which poetry and music helped to determine each other's development. We have seen how both the great musical forms of the English Renaissance were affected by literary ideas, and how the singing of lyrics caused their structure and content to be adapted to the requirements of music. Men of letters and musicians felt there was a union between their two arts, and the traditions they inherited helped them to realize the implications of such a union. But every period carries within it the seeds of a new age. In the seventeenth century poetry and music were to separate by the very logic of their own natures. Each was to develop its own characteristics and its own resources. The poetry of Dryden and the music of Purcell may join forces for an opera or a song, but each has its own appeal and its own technique. In the style of the classical period of music literary pre-occupations played small part ; nor has music anything to do with the poetry of the Augustan age. These changes were being prepared during the Renaissance itself. When the union between music and poetry was closest each was beginning to feel round for methods of expression that were to estrange it from its sister.

All the music with which we have been concerned in the preceding chapters was built on song-form, and the poetry sung to it to some extent determined the shape of the music. The possibilities of that form were exhausted by the end of the sixteenth century. The madrigal had found in the fugal principle an ingenious way of turning song-form into compositions of considerable length and musical interest, though the structure remained dependent on that of the verse. Each line of the poem was taken in turn, and the development of the musical material did not entirely govern the dimensions or elaboration of the composition, which were largely fixed by the length and character of the poem. Instrumental music, on the whole, merely reproduced what had been written for voices : madrigals were often performed with viols instead of voices. But the fugal principle did greatly assist in freeing music from the restrictions of song-form by providing, if not an alternative principle of form, at least a purely musical method of development. The instrumental fantasia handled points of imitation and other features of contrapuntal technique without any of the limitations imposed by a text. Morley emphasized that one of its chief merits was its liberty to explore the material on which it was based.

The most principall and chiefest kind of musicke which is made without a dittie is the fantasie, that is, when a musician taketh a point at his pleasure, and wresteth and turneth it as he list, making either much or little of it according as shall seeme best in his own conceit. In this may more art be showne then in any other musicke, because the composer is tide to nothing but that he may adde, deminish, and alter at his pleasure. And this kind will beare any allowances whatsoeuer tolerable in other musick, except changing the ayre & leauing the key, which in fantasie may neuer be suffered. Other thinges you may vse at your pleasure, as bindings with discordes, quicke motions, slow motions, proportions, and what you list. Likewise, this kind of musick is with them who practise instruments of parts in greatest vse, but for voices it is but sildome vsed.[1]

The restriction of key was inevitable in a style derived ultimately from the modes. The key system of the classical period, the great secret of much of the new form, grew slowly from homophonic music, in which the cadences were clear. Instrumental dance music provided such a texture, and the dance figures imposed on it a certain kind of pattern. The pavan and the galliard usually consisted of three repeated sections—AABBCC—and sometimes each section was varied in repetition, producing the form AA'BB'CC'. To underline the structure with different cadences or modulations to different keys was a natural step. The slow pavan and the quicker galliard on the same theme were generally associated, and the alternation of fast and slow movements, with a key system to clarify the structure, soon produced the suite during the seventeenth century. Another method of development had also been discovered by the English composers. The variation, which virginals and lute composers often wrote on popular songs, was still very primitive, but it promised great future possibilities.

The feeling for purely musical form, stimulated by instrumental composition, is discernible even in vocal music. One of the minor forms associated with the madrigal had a structure that was musical rather than literary and was in fact derived from the dance. The ballet was strophic, each stanza consisting of two

[1] op. cit., pp. 180–1.

repeated sections. The words of both sections of the stanza were
followed by a refrain, set to ' fa-la '. The text was set more or
less homophonically, and the refrain was usually more contrapuntal. In its simplest form each half consisted of a couplet
followed by ' fa-la 's.

> Now is the month of maying,
> When merry lads are playing.
>   Fa-la.
> Each with his bonny lass
> Upon the greeny grass.
>   Fa-la.[1]

The poetic structure is not rigid. Sometimes the text has three
lines and cannot be divided into two equal halves.

> Singing alone sat my sweet Amaryllis ;
> The satyrs danced, all with joy surprised.
> Was never yet such dainty sport devised.[2]

The character of the words and the rime-scheme decide which
line is to be treated by itself. The first line constitutes the first
section of the composition, followed by ' fa-la 's and repeated.
Even when the stanza seems to divide into two equal halves, the
music may be differently arranged. In the following ballet the
text, read alone, would seem to divide into two quatrains.

> Shoot, false Love, I care not.
> Spend thy shafts and spare not.
> I fear not, I, thy might ;
> And less I weigh thy spite.
> All naked I unarm me ;
> If thou canst, shoot, and harm me.
> So lightly I esteem thee,
> As now a child I deem thee.[3]

Morley actually takes the first couplet only for the first section
of the composition. The constant factor in the ballet, then, is
the musical structure, which is what the text-books call ' binary
form '.

One of the madrigal composers, Thomas Weelkes, used the
form of the ballet in the structural framework for one or two
madrigals. In his 1597 volume some of the texts consist of
quatrains whose rhythm suggests the ballet, and Weelkes has set
them as two repeated couplets, the parts sometimes interchanging

---

[1] Morley's *Ballets*, No. 3.   [2] ib., No. 5.
[3] ib., No. 2.

in the repeat (Nos. 13, 15, 16, 17). There are no nonsense syllables at the end of each half, and the texture is that of the madrigal rather than that of the ballet, though the binary form comes from the dance song. Two of Weelkes's actual ballets are included in the 1600 volume of madrigals, and in texture again they are really madrigals rather than ballets. Weelkes has retained the 'fa-la' refrain, and the texts have the familiar quatrain. The two pieces are consecutive stanzas of the same poem, and the settings are parallel. The first madrigal opens with slow-moving suspensions to depict 'O care, thou wilt dispatch me'. A brisker but still heavy-footed phrase enters on the second line, 'If music do not match thee', which passes into half-hearted 'fa-la's—a brave but hopeless attempt to whistle and keep one's courage up. The heaviness returns in the third line, 'So deadly dost thou sting me', and on the word 'deadly' is a clash of major and minor thirds. Once more music is invoked to banish care, and the line 'Mirth only help can bring me' passes into 'fa-la's of forced cheerfulness. The second madrigal is constructed in the same way. It opens with a remarkable chromatic passage on 'Hence, Care, thou art too cruel', and the tantalizing of care is reflected in the continual frustration of an expected full close. The next line, the invocation of music, 'Come, music, sick man's ewel', is this time an anticipation of the refrain in augmentation. The 'fa-la's are heavy and forced, and the third line, 'His force had well nigh slain me', is another chromatic episode. The weary movement of the last line and the lugubrious heaviness of the refrain depict the failure of music to banish care. In both compositions the ballet form has been used with exceptional originality. In them and in the four madrigals of the 1597 volume just mentioned Weelkes has in effect constructed madrigals round the musical form of the ballet.

A purely musical principle sometimes found in madrigals is the assimilation of several of the themes set to the different lines of poetry, so that the composition as a whole appears like variations on one melodic idea. The most extended use of this device is Morley's elegy on Henry Noel (No. 21 in the *Canzonets to Five and Six Voyces*), which is entirely built up from one theme. Morley frequently sets a number of lines to musical phrases that are melodically related. A great deal of the three-part canzonet, 'Hold out, my heart', is composed of phrases that are variants of a series of notes descending a fifth. They appear in such forms as these (their statement being sometimes at the fifth) :

'Love's folk in green arraying', in the five- and six-part canzonets, consists of phrases rising and falling within the compass of a fifth:

Wilbye's madrigals often have the same kind of assimilation of phrases. 'Away, thou shalt not love me' in the first set is mainly founded on a series of descending notes very like the one just quoted from Morley. They occur in different rhythmical representations to suit the different lines of the text.

'Why dost thou shoot?', in the same set, is constructed from these phrases, all versions of the same melodic idea.

In 'Ah cruel Amaryllis', in the second set, the repetition of the opening words in the last line has suggested the repetition of the music set to them.

There is an interesting use of *da capo* form in Morley's two-part canzonet 'Miraculous love's wounding'. The first line of the text is treated very fully. It is followed by a middle section in which several themes occur, and then the first line is repeated to the same music as before. This is exactly the classical *da capo* form, not merely an anticipation of it. It must be added, however, that Morley deserves no credit for it. His text translates one of Anerio's, and the *da capo* form is borrowed from him too. The very melodic ideas and the entries are suspiciously like Anerio's. One must hesitate to ascribe much originality to Morley, master of madrigal technique as he was.

The madrigal composers, then, although they practised a particularly literary form of music, were casting round for purely

musical principles of organization.   It is significant that several of
them should have tried means of co-ordination that recalled dance
patterns and the variations and *da capo* forms.   Instrumental music
intensified the problem of finding satisfactory formal principles.
In working out the new possibilities music had a path of its own
to follow, and the fact that even the madrigal composers were
affected by the desire for purely musical form was a symptom
that the interests of musicians were taking them further from
literary points of view.   The New Poetry had done much for
music ;   it had inspired it to fresh dramatic and emotional effect.
The technique of 'word-painting' had made music a complete
language of emotional expression, and in doing so had obviated
the need for further literary inspiration.   Instrumental pieces were
often given impressionist names—'Il doloroso', 'La Serena',
'Giles Farnaby his Reste', and 'His Dreame'.   Only a wider
conception of form was necessary to make music a completely
self-sufficient art able to appeal directly to both intellect and
emotions.

Indeed, composers had to decide either to work out the independent possibilities of their own art or else to become completely
subservient to the poet.   The madrigal had allowed musical
ingenuity free play, but criticism of counterpoint and the new
attention to monodic music could logically lead only to a sov-
ereignty of speech rhythms over musical values.   The Italians had
tried to stylize natural speech into recitative :   only thus could
literary values be further applied to music.   The Italian declamatory style had already made some impression on the English airs.
The English themselves were trying to use the vigour and natural-
ness of ordinary speech, together with music to create an atmosphere.   In the *Lords Maske* (1613) Campion attempted this by
providing a musical background to spoken verse.   '. . . the musick
changed into a very solemne ayre, which they softly played, while
Orpheus spake.'[1]   Not being able to devise a satisfactory convention for themselves, the English soon turned to Italian methods.
Lanier set two of Jonson's masques in the Italian manner in 1617.
A great deal of seventeenth-century effort was expended on the
creation of an English opera from these slight entertainments.[2]
The leading composers of the next generation, the brothers Lawes,
applied the declamatory style to the setting of lyrics.   They are

[1] *Works*, ed. Vivian, p. 90.
[2] A full account of English attempts to create an opera is given by E. J. Dent,
Foundations of English Opera.

fairly successful in reproducing the accentuation of the verse, though they are hampered by a stricter bar-line than the Elizabethans, a product of the large instrumental combinations necessary in elaborate entertainments like the masque. Some attempt is made to vary the speed of the declamation in accordance with the sentiments of the words, and the rise and fall of the melody is largely governed by the stresses required by the verse. Poets praised such fidelity to their poetry. With one accord they acclaimed Henry Lawes as their ideal partner. To Milton he was

> Harry, whose tuneful and well-measured song
> First taught our English music how to span
> Words with just note and accent, not to scan
> With Midas' ears, committing short and long.

One cannot help reflecting that poets liked Lawes because his music has insufficient intrinsic interest to distract attention from their verse. He is at his best when he forgets to be declamatory and composes graceful little tunes in triple time that recall Campion. But his art is very miniature, and there was no future for music along his lines. Instrumental composers were busy creating a technique that owed nothing to poetry, and it was their achievements that opened a new realm for music and laid the foundations for the art of Bach and Handel.

If music had reached a point at which it could not profitably gain much further from literary inspiration, poetry was developing in a way that left the musician little scope. The lyric was ceasing to trouble about singing qualities and appealing to the reader. The *Songs and Sonets* of John Donne, written some time round the turn of the century, reveal a novel temper and outlook and break with the traditional values of lyric poetry. It is doubtful whether Donne himself realized how revolutionary they were in their effect on the relations of music and poetry. He was very fond of music. Walton records in his *Life* that, having written his Hymn to God the Father,

he caused it to be set to a most grave and solemn tune, and to be often sung to the organ by the choristers of St. Paul's Church, in his own hearing ; especially at the evening service ; and at his return from his customary devotions at that place, did occasionally say to a friend, ' The words of this hymn have restored to me the same thoughts of joy that possessed my soul in my sickness, when I composed it. And, O the power of church-music ! that harmony added to this hymn has raised the affections of my heart, and quickened my graces of zeal and gratitude ; and I observe that I always return from paying this public duty of praise and prayer to God, with an unexpressible tranquillity of mind, and a willingness to leave the world.

What is more remarkable, Donne expected his *Songs and Sonets* to be set to music. The title itself is a common one for song lyrics in that period. In 'The Triple Foole' he exclaims:

> I am two fooles, I know,
> For loving, and for saying so
> In whining Poetry,

and adds that poetry makes him a third fool when he has penned it, for

> . . . When I have done so
> Some man, his art and voice to show,
> Doth *set and sing* my paine,
> And, by delighting others, frees againe
> Grief, which verse did restraine.

Some of the *Songs and Sonets* have a singing quality; but comparatively few of them have been found with musical settings, and their general character does not make this surprising. Most of them have a speech rather than a song rhythm. The first poem in the volume indicates the tone, and its rime does not disguise its affinity with dramatic blank verse.

> I wonder by my troth, what thou, and I
> Did, till we lov'd? were we not weaned till then?
> But sucked on countrey pleasures, childishly?
> Or snorted we in the seaven sleepers den?
> 'Twas so; But this, all pleasures fancies bee.
> If ever any beauty I did see,
> Which I desir'd, and got, 'twas but a dreame of thee.

The line is no longer the rhythmical unit. Speech periods are freely counterpointed on the metrical base. Marlowe's 'mighty line', a free and flexible medium for speech on the stage, unfettered by the musical ancestry of earlier verse, with its end-stopping and caesura where the cadences used to come—this speech verse has entered the lyric. When Jonson censured Donne's 'not keeping of accent' he pointed to the absence of metrical tune in Donne's lyric verse. M. Pierre Legouis has shown that many of Donne's lyrics begin with a stanza freely constructed from the natural prose rhythm of passionate speech, and the following stanzas are fitted to the pattern so created. The strophic form tends to be obliterated by the flow of free speech rhythm. Moreover, the thought and the imagery, drawn from a dozen sciences and from common experience, tend to be more intellectual than those of Elizabethan lyrics. Feeling and reflection are fused together, and there is a curious blend of sincerity and sardonic wit. Atmosphere and mood are exceedingly complex. None of these qualities can be readily translated into music. The full experience of the poet is inseparable from his words, and to simplify it into a mood suitable for musical treatment would be to distort it beyond recognition.

Donne initiates a separation between music and poetry that widens as the seventeenth century advances. The metaphysicals intended their verses to be read, not sung. The earlier lyric tradition, however, was not dead. Herrick continues the ease and grace of Campion. It is still possible in the seventeenth century to find lyrics headed ' Set by Mr. ——'. Social contacts between poets and musicians were still very close. Most of the poets were musical. Walton tells us that George Herbert used to attend a private music-meeting at Salisbury every week, and ' His chiefest recreation was music, in which heavenly art he was a most excellent master, and did himself compose many divine hymns and anthems, which he set and sung to his lute or viol.' Most of the other leading poets of the seventeenth century shared his appreciation of the art. Lovelace, for instance, to cite a poet of quite different kind, frequently refers to his musical friends. In one poem he writes complimentary verses on the singing and dancing of a lady he knew. In another he replies ' To a Lady that desired me I would beare my part with her in a Song.' With the assumed timidity of the amateur he assures her

> This is the Prittiest Motion :
> Madam, th'Alarums of a Drumme
> That calls your Lord, set to your cries,
> To mine are sacred Symphonies.

He is forced, however, to admit his reputation as a singer :

> What, though 'tis said I have a voice ;
> I know, 'tis but that hollow noise ;
> Which (as it through my pipe doth speed)
> Bitterns do Carol through a Reed.

Musical analogies spring readily to his lips. Finding Elinda's glove, he declares he leaves it

> Five kisses, one unto a place :
> For though the Lute's too high for me ;
> Yet Servants knowing Minikin nor Base,
> Are still allowed to fiddle with the case.

In another mood, affecting an amorous melancholy, he can imagine that

> Grief, Despair, and Fear, dance to the Air,
> Of my despised Prayer.
> A pretty Antick Love does this
> Then strikes a Galliard with a kiss ;
>   As in the end
>   The chords they rend ;
> So you with but a touch from your fair Hand
>   Turn all to Saraband.

To compliment his cousin, Thomas Stanley, on the *Ayres and Dialogues* in which he collaborated with John Gamble, Lovelace summons an array of contemporary musical terms to a display of wit typical of the period.

Though poets were still knowledgeable about music, it was the result of social contacts rather than any close ties between the two arts. The gulf between them was widening. Poetry was exploiting speech rhythm, and music was perfecting its own formal principles. Both were following the inner necessities of their own natures. Vocal music would still bring poet and composer together from time to time ; but the poet tended to present his composer with something that had not necessarily been created for singing, and the composer used the poet's work as a starting-point for a composition that was quite self-sufficient. Dryden was impatient that he had had to leave his verses rough in *King Arthur* to allow the composer more scope. Purcell's music depends little on the poetry he set. From reading ' I attempt from love's sickness to fly ' one could not deduce that the music would be in rondo form ; nor has Purcell's fondness for a ground-bass anything to do with the texts of his songs. He is not dependent, as the Elizabethans were, on the poetic structure, and he can transform even indifferent texts into marvels of imagination. In the eighteenth century independence became contempt. Three lines of Pope, detached from their context, sufficed to supply Handel with words for an aria of considerable length. In fact, music had become instrumental in conception. The general sentiments of the poem may have coloured the texture of the music, but the form of the poetry was quite lost in the form of the music. Being a mere convenience of the composer, the poet ceased to trouble about the demands of music, even in lyrics. Changes in social custom, and the bad luck that few of the Augustan poets knew much about music, accentuated the divorce. But in the main it was a natural development. The Renaissance brought a rapprochement between poetry and music that could neither last nor be repeated. Social practise, the degree of technical development already attained, and neo-classical precedent, all united to make the relationship of the two arts a natural expression of the age. Only a particular society at a particular moment could have produced such interdependence, and ' the sister and the brother ' were bound to outgrow it and become adults with lives of their own.

BIBLIOGRAPHY

The Actors Remonstrance, 1643.

ADAM DE LA HALLE, *Œuvres complètes*, ed. E. de Coussemaker, Paris, 1872.

ADLER, G., *Handbuch der Musikgeschichte*, Berlin, 1930.

ALFRED, KING, *Pastoral Care*, ed. H. Sweet (Early English Text Society), 1871.

ALISON, R., *An Howres Recreation in Musicke*, 1606 (ed. E. H. Fellowes, *English Madrigal School*, Vol. 33).

Psalmes, 1606.

AMBROS, A. W., *Geschichte der Musik*, Leipzig, 1887 (revised H. Leichentritt, Leipzig, 1919).

ANERIO, F., *Canzonette a Quattro Voci*, Venice, 1607.

The Ancren Riwle, ed. J. Morton (Camden Society), 1853.

ANGLADE, J., *Les troubadours*, Paris, 1919.

ARBER, E., *A Transcript of the Registers of the Stationers' Company of London, 1554–1640*, 1875–94.

ARKWRIGHT, G. P. E., *Early Elizabethan Stage Music* (*Musical Antiquary*, Vol. I), 1909–10.

Elizabethan Choir-boy Plays and their Music (*Proceedings of the Musical Association*, Vol. XL), 1914.

Notes on the Ferrabosco Family (*Musical Antiquary*, Vols. III–IV), 1911–12.

Old English Edition, 1889–1902.

ASCHAM, R., *The Scholemaster* (1570), ed. J. E. B. Mayor, 1934.

ASSER, J., *De Rebus Alfredi Magni*, ed. T. D. Hardy (*Monumenta Historica Britannica*), 1848.

ATTEY, J., *The First Booke of Ayres*, 1622.

AUDIAU, J., *Les troubadours et l'Angleterre*, Paris, 1927.

AULT, N., *Elizabethan Lyrics*, 1925.

Seventeenth Century Lyrics, 1928.

Bagford Ballads, ed. J. W. Ebsworth (Ballad Society), 1876–80.

BALE, J., *Scriptorum Illustrium maioris Britanniae Catalogus*, Basle, 1557–9.

BANDINI, A. G., *Commentariorum de vita et scriptis Ioannis Bapt. Doni . . . Libri Quinque*, Florence, 1755.

BARLEY, W., *A newe booke of tabliture*, 1596.

BARTLET, J., *A Book of Ayres*, 1606.

BASKERVILL, C. R., *The Elizabethan Jig*, Chicago, 1929.

BATESON, T., *The first set of English Madrigales*, 1604 (ed. E. H. Fellowes, *The English Madrigal School*, Vol. 21).

The Second set of Madrigales, 1618 (ed. E. H. Fellowes, *The English Madrigal School*, Vol. 22).

BECK, J. B., *La Musique des Troubadours*, Paris, 1928.

BEDE, THE VENERABLE, *Historiae Ecclesiasticae gentis Anglorum libri quinque* (*Monumenta historica Britannica*), 1848.

BEMBO, P., *Opere*, Milan, 1808–10.

BENNET, J., *Madrigalls to fovre Voyces*, 1599 (ed. E. H. Fellowes, *English Madrigal School*, Vol. 23).

Beowulf, ed. A. J. Wyatt and R. W. Chambers, 1920.

BERDAN, J. M., *Early Tudor Poetry*, New York, 1920.

BONTOUX, G., *La Chanson en Angleterre au temps d'Elisabeth*, Paris, 1936.

BRENET, M., *Musique et musiciens de la vieille France*, Paris, 1911.

BRETON, N., *The Arbor of amorous Devises* (1597), ed. H. E. Rollins, Harvard, 1937.
    Brittons Bowre of Delights (1591 and 1597), ed. H. E. Rollins, Harvard, 1933.
    Melancholike Humours (1600), ed. G. B. Harrison, 1929.

BRIGGS, H. B., *Songs and Madrigals by English Composers of the End of the Fifteenth Century* (Plainsong and Medieval Music Society), 1891 and 1893.

BROWN, J., *A Dissertation on the Rise, Union and Power of Poetry and Music*, 1763.

BULLEN, A. H., *Lyrics from the Song-Books of the Elizabethan Age*, 1887.
    More Lyrics from the Song-Books of the Elizabethan Age, 1889.

BURNEY, C., *A General History of Music* (1789), ed. F. Mercer, 1935.

BYRD, W., *Gradualia*, 1607 (*Tudor Church Music*, Vol. VII, 1927).
    Psalmes, Sonets, and Songs of Sadnes and Pietie, 1588 (ed. E. H. Fellowes, *English Madrigal School*, Vol. 14).
    Songs of sundrie natures, 1589 (*English Madrigal School*, Vol. 15).
    Psalmes, Songs, and Sonnets, 1611 (*English Madrigal School*, Vol. 16).

BYRNE, M. ST. CLARE, *The Elizabethan Home*, 1930.

CACCINI, G., *Nuove Musiche*, Venice, 1602.

Calendar of Letters and Papers of the Reign of Henry VIII, ed. J. S. Brewer and J. Gairdner, 1862–1910.

Calendar of Letters and State Papers, relating to English Affairs, preserved principally in the Archives of Simancas, 1892–9.

Calendar of State Papers and MSS. relating to English Affairs existing in the Archives and Collections of Venice, 1202–1603, 1864–98.

Calendar of State Papers, Domestic Series, ed. R. Lemon and M. A. E. Green, 1856–72.

The Cambridge History of English Literature, 1909. Vol. IV, Chap. VI, 'The Song-Books and Miscellanies'; Chap. VIII, 'Thomas Campion'.

The Camden Miscellany, II (Camden Society Publications, Vol. LV), 1853.

CAMPION, T., *Two Bookes of Ayres*, n.d.
    Third and Fovrth Booke of Ayres, n.d.
    Works, ed. S. P. Vivian, 1909.

CARLTON, R., *Madrigals to Fiue voyces*, 1601 (ed. E. H. Fellowes, *English Madrigal School*, Vol. 27).

CASE, J., *Praise of Musicke*, 1588.

CASSIODORUS, M. A., *Variarum Epistolarum Libri XII* (*Monumenta Germaniae Historica, Auctores*, ed. T. Mommsen, Vol. 12), Berlin, 1894.

CASTIGLIONE, B., *The Book of the Courtyer*, trans. T. Hoby (1561), Everyman Library ed.

CAVENDISH, M., *14. Ayres in Tabletorie to the Lute. . . . And 8. Madrigalles to 5. voyces*, 1598.

CESARI, G., *Le origini del madrigale cinquecentesco* (*Rivista musicale italiana*, Vol. XIX), 1912.

CHADWICK, H. M., and N. K., *The Growth of Literature*, 1932.

CHAMBERS, E. K., *The Elizabethan Stage*, 1923.
    The Mediaeval Stage, 1903.
    Sir Thomas Wyatt and Other Studies, 1933.

— and SIDGWICK, F., *Early English Lyrics*, 1907.

CHAPPELL, W., *Popular Music of the Olden Time*, 1855—rev. E. H. Wooldridge, 1893.

CHAUCER, G., *Works*, ed. W. W. Skeat, 1895.

CHAYTOR, H. J., *The Troubadours*, 1912.
The Troubadours and England, 1923.

CHETTLE, H., *Kind-harts Dreame*, ed. G. B. Harrison, 1923.

CHILD, F. J., *English and Scottish Popular Ballads*, Boston, 1882–98.

CHILESOTTI, O., *Les maitres musiciens de la Renaissance française* (*Rivista musicale italiana*, Vol. VI), 1899.

The Complaynt of Scotland, ed. J. A. H. Murray (Early English Text Society), 1872.

COPLAND, W., *The seuen sorowes that women haue* [1560 ?].
The Manner to Dance Boer Dances (Pear Tree Press ed.), 1937.

COPRARIO, J., *Fvuneral Teares*, 1606.
Songs of Mourning, 1613.

CORKINE, W., *Ayres*, 1610.
The Second Booke of Ayres, 1612.

COWLING, G., *Music on the Shakespearian Stage*, 1913.

DANIEL, S., *Complete Works*, ed. A. B. Grosart, 1883.

DANTE, C. ALIGHIERI, *De Vulgari Eloquentia*, trans. A. G. Ferrers Howell, 1890.

DANYEL, J., *Songs*, 1606.

Daurel et Béton, ed. P. Meyer (*Société des anciens textes français*), Paris, 1880.

DAVEY, H., *History of English Music* (1895), 1921.

DAVID, E., *Études Historiques sur la Poésie et la Musique dans la Cambraie*, Paris, 1884.

DAVIES, SIR J., *Orchestra* (1596), ed. R. S. Lambert, 1922.

DELONEY, T., *Works*, ed. F. O. Mann, 1912.

DENT, E. J., *Foundations of English Opera*, 1928.
Notes on the Amfiparnasso of Orazio Vecchi (*Sammelbande der Internationalen Musikgesellschaft*, Vol. XII), Leipzig, 1911.
William Byrd and the Madrigal (*Festschrift für Johannes Wolf*), Berlin, 1929.

DESCHAMPS, E., *Œuvres*, ed. Marquis de Queux de St. Hilaire and G. Raynaud (*Société des anciens textes français*), Paris, 1878–1903.

Documents and Accounts in Manners and Household Expenses in England, ed. B. Botfield (Roxburgh Club), 1841.

DONNE, J., *The Complete Poetry and Select Prose*, ed. J. Hayward, 1929.

DOWLAND, J., *The First Booke of Songes or Ayres*, 1597.
The Second Booke of Songs or Ayres, 1600.
The Third and Last Booke of Songs or Aires, 1603.
A Pilgrimes Solace, 1612.
Lachrimae, 1605.

DOWLAND, R., *A Musicall Banquet*, 1610.

DOWLING, M., *The Printing of John Dowland's Second Booke of Songs or Ayres* (*The Library*, 4th Series, Vol. XII, No. 4), 1932.

DRAYTON, M., *Complete Works*, ed. J. W. Hebel, 1931–41.

DRYDEN, J., *Poetical Works*, ed. J. Sargeaunt, 1925.

D'URFEY, T., *Pills to Purge Melancholy*, 1719–20.

EARLE, T., *Microcosmographie* (1628), ed. G. Murphy, 1928.

EAST, M., *Madrigals to 3. 4. and 5. parts*, 1604 (ed. E. H. Fellowes, *English Madrigal School*, Vol. 29).

The second set of Madrigals, 1606 (ed. E. H. Fellowes, *English Madrigal School*, Vol. 30).

The Third Set of Bookes, 1610 (*English Madrigal School*, Vol. 31).

The Fovrth Set of Bookes, 1619 (*English Madrigal School*, Vol. 31).

EGINHARD, —, *Vita Karoli Magni* (*Monumenta Germaniae Historica, Auctores*, ed. G. H. Perts, Vol. 2), Berlin, 1826.

EINSTEIN, A., *Augenmusik im Madrigal* (*Zeitschrift der Internationalen Musikgellschaft*, Vol. XIV), Leipzig, 1921.

Italian Madrigal Verse (*Proceedings of the Musical Association*, Vol. LXIII), 1937.

EITNER, R., *Biographisch-Bibliographisches Quellen-Lexikon der Musiker und Musikgelehrten*, Leipzig, 1900.

ELYOT, T., *The Boke Named the Governour* (1531), Everyman Library ed., 1907.

Emaré, ed. E. Rickert (Early English Text Society), 1908.

Englands Helicon (1600), ed. H. E. Rollins, Harvard, 1935.

ERASMUS, D., *Opera*, ed. J. le Clerc, Lyons, 1703–6.

EXPERT, H., *Les maitres musiciens de la Renaissance Française*, Paris, 1894.

Monuments de la Renaissance française, Paris, 1924.

FARAL, E., *Les Jongleurs en France au moyen age*, Paris, 1869.

FARMER, J., *The First Set of English Madrigals*, 1599 (ed. E. H. Fellowes, *The English Madrigal School*, Vol. 8).

FARNABY, G., *Canzonets to Fowre Voyces*, 1598 (ed. E. H. Fellowes, *The English Madrigal School*, Vol. 20).

FELLOWES, E. H., *The English Madrigal*, 1925.

English Madrigal Composers, 1921.

The English Madrigal School, 1913–24.

The English School of Lutanist Song-Writers, 1920–6.

English Madrigal Verse, 1920.

FERRABOSCO, A. (the elder), *Nine Madrigals to Five Voices, from Musica Transalpina, 1588*, ed. G. P. E. Arkwright (Old English Edition, No. XI), 1894.

FERRABOSCO, A. (the younger), *Ayres*, 1609.

FEUILLERAT, A., *Documents relating to the Revels at Court in the Time of King Edward VI and Queen Mary* (W. Bang, *Materialien zur Kunde des alteren englischen Dramas*, No. XLIV), 1914.

FILMER, E., *French Court Ayres*, 1629.

The Fitzwilliam Virginals Book, ed. J. A. Fuller-Maitland and W. Barclay Squire, Leipzig, 1894–9.

FLOOD, W. H. GRATTAN, *Early Tudor Composers*, 1926.

Master Sebastian of St. Paul's (*Musical Antiquary*, Vol. III), 1911.

FORBES, J., *Cantus, Songs and Fancies*, 1666.

FORD, T., *Musicke of Sundrie Kindes*, 1607.

FOXWELL, A. K., *A Study of Sir Thomas Wiat's Poems*, 1911.

FULLER, R., *History of the Worthies of England*, 1662.

FURNIVALL, F. J., and MORFILL, W. R., *Ballads from Manuscripts* (Ballad Society), 1868–73.

GAIMER, G., *Lestorie des Engles*, ed. T. D. Hardy and C. T. Martin (Rolls Series), 1888.

GALILEI, V., *Dialogo . . . della musica antica e della moderna*, Florence, 1581.

GASGOIGNE, G., *Works*, ed. J. W. Cunliffe, 1907.

GASTOLDI, G. G., *Ballette a Cinque Voci*, Antwerp, 1601.

GENNRICH, F., *Grundriss einer Formenlehre der mittelalterlichen Liedes*, Halle, 1932.

GIBBON, J. MURRAY, *Melody and the Lyric*, 1930.
GIBBONS, O., *The First Set of Madrigals*, 1612 (ed. E. H. Fellowes, *English Madrigal School*, Vol. 5).
Keyboard Works, ed. M. H. Glyn.
GIRALDUS CAMBRENSIS, *Works*, ed. J. S. Brewer, J. F. Dunock and G. F. Warner (Rolls Series), 1861–91.
GOOGE, B., *Eglogs, Epitaphes, and Sonettes*, 1563.
GORDON, R. K., *Anglo-Saxon Poetry*, 1927.
A gorgious Gallery of Gallant Inventions (1578), ed. H. E. Rollins, Harvard, 1926.
GOSSON, S., *An Apologie for the Schoole of Abuse* (1597), ed. E. Arber.
GOWER, J., *Works*, ed. G. C. Macaulay, 1899–1902.
GREENE, R. L., *Early English Carols*, 1935.
Gude and Godlie Ballatis (1567), ed. A. F. Mitchell (Scottish Text Society), Edinburgh, 1897.
GUI D'AMIENS, *Carmen de Hastingae proelio*, ed. F. Michel (*Chroniques anglo-normandes*, Vol. III), 1836.
HADDAN, A. W., and STUBBS, W., *Councils and Ecclesiastical Documents*, 1869–78.
HALLIWELL-PHILLIPS, J., *A catalogue of an unique collection of English Broadside Ballads*, 1856.
A Handeful of pleasant delites (1584), ed. A. Kershaw, 1926.
HARVEY, P., *The Oxford Companion to English Literature*, 1938.
Havelok the Dane, ed. W. W. Skeat, rev. K. Sisam, 1915.
HAWKINS, J., *A General History of the Science and Practice of Music*, 1776.
HERBERT, LORD, OF CHERBURY, *Poems*, ed. G. C. Moore Smith, 1923.
HERBERT, G., *The English Works*, ed. G. H. Palmer, 1905–15.
HESELTINE, P., and GRAY, C., *Carlo Gesualdo*, 1926.
HEYWOOD, J., *Works*, ed. J. S. Farmer, 1905–6.
HILLEBRAND, H. N., *The Child Actors* (University of Illinois Studies in Language and Literature), Urbana, 1926.
HILTON, J., *Ayres*, 1627.
Historical Manuscripts Commission, Reports on the MSS. at Belvoir Castle and Hatfield House.
HOLBORNE, A., *The Cittharn Schoole*, 1597.
HOLYBAND, C., *The French Schoole maister*, 1573.
HOWELL, T., *The Arbor of Amitie* (1568), ed. A. B. Grosart, 1879.
Newe Sonets, and pretie Pamphlets (1567–8), ed. A. B. Grosart, 1879.
HUME, T., *Musicall Humors*, 1605.
Poeticall Musicke, 1607.
HUTH, H., *Ancient Ballads and Broadsides*, 1867.
JEANROY, A., *Les Origines de la Poesie Lyrique en France au Moyen Age*, Paris, 1925.
JEBB, R. C., *Homer: An Introduction to the Iliad and the Odyssey*, Glasgow, 1887.
JOHNSON, R., *A Crowne Garland of Golden Roses* (1612), ed. W. Chappell, 1842.
JONES, R., *The First Set of Madrigals*, 1607 (ed. E. H. Fellowes, *The English Madrigal School*, Vol. 35).
The First Booke of Songes and Ayres, 1600.
The Second Booke of Songes and Ayres, 1601.
Ultimum Vale, 1608.
A Musicall Dreame, 1609.
The Muses Gardin for Delights, 1610.
JONSON, B., *Works*, ed. C. H. Herford and P. Simpson, 1925–37.

JORDANIS, *De Getarum origine* (*Monumenta Germaniae Historica, Auctores*, ed. T. Mommsen, vol. 5), Berlin, 1882.

JUSSERAND, J. J., *Wayfaring Life in the Middle Ages*, trans. L. T. Smith, 1889.

KEMP, W., *Kemps nine daies wonder* (1600), ed. G. B. Harrison, 1923.

King Horn, ed. J. Hall, 1901.

KIRBYE, G., *The first set of English Madrigalls*, 1597 (ed. E. H. Fellowes, *English Madrigal School*, Vol. 24).

KROYER, T., *Die Anfange der Chromatik im italienischen Madrigal des 16. Jahrhunderts* (Beiheft der Internationalen Musikgesellschaft), Leipzig, 1912.

LANGLOIS, M. E., *Receuils d'arts de seconde Rhetorique*, Paris, 1902.

LAWES, H., *The Treasury of Musick*, 1669.

LICHFIELD, H., *The First Set of Madrigals*, 1613 (ed. E. H. Fellowes, *English Madrigal School*, Vol. 17).

The Losely Manuscript, ed. A. Feuillerat, 1914.

LOVELACE, R., *Poems*, ed. C. H. Wilkinson, 1925.

LYLY, J., *Complete Works*, ed. R. W. Bond, Oxford, 1902.

MACDONAGH, T., *Thomas Campion and the Art of English Poetry*, Dublin, 1913.

MACHAUT, G. DE, *Œuvres*, ed. E. Hoeffner (*Société des anciens textes français*), Paris, 1926.

Musikalische Werke, ed. F. Ludwig, Leipzig, 1926.

MACHYN'S *Diary*, ed. J. G. Nichols (Camden Society), 1848.

MALMESBURY, WILLIAM OF, *De Gestis Pontificum Anglorum*, ed. N. E. S. A. Hamilton (Rolls Series), 1870.

MANNYNG, R., of Brunne, *Handlyng Synne*, ed. F. J. Furnivall (Roxburgh Club), 1862.

MARENZIO, L., *Samtliche Werke*, ed. A. Einstein, Leipzig, 1929.

MARLOWE, C., *Poems*, ed. L. C. Martin.

MEI, G., *Discorso sopra la musica antica e moderna*, Venice, 1602.

The Melvill Book of Roundels, ed. G. Bantock and H. O. Anderton (Roxburgh Club), 1916.

MIGNE, J. P., *Patrologiae Latinae cursus completus*, 1844–64.

MILTON, J., *Poetical Works*, ed. H. J. C. Grierson.

MONTEVERDI, C., *Tutti le Opere*, ed. G. F. Malipiero, Asolo, 1926.

MORLEY, T., *A Plaine and Easie Introduction to Practicall Musicke*, 1597.

Canzonets or Little Short Songs to Three Voyces, 1593 (ed. E. H. Fellowes, *English Madrigal School*, Vol. 1).

Madrigalls to Foure Voyces, 1594 (ed. E. H. Fellowes, *English Madrigal School*, Vol. 2).

The first booke of Canzonets to Two Voices, 1595 (ed. E. H. Fellowes, *English Madrigal School*, Vol. 1).

The First Booke of Balletts to Fiue Voyces, 1595 (ed. E. H. Fellowes, *English Madrigal School*, Vol. 3).

Il Primo Libro delle Ballette, 1595.

Canzonets or Little Short Aers to fiue and sixe Voyces, 1597 (ed. E. H. Fellowes, *English Madrigal School*, Vol. 4).

Canzonets or Little Short Songs to Foure Voyces : celected out of the best approued Italian Authors, 1597.

Madrigals to fiue voyces. Celected out of the best approued Italian Authors, 1598.

Madrigales, The Triumphes of Oriana, 1601 (ed. E. H. Fellowes, *English Madrigal School*, Vol. 32).

MORRIS, R. O., *Contrapuntal Technique in the Sixteenth Century*, 1922.

MORYSON, FYNES, *Itinerary* (1617). James MacLehose & Sons, Glasgow, 1907–8.

MULCASTER, R., *Positions*, ed. R. H. Quick, 1887.

MUNDAY, A., *A Banquet of daintie Conceits*, 1588.

MUNDY, J., *Songs and Psalms*, 1594 (ed. E. H. Fellowes, *English Madrigal School*, Vol. 35).

NASHE, T., *Works*, ed. E. B. McKerrow, 1904.

NETTLESHIP, H., *Ancient Lives of Virgil*, 1879.

NICHOLS, J., *The Progresses and Public Processions of Queen Elizabeth*, 2nd ed., 1823.

NOBLE, R., *Shakespeare's Use of Song*, 1923.

The Northumberland Household Book—i.e. *The Regulations and Establishment of the Household of Henry Algernon Percy, the fifth Earl of Northumberland*, ed. T. Percy, 1770.

The Oxford History of Music, rev. ed., 1933–

PADELFORD, F. M., *Early Sixteenth Century Lyrics*, Boston, 1907.

    Old English Musical Terms, Bonn, 1899.

The Paradise of daynty devises (1576), ed. H. E. Rollins, Harvard, 1927.

Parthenia (1611), ed. Musical Antiquarian Society, 1847.

PAULUS DIACONUS, *Historia Langobardorum* (*Monumenta Germaniae Historica, Scriptores Rerum Langobardicarum et Italicarum*), ed. G. Waitz, Hanover, 1878.

PEELE, G., *Works*, ed. A. H. Bullen, 1888.

PEERSON, M., *Priuate Musicke*, 1620.

The Pepys Ballads, ed. H. E. Rollins, Harvard, 1929–32.

PERCY, T., *Reliques of Ancient English Poetry* (1765–94), Everyman ed.

The Percy Folio Manuscript, ed. J. W. Hales and F. J. Furnivall, 1867–8.

PETRARCH, F., *Opera*, Basle, 1554.

The Phoenix Nest (1593), ed. H. E. Rollins, Harvard, 1931.

Piers Plowman, ed. W. W. Skeat, 1906.

A Pilgrimage to Parnassus (1600)—Tudor Facsimiles, ed. J. S. Farmer.

PILKINGTON, F., *The First Booke of Songes or Ayres*, 1605.

    The First Set of Madrigals, 1613 (ed. E. H. Fellowes, *English Madrigal School*, Vol. 25).

    The Second Set of Madrigals, 1624 (ed. E. H. Fellowes, *English Madrigal School*, Vol. 26).

A Poetical Rhapsody (1602), ed. H. E. Rollins, Harvard, 1932.

POUND, L., *Poetic Origins and the Ballad*, New York, 1921.

PRUNIERES, H., *Monteverdi* (English ed.), 1926.

RALEIGH, W., *Poems*, ed. M. C. Latham, 1929.

RAVENSCROFT, T., *A Briefe Discovrse*, 1614.

    Deuteromelia, 1609.

    Melismata, 1611.

REED, A. W., *Early Tudor Drama*, 1926.

The Return from Parnassus (1606)—Tudor Facsimiles, ed. J. S. Farmer.

REYHER, A., *Les Masques anglais*, Paris, 1909.

RITSON, J., *Ancient Songs and Ballads*, ed. W. C. Hazlitt, 1877.

ROBINSON, T., *New Citharn Lessons*, 1609.

ROGER OF HOVEDON, *Chronicon*, ed. W. Stubbs (Rolls Series), 1868–71.

ROLLAND, R., *Some Musicians of Former Days*, 1915.

ROLLINS, H. E., *An Analytical Index of the Ballad Entries, 1557–1706, in the Registers* of the Company of Stationers (Studies in Philology, N. Carolina, Vol. XXI), 1924.

A Pepysian Garland.

Old English Ballads, 1553–1625, 1920.

RONSARD, P., Œuvres, 1609, and ed. H. Vaganay, Paris, 1923–4.

ROPER, W., Life of Sir Thomas More, ed. E. V. Hitchcock (Early English Text Society), 1935.

ROSSETER, P., A Booke of Ayres, 1601.

ROWLANDS, S., Works, ed. Hunterian Club, Glasgow, 1880.

Roxburgh Ballads, ed. W. Chappell and J. W. Ebsworth (Ballad Society), 1869–97.

SAINTSBURY, G., Minor Poets of the Caroline Period, Oxford, 1905–21.

SANDBERGER, A., Roland Lassus's Beziehungen zur italienischen Literatur (Sammelbande der Internationalen Musikgesellschaft, Vol. V), Leipzig, 1904.

SANDERSON, J., Travels, ed. W. Foster (Hakluyt Society), 1931.

SCHWARTZ, R., Die Frottole im 15. Jahrhunderts (Vierteljahrbuch für Musikwissenschaft, Vol. II), 1886.

SCHOLES, P., The Puritans and Music, 1934.

SELDEN, J., Table Talk, ed. S. H. Reynolds, Oxford, 1892.

SERAFINO DEL'AQUILA, Opere, Venice, 1505.

SHAKESPEARE, W., Works, ed. W. J. Craig, 1891.

SHARP, C., English Folk-Song : Some Conclusions, 1907.

Shirburn Ballads, 1585–1616, ed. A. Clark, 1907.

Sidneiana (Roxburgh Club), 1837.

SIDNEY, P., Works, ed. A. Feuillerat, 1912–16.

Sidney Papers, ed. A. Collins, 1746.

SIDONIUS APOLLINARIS, Carmina (Monumenta Germaniae Historica, Auctores, vol. VIII, ed. C. Luetjohann), Berlin, 1887.

SISAM, K., Fourteenth Century Verse and Prose, 1921.

SKELTON, J., Poems, ed. A. Dyce, 1843.

SMITH, C. GREGORY, Elizabethan Critical Essays, 1904.

SPENSER, E., Poetical Works, ed. E. de Selincourt, 1926.

STAINER, J., Early Bodleian Music, 1901.

    Dufay and his Contemporaries, 1898.

Stationers' Registers—see Arber, E.

STOPES, C. C., William Hunnis (W. Bang, Materialen zur Kunde des älteren englischen Dramas, no. XXIX), Bonn, 1902.

SUCKLING, H., Works, ed. A. Hamilton Thompson, 1910.

STOW, J., A Survey of London (1603), ed. H. B. Wheatley (Everyman Library), 1912.

STUBBS, W., Memorials of St. Dunstan (Rolls Series), 1874.

TIERSOT, J., Ronsard et la musique de son temps (Sammelbande der Internationalen Musikgesellschaft, Vol. IV), Leipzig, 1903.

TIRABOSCHI, G., Storia della letteratura italiana, Milan, 1822–6.

TORCHI, L., L'Arte musicale in Italia, Milan, 1898–1907.

TOMKINS, T., Songs, 1622 (ed. E. H. Fellowes, English Madrigal School, Vol. 18).

TOTTEL's Miscellany (1557), ed. H. E. Rollins, Harvard, 1929.

TREFUSIS, M., Songs, Ballads and Instrumental Pieces by Henry VIII, 1912.

TURBERVILLE, G., Epitaphes, Epigrams, Songs and Sonets, 1570.

TUSSER, T., A Hundreth good points of Husbandrie (1557), ed. D. Hartley, 1931.

VALERIUS, A., Neder-Landtsche Gedenck-Clancke, Haarlem, 1626.

VAUTOR, T., *The First Set*, 1619 (ed. E. H. Fellowes, *English Madrigal School*, Vol. 34.).

VENANTIUS FORTUNATUS, *Carmina* (*Monumenta Germaniae Historica*, *Auctores*, vol. 4, ed. F. Leo), Berlin, 1877.

La Vie de St. Alexis, ed. L. Panier and G. Paris, Paris, 1872.

VISING, J., *Anglo-Norman Language and Literature*, 1923.

Volsunga Saga, trans. M. Slauch, 1930.

VOGEL, E., *Bibliothek der gedruckten Weltlichen Vocalmusik Italien aus den Jahren 1500–1700*, Berlin, 1892.

WACE, *Roman de Rou*, ed. H. Andreson, Bonn, 1877–9.

WALKER, E., *A History of Music in England* (1907), 1924.

WALLER, E., *Poems*, ed. G. Thorn Drury, 1893.

WALTON, I., *Lives*, ed. G. Saintsbury, 1927.

    The Compleat Angler (1676), ed. J. Buchan, 1901.

WARD, J., *The First Set of English Madrigals*, 1613 (ed. E. H. Fellowes, *English Madrigal School*, Vol. 19).

WARLOCK, P., *The English Ayre*, 1926.

    Elizabethan Songs, that were originally composed for one voice to sing and four stringed instruments to accompany, 1926.

WATSON, FOSTER, *The Grammar Schools to 1660*, 1898.

WATSON, T., *Hecatompathia or the Passionate Centurie of Love*, 1582.

    Italian Madrigalls Englished, 1590.

    The Teares of Fancie, 1593.

WEELKES, T., *Madrigals*, 1597 (ed. E. H. Fellowes, *English Madrigal School*, Vol. 9).

    Balletts and Madrigals, 1598 (ed. E. H. Fellowes, *English Madrigal School*, Vol. 10).

    Madrigals of 5. and 6. parts, 1600 (ed. E. H. Fellowes, *English Madrigal School*, Vol. 11).

    Madrigals of 6. parts, 1600 (ed. E. H. Fellowes, *English Madrigal School*, Vol. 12).

    Ayeres or Phantasticke Spirites, 1608 (ed. E. H. Fellowes, *English Madrigal School*, Vol. 13).

WELSFORD, E., *The Court Masque*, 1927.

WHITELOCKE, J., *Liber Famelicus* (Camden Society Publications, LXX), 1858.

WHYTHORNE, T., *Songs*, 1571.

WILBYE, J., *The First Set of English Madrigals*, 1598 (ed. E. H. Fellowes, *English Madrigal School*, Vol. 6).

    The Second Set of Madrigales, 1609 (ed. E. H. Fellowes, *English Madrigal School*, Vol. 7).

WITHER, G., *Works*, ed. A. B. Grosart, 1871–3.

WILSON, J., *Cheerfull Ayres or Ballads*, 1660.

WOLF, J., *Geschichte der Mensural-Notation*, Berlin, 1904.

    Italian Trecento Music (*Proceedings of the Musical Association*, Vol. LVIII), 1932.

WOOLDRIDGE, E. H., *Early English Harmony*, 1897, 1913.

WYATT, T., *Poems*, ed. A. K. Foxwell, 1913.

YOULL, H., *Canzonets*, 1608 (ed. E. H. Fellowes, *English Madrigal School*, Vol. 28).

YONGE, N., *Musica Transalpina*, 1588 and 1597.

ZANDERVOORT, R. W., *Sidney's Arcadia. A Comparison between the two Versions*, Amsterdam, 1928.

INDEX

15

Printed in Great Britain by Butler & Tanner Ltd., Frome and London